Humans

Humans

An Introduction to Four-Field Anthropology

Alice Beck Kehoe

Routledge
New York and London

Published in 1998 by
Routledge
29 West 35th Street
New York, NY 10001

Published in Great Britain by
Routledge
11 New Fetter Lane
London EC4P 4EE

The text was set in Galliard

Library of Congress Cataloging-in-Publication Data
Kehoe, Alice Beck, 1934–
    Humans : an introduction to four-field anthropology / Alice Beck
Kehoe.
        p.   cm.
    Includes bibliographical references and index.
    ISBN 0-415-91984-3 (hb). — ISBN 0-415-91985-1 (pbk.)
    1. Anthropology.   I. Title.
GN25.K45   1998
301—dc21   97-40017
                                                                       CIP

Cover Photo: Ekeko is a sprite who comes to Bolivia on January 24, bringing people what they are
hoping to get—house, car, bountiful potato harvest, cooking pot always full of food, money, air-
plane ticket. Ekeko is pictured as a mestizo, part Indian but living in Bolivia's urban "modern"
style. Ekeko typifies today's global society.

Acknowledgments

The assistance, and friendship, of the following colleagues have directly benefited the following sections:

Chapter 3, James B. Courtright, Professor of Biology, Marquette University, critical reading.

Chapters 4–6, Andrew J. Petto, primatologist, University of Wisconsin-Madison, and editor, National Center for Science Education *Reports,* critical reading and selection of photographs.

Chapter 10, discussions with Barry L. Isaac, editor, *Research in Economic Anthropology;* and Rhoda H. Halperin, Professor of Anthropology, University of Cincinnati.

I am grateful also to the staff at Routledge, New York, for their spirited common sense and efficiency. It's been a real pleasure to work with editor William Germano, his assistants Alexandria Giardino and Nick Syrett, and production editor Brian Phillips.

Contents

Preface

Students introduced to a subject need a broad general outline of topics and approach to integrate what is presented into an intelligible picture. If an introductory textbook overwhelms students with details, most will respond by cramming for tests, while the few seriously interested will struggle for comprehension of the field. In my experience with thousands of students, in the long run, less becomes more of real learning.

Instructors for introductory anthropology courses face more than the challenge of presenting an overview of a complex field at a level comprehensible to students who may be ill-prepared or uninterested in intellectual questions. Instructors also wish to use their own preparation and experience to strengthen their teaching. Instructors who are excited by their own graduate coursework and their research, who are eager to share their fascination with anthropology, are likely to be most effective in transmitting the worldview that is the essence of anthropology. Hobbling an instructor with a six-hundred-page textbook hinders real teaching.

This is a concise, introductory textbook minimizing the number of technical terms and names. I wanted a textbook that freed me, in lecturing, from plowing through each of the major points every student ought to encounter in an introduction to anthropology; I wanted to be able to simply refer to some material available in the text. Accustomed as we are to the method of apt illustration characteristic of anthropological discourse, I needed a textbook short enough to permit assigning students, in addition, good illustrative reading. Six-hundred-page books with boxed illustrative ethnographies force us to repeat other fieldworkers' conclusions instead of building upon our own experience. When it appeared that no one else was going to sit down and write the concise textbook I needed, I did. This is the outline I have found effective in conveying the essence of contemporary American anthropology to a wide range of under-graduates.

There is a great deal that is not in this book. That is by design. The preponderance of students taking an introductory course are already in programs that do not give them much option to continue into anthropology, even if this course attracts them. What students are likely to absorb are concepts they can quickly link to their own lives. Rather than construct a text presenting each subfield equally, I have weighted this one with aspects of anthropology useful in reflecting upon one's life in our society. I have been concerned to winnow out those facets of traditional anthropology that are now appraised to stem from the nineteenth-century, imperial, colonial foundation of the discipline, e.g., the emphasis on the "domain" of kinship and the false contrast between "kin-based" and "contract" societies.

This textbook is for creative instructors who are concerned with tailoring the introductory course to their students, in their colleges. I anticipate instructors individualizing their courses through ethnographic and archaeological case studies, projects, or readers reflecting the instructors' enthusiasms. I have avoided expositions of formal approaches such as kinship studies or functionalism so that instructors are not burdened with material they may find unpalatable, misguided or inappropriate. I mention by name only a few historically highly influential anthropologists, giving instructors opportunity to introduce their own admired leaders.

References in the text have been kept to a minimum, in line with reducing citations of anthropologists in order to free instructors to introduce or emphasize those they themselves most respect. Apt illustrations not in the end-of-chapter publications have been drawn out of my own and close colleagues' experiences. For example, the description of Bolivian peasant life in Chapter 10 comes from my 1988 fieldwork in the village of Lakaya, on the Lake Titicaca pampa, and overall, the material in the chapter reflects many discussions with Barry L. Isaac, editor of *Research in Economic Anthropology*. This text is not designed to be a bland compendium of traditional academic anthropology, a liturgy, as it were, for the ritual practitioner. Drawing upon my own students' reactions—not discounting apathy!—to efforts to awaken them to the worthwhile insights from anthropology, I am convinced that instructors who make a real impact on student thinking are propelled by the excitement of their own work in the discipline.

Using this textbook, students who may not take any more anthropology should conclude the course with an understanding of the unity of the human species, the adaptation of societies to their environments (physical and political), and an appreciation of the power of socialization into a culture. Those students who may major in anthropology should obtain the framework for pursuit of the discipline's subfields. Instructors should welcome the opportunity to challenge stereotypes and biases through a combination of a truly basic text and their own assignments, maximizing the value of both students' and instructors' background.

References

In winnowing out the material in traditional anthropology that stems from the discipline's nineteenth-century, European/Euroamerican origins, I have used, among others, the books and edited volumes by George A. Stocking, Jr., and Adam Kuper, Hobsbawm and Ranger's *Invention of Tradition*, Schneider's *Critique of the Study of Kinship*, and Adrian Desmond's and James Moore's works on Darwin and nineteenth-century evolutionism. See also these publications by Kehoe:

1981 "Revisionist Anthropology: Aboriginal North America." *Current Anthropology* 22:503–509, 515–516.

1985 "The Ideological Paradigm in Traditional American Ethnology." In *Social Contexts of American Ethnology, 1840–1984*, ed. J. Helm. Washington: American Ethnological Society, pp. 41–49.

1989 " 'In Fourteen Hundred and Ninety-two, Columbus Sailed . . .': The Primacy of the National Myth in American Schools." In *The Excluded Past*, ed. P. Stone and R. MacKenzie. London: Unwin Hyman, pp. 201–216.

1990 "Primal Gaia: Primitivism and Plastic Medicine Men." In *The Invented Indian*, ed. J. A. Clifton. New Brunswick, NJ: Transaction Books, pp. 193–209.

1991 "The Invention of Prehistory." *Current Anthropology* 32(4):467–476.

1991 "The Centro de Madres in the Village of Lakaya, Bolivia." In *Marxist Approaches in Economic Anthropology*, ed. Alice Littlefield and Hill Gates. Society for Economic Anthropology, Monographs in Economic Anthropology, No. 9. Washington: University Press of America, pp. 119–133.

1992 "The Paradigmatic Vision of Archaeology: Archaeology as a Bourgeois Science." In *Rediscovering Our Past: Essays in the History of American Archaeology*, ed. Jonathan E. Reyman. Aldershot: Avebury. pp. 23–27.

1998 *The Land of Prehistory: A Critical History of American Archaeology*. New York: Routledge.

C·H·A·P·T·E·R   1

Anthropology—A General Introduction

Anthropology studies humans. Anthropology is unique in seeing humans whole, as biological organisms and as thinking, social beings: anthropology's *holistic perspective* brings together in an integrated study the physical, environmental, social, historical, and intellectual facets of human life. Humans survive and prosper through group living, and the characteristic behavior of people in socieities, their *cultures,* is the focus of anthropology.

Our society is accustomed to separate aspects of human life according to a supposed contrast between nature and human civilization. Our physical bodies and the natural world in which we live are studied in the natural sciences—physics, chemistry, and biology; our thinking and our behavior are studied in the humanities and social and behavioral sciences—philosophy, literature, history, sociology, political science, economics, law, psychology, and business. All of these come into anthropology. These customary divisions are constructed within our particular cultural tradition. Anthropologists work to reach an understanding of humans that goes beyond the limited vision of restricted studies, of conventional focus on politically powerful nations, and of documented history.

holistic perspective

Within their holistic perspective, individual anthropologists usually concentrate on one or another area of human experience. *Biological anthropologists* (sometimes called *physical anthropologists*) become especially knowledgeable about human genetics, health, and nutrition, or fossils of ancestor species. *Archaeologists* study evidence preserved in ruins and in the ground to learn about human life in the past. *Anthropological linguists* study languages and their use. *Cultural* or *social* anthropologists—the most numerous kind—observe contemporary societies, our own and others around the world. Some anthropologists who work in corporations or agencies suggest *applied anthropology*

four fields of anthropology

1

should be considered a fifth field, and they refer to themselves as *practicing anthropologists.*

Anthropologists may teach in universities, but an increasing number make their living as staff members or consultants to businesses, institutions, and agencies. One anthropologist is a troubleshooter for the U. S. Navy; another advises the U. S. Department of State on how to interpret events in the Middle East; one helps a Florida public health agency to bring medical aid to impoverished mothers and children; a fourth is in Latin America assisting villagers to revive ancient agricultural methods that will return ruined fields to crop production. Anthropologists prize a flexible approach that highlights human values.

Basic Concepts

Two statements will guide us through this book:

> *Humans are gregarious mammals adapted to a wide range of habitats through a large and complex brain.*
>
> *Cultures are sets of patterned behavior learned by humans as members of particular societies.*

These statements are like suitcases with several compartments. Let's unpack them.

- Humans are *mammals.* We are living organisms with backbones, brains, four limbs, warm blood, hair. We reproduce by copulation between males and females, the female carrying the young inside her body during its early growth and then nourishing it with milk from her mammary glands.

- Humans are *gregarious* mammals. We live in groups with other people. No human has ever grown up alone—human babies die if left without human caretakers. (Plants can grow up alone, so can many insects, fishes, and reptiles, but not mammals.) "Gregarious" means social.

- Humans are *adapted to a wide range of habitats.* People are found living in a greater variety of places than any other creature. People live in deserts and jungles, islands and high mountain valleys, on the water and now in spaceships.

- Humans are adapted to a wide range of habitats *through a large and complex brain.* The human brain is one of the largest of animal brains, especially when you consider its size relative to the body. (Whale brains

Humans are gregarious mammals who learn patterned behavior as they grow up in their societies. Nurturing adults are vital to humans' survival.
Photo credit: Aldis Strazdins

are larger, but whale bodies are vastly larger, too.) The human brain is not only large, it is also unusually complex, with millions of neurons in intricate networks. This large and also complex brain is the basic instrument by which we humans have been able to invent means to survive in our wide range of habitats, spreading throughout the world and into space.

- Cultures are *sets* of patterned behavior. Cultures are not single "things," but rather many habits, customs, and expectations carried by people in communities. People grow up imitating the behavior of older members of their communities, learning to accomplish tasks and to express emotions and talents in accustomed ways. Through this process human behavior is *patterned* in customary ways, and the *sets* of patterned behavior may be said to be the *culturally patterned* behavior characteristic of members of a particular community.

- Cultures are sets of *patterned behavior*. What the anthropologist actually *sees* is behavior. We can't see thoughts, laws, or beliefs, we can only infer them from people's behavior (including speaking and writing).

Gregarious humans, hundreds together for Milwaukee Public Museum's annual "fun race."
Photo credit: Milwaukee Public Museum of Milwaukee County

When we observe certain patterns of behavior again and again in many members of a community, we conclude the patterned behavior has been *learned by humans as members of particular societies.*

Very little that adult humans do is instinctive. Babies will suck and will move quickly if startled, then very soon begin to look intently at people around them to learn to behave as persons in their social group. Most of our behavior we learn while very young, from our family and neighbors. How people talk, how they usually move, how they sit, eat, sleep, play, make love—everything is learned in society. Patterns of behavior passed along in this way differ from place to place and even within larger social groups, some patterns being learned as proper to men, others as proper to women, or some as proper to upper-class people, others as proper to lower class. In this way, societies will demonstrate sets of patterned behavior.

The Anthropological Method

Every field of study has its methods of study and also its mode of discourse, that is to say, its accepted form of presentation. For its *mode of discourse,*

Mombasa, Kenya, 1928, annual public dance.
Photo credit: Milwaukee Public Museum.

anthropology favors *apt illustration:* a general idea is stated, then an example is described. These examples are always real cases actually observed by anthropologists. Hypothetical examples, such as philosophers give, are not acceptable in anthropological discourse. Neither are experimental situations such as those psychologists often set up. The anthropologist's apt illustrations may seem like anecdotes, but they are vital demonstrations of the general principle or idea presented.

| anthropologists present ideas through apt illustrations |

    Anthropologists' basic *method* is to be a *participant observer* in an existing social group, trying to be with the people without interfering with their activities.

| participant observer method |

After months or years of living with the observed people, the anthropologist has enough experience to see and describe the patterns of their behavior: this is *ethnography*.

| *ethno* ("nation, people") + *graphy* ("writing") |

Then comparisons are made with other peoples, observed by the same or by other anthropologists, to work out basic human needs and societies' answers to these needs. Our physical nature requires food, drink, shelter, social groupings committed to child care. Differing environments, population sizes and historical heritages result in diverse societal responses to these

Cameroons, Africa, 1959. Anthropologist observing Bafut diviner.
Photo credit: Milwaukee Public Museum.

basic needs—diverse cultures. Out of anthropologists' *cross-cultural compar-isons* come the general statements about humans that guide us to understand particular societies and their members.

> cross-cultural comparisons

   Now, how can an archaeologist or a biological anthropologist be a partic-ipant observer? Archaeologists work in the actual sites where ancient commu-nities lived. By closely observing the present conditions and analyzing the clues to past climate, land form, vegetation, animal life, structures, unusual events, and daily living, an archaeologist mentally reconstructs the society in the past and compares what is discovered about it to knowledge of other societies, pre-sent and historic. Archaeologists dig to recover stains in soil from house walls, discarded tools, broken pottery—garbage from long-ago activities. The decay of so much of a past community's material, not to mention the gone-in-a-breath speaking and actions of its people, forces the archaeologist to outline general cultural patterns of behavior persisting over a century or so. Although this isn't quite the same as ethnography of a living community, it broadens cross-cultural comparisons through at least partial knowledge of humans of the past.

Biological anthropologists may spend much of their research time in laboratories, but what they seek is a picture of how the physical features being scrutinized affected human behavior. They may measure and record other physical traits of living people or of skeletons, aiming toward better understanding of how individuals and population groups are affected by living conditions including climate, nutrition, disease, and work stresses. Biological anthropologists may collaborate with medical researchers in large-scale studies, or go alone to a community to observe how its conditions relate to health. Some patiently watch nonhuman primates in their wild homes or work with them in laboratories to discover their manual and cognitive capabilities. Biological anthropologists

> primates: humans, apes, monkeys, prosimians (see Chapter 4)

may work as forensic anthropologists identifying human remains for police or military investigations. Archaeologists and biological anthropologists who work in laboratories are not strictly speaking participant observers, yet their training in general anthropology and holistic perspective permits them to use cross-cultural comparisons to understand the material they study. Those "primatologists" who do observe natural groups of apes, monkeys, or prosimians enable us to see humans against a background of our closest genetic relations, another angle on the age-old question, "What is it, to be human?"

Cross-cultural comparisons are a kind of experiment. Anthropology is a science, which is to say that anthropologists restrict themselves to actually occurring, real-world data and try to recognize what is similar, what different, and what may be the reason for these observations. Because anthropologists will not construct artificial situations, they plan research where many conditions are similar for two societies (or sites of ancient societies) but what are hypothesized to be key factors seem to differ. In other words, anthropologists seek *natural experiments,* already existing societies or sites or biological specimens that have features that test postulated hypotheses. Some anthropologists plan their natural experiment from the beginning, many others find themselves engaged to analyze a community or site or specimen and then look for good comparisons. The basic method remains cross-cultural comparison, as other scientists make comparisons between their data, whether observed in natural settings or in laboratories.

Responding to greatly increased opportunities to travel abroad and to the realization that constitutional guarantees of freedom of religion and expression extend beyond conventional Anglo-American churches and dress, Americans have begun celebrating "multiculturalism." Anthropologists have been amused by incidents of members of multicultural studies committees being surprised to discover that we've been "doing multiculturalism" for more than a century, and doing it in more depth than just school exhibits of dancing, costumes, and special foods. Sometimes anthropologists have come into conflict with well-intentioned teachers who assign for "multicultural understanding," literature by highly educated American professional writers expressing their personal reflections on their ethnic heritage. These works in western literary forms are generally quite different from collaborative efforts between anthropological linguists and word artists from nonwestern societies to present their literatures in publishable form. True multiculturalism jerks a person into what at first seems an alien world. The reward comes not from feeling good about oneself and others, but from feeling more keenly one's own experiences and heritage as well as others.

We expect you will read case studies by anthropologists in conjunction with this textbook. The book is designed to help you make cross-cultural comparisons between the societies you read about and your own. Try some participant-observation anthropology in your everyday life. Watch for patterned behavior and check it against the general statements in the chapters of this book. Use the holistic perspective to catch the physical, environmental, and social influences on the pattern of behavior. We'll bet you discover everyday life is surprisingly rich and complex. We humans are fascinating.

Anthropology in Our Lives

Anything having to do with humans can be studied by anthropology, and anthropological studies have contributed to a great many aspects of our lives.

Are you wearing clothes bought at stores or from catalogs? The sizes that standardize clothing proportions, making it possible to mass produce and merchandise properly fitting clothes, were developed primarily by a few anthropologists hired by the U. S. Air Force early in World War II to enable both clothing and equipment required by the armed forces to adequately fit the fighting men and women. Hundreds of measurements were made on each of thousands of people, the results compiled and analyzed statistically (anthropologists creating some of the necessary statistical methods), and recommendations prepared. Not only clothing—including the pressurized suits later developed for space travel—and ejection seats, but also the dimensions of gun turrets were drawn from anthropologists' studies of real human variation.

Advertising, management, international business, urban planning, and criminology are other fields utilizing anthropologists. Their training in viewing subjects from the holistic perspective gives anthropologists the capability to bridge more limited contributions to produce "the big picture." At the same time, anthropologists' sensitivity to cultural traditions and human variation often alerts agencies to problems. It was an anthropologist who years ago pointed out that Americans are accustomed to standing farther apart when talking than are people in many other societies: Middle Eastern businessmen, for example, will stand so close that American businessmen feel uncomfortable, while the distance that keeps Americans comfortable indicates coldness and discourtesy to a Middle Easterner. Once this was realized, American business travelers could remember to allow Middle Eastern colleagues to stand closer, keeping the atmosphere friendly and productive.

Most people think anthropologists only deal with exotic peoples. This is not entirely mistaken, for anthropologists are more likely to be hired to work with people from nonwestern cultures. This experience has made anthropologists particularly valuable in today's global economy, where multinational corporations, international markets, and foreign investors are critical to our society. Within our nation, the settlement of refugees from Asia, Latin America, the Caribbean, and Eastern Europe calls up anthropologists' knowledge of the cultures of these areas to ease the immigrants' adjustment. Anthropologists' training for understanding different cultures and their technique of participant observation are often critical in developing and testing programs assisting many segments of our society. Anthropologists were among the first to work with the elderly, sharing the days in nursing homes and retirement communities to identify ways to make those days more pleasant, less frustrating. Anthropologists hung out in low-income housing projects and the schools and clinics serving them, working out strategies to effectively deliver the allocated services. Medical anthropologists are part of teams improving hospitals as well as members of disease research programs.

Archaeologists have increasingly become involved with the public. With biological anthropologists, archaeologists have lent their skills to crime investigation: finding clues to past events is the archaeologists' job, and sometimes the past event is a recent murder. More archaeologists work in "culture resource management" (CRM), checking localities for evidence of past settlements before construction may destroy them. If evidence is found and the construction can't be rerouted, the archaeological crews work ahead of the bulldozers, recording the evidence so it won't be forever lost. Settlements thus preserved may be historic or ancient; both are part of our heritage.

Anthropological linguists are active in bilingual programs. Their work has made it possible for hundreds of thousands of children to learn in both their families' native language and the national language such as English, French, or Spanish. Much research has shown that children usually do better in school if they are not forced to give up the language of their home. Hundreds of languages that had not developed written form have been analyzed by anthropological linguists who have advised native speakers creating modern communication systems operating in the peoples' own tongues. Anthropological linguists observe people talking in many situations—in law courts and medical clinics, for example—and pinpoint misunderstandings, suggesting how effective communication may be facilitated. Probably the most familiar contribution of anthropological linguists is description of culturally patterned differences between men's manner of talking and women's. Marriage counselors have used this research to assist couples to better understand and accept each other.

Africa, 1928, early anthropologists in the field with their native servants. This Hollywood B-movie image won't fit contemporary anthropologists.
Photo credit: Milwaukee Public Museum.

A popular image of an anthropologist is the dashing archaeologist slashing his way into the Temple of Doom. That's not quite (not quite!) altogether wrong—we know an archaeologist (a woman) who was nearly blown up by a land mine in Guatemala on her way to record ancient religious paintings deep in a cave, and a biological anthropologist threatened by gangsters who didn't want a certain body found, and I've dealt with bears and suspicious pistol-toting ranchers—but by and large, anthropologists do their best to get on with their work with the least fuss. Spending months in remote villages without electricity and flush toilets is not an adventure, just participant observation. In this book we want to bring you along with us, to show you that anthropology is *not* about stealing exotic treasures, it's about extending our knowledge of our own kind, humans.

RECOMMENDED READINGS

Coming to Light: Contemporary Translations of the Native Literatures of North America, edited by Brian Swann (Vintage paperback, New York: Random House, 1994), is a good introduction to literature from American Indian societies translated in collaboration with anthropologists—multicultural literature as close to indigenous forms as can be managed in English.

Deborah Tannen's *You Just Don't Understand: Women and Men in Conversation* (New York: William Morris, 1990) popularized recognition of cultural patterns differentiating men's and women's speaking.

Edward T. Hall, *The Silent Language* (Garden City: Doubleday, 1959) is the classic presentation of cultural differences in nuances of position and gesture.

Eliot D. Chapple pioneered holistic anthropological analyses of contemporary American behavior, particularly in organizations and therapy procedures; see his *Culture and Biological Man* (Fort Worth: Holt Rinehart Winston, 1970). Although neither Hall nor Chapple has been a central figure in academic anthropology, their researches have deeply influenced business management principles.

2

Knowing What We Know

Anthropologists aim to understand human nature and human societies. None of us can begin anthropological study without first confronting what we think we already know about this most vital and fascinating subject. It's useful to clear the decks of outmoded baggage to avoid confusing popular stereotypes and erroneous information with what anthropologists have actually discovered.

Science

Science is a method of seeking to understand the natural world. Science has two important characteristics: (1) it is based on *observing what happens,* and (2) it puts together observations and possible explanations in a *systematic* way. The most important characteristic is the first, the limitation of the scientist to *what may be actually observed,* and this means observed by *anyone.* A person may need training or instruments to observe some phenomena, such as microscopic organisms or structures, or even a means of observation not yet practical (such as a telescope more powerful than any yet built), but it is essential that the phenomena are judged to be at least potentially observable. Something such as God, which is believed to transcend human capacity to observe, cannot be studied by scientists as scientists, whatever their personal faith. Something that is supposed to be knowable only by means of a magical or spiritual power cannot be considered within science.

The second characteristic of science—the systematic way in which the observations made by scientists are collected together—is the difference between ordinary everyday knowledge and science. What we ordinarily know, we have learned over the course of our lives, beginning even before we were born when we could sense vibrations as we lay curled up in our mothers' wombs. In our families, neighborhoods, playgrounds, schools, through television, films, radio, printed materials, we pick up knowledge. Some of what we are told we know is not true, for example the claim that "PUTZ BEER is the BEST in the WORLD!" Some we may not be sure of, such as the claim that Wonder Bread builds strong bodies twelve ways. (What are the twelve ways?) Some we know is just wishful thinking, but it feels good to think it: my family is the greatest. Some "knowledge" is harmful propaganda, like the Nazi claim that only blond, blue-eyed "Aryans" are fit to rule the world. Whatever the value, or danger, of all these bits of knowledge we pick up during the course of our lives, such ordinary knowledge differs from science in that ordinary knowledge is not carefully *systematized*. In science, we must clearly set out what are the basic assumptions we are taking for granted as true, what are the observations we have made, what question are we asking of our observations, what are we considering relevant to the question and what are we excluding, what explanation are we testing to see whether it seems consistent with new observations. Consciously fitting together observations, questions, and further observations enables the person thinking as a scientist to evaluate how sound our knowledge may be. In contrast, ordinary knowledge piles up as bits from here and there, and people seldom take the time to reflect whether the kid in our grade school class that we saw eat Wonder Bread every day really did develop a strong body. Whether one bit of knowledge contradicts another is not necessarily noticed.

> *Ordinary* knowledge can be full of contradictions we don't notice.
> *Scientific* knowledge is *systematized* to show up inconsistencies.

It is the goal of anthropology, as a science, to *systematize* observations about human behavior in order to discover what knowledge is supported by actual observations of behavior, and what is only supposed to be so.

Obstacles to Anthropology

Because we have survived by learning to live in a human society, we have each accumulated a great deal of knowledge. We have learned what to pay attention to and what we can safely ignore. Unhappily, in our unsystematic, accumulated knowledge there is propaganda ("our athletes are real champs") and misinformation ("people who live in poor housing are all lazy and promiscuous").

We in America have been socialized to pay attention to the color of a person's skin and to ignore the shape of their ears. Using artifacts made of metal and plastic and driven by electricity is a sign of intelligence, we are led to believe. Walking is a sign of backwardness. Eating cooked insects or worms is horrible. Lacking a permanent address in a long-lasting building is animal-like. All these and many more bits are learned by Americans as they are socialized to value American social structure and styles.

When students come into an anthropology class, they must be prepared to reject stereotypes that are not supported by actual observations. One major purpose of an anthropology course is to distinguish between false notions and well-supported knowledge. It is a false notion that the color of a person's skin is a clue to superior, or inferior, brain power or moral standards. It is well-supported knowledge that all living humans are part of a single species in which there are no true races, as biologists would use the term. Distinguishing between false notions and valid knowledge often has significant bearing on questions of human rights, as in the 1954 Supreme Court ruling against segregated educational facilities. Rejecting false notions may cost taxpayers money, or take away wealthy people's enjoyment of privileged treatment. Americans often find it hard to reject stereotypes, such as America's "manifest destiny" to be the leading nation in the world. You must be prepared to lose some treasured notions of superiority if you reflect upon anthropologists' discoveries.

"Primitive" and "Civilized"

Peoples around the world are convinced that their own particular way of life is morally good and worthwhile. They usually hear their language as melodious and see the countryside around their homes as beautiful. Their style of dress is properly modest, their usual foods and cooking good tasting, their homes adequate shelter. Foreign peoples look ugly, their costumes are bizarre, their food is weird and cooking unpalatable, their language sounds like monkey gibberish, and even their landscape may appear forbidding. *Ethnocentrism* is the practice of believing one's own ethnic group is superior, of centering one's good opinion on one's own group. All over the world, and from the beginning of historic times, foreign peoples are described as "primitive" in technology, morals, or both. The word "primitive" has so often been a label applied from ethnocentric prejudice that anthropologists today shudder when they hear it. The term really means "early" in the sense of "ancient" and so cannot be applied to any living or historic people.

Ethnocentrism creates prejudice against other ethnic groups.

The next chapter explains how evolution once was thought to show that educated European men are superior to anyone else on earth. This was done by arranging organisms in a line from smallest one-celled creatures, through multi-celled organisms depending on their body parts to gain what they need, to small nomadic human groups, and finally large populations in cities with elaborate material goods. The conclusion was that the more metal machinery manufactured by a society, the higher it is on the Scale of Nature. What it came down to was really a Scale of Weapon Effectiveness, with nations commanding large long-range gunnery rated superior, on this Scale, to countries lacking the resources to manufacture powerful weapons. Educated European (and Euro-American) men were the generals and admirals in charge of the long-range gunnery. Men of other countries, and all women, must be inferior because they could be gunned down by the "superior" men, the only people permitted advanced education and citizens' rights. The "inferiors" were denied the rights of citizens. The idea of "civilized" was perverted, just as the term "primitive" was misapplied.

Originally, "civilized" meant "being a citizen of a city." Its modern sense refers to the *qualities* admired by good citizens: consideration for others ("being civil") and intelligent obedience to lawful government. These qualities are evident in people in all sorts of societies, whatever their technology. Being "civilized" should mean recognizing and obeying moral standards; acting thoughtfully rather than upon impulse; valuing art, music, and beauty; restraining oneself from violence and injustice. It should not mean possessing a great quantity of manufactured objects—a dog left a fortune by a doting owner is not civilized.

Technology enables humans to adapt to their environments. Where there is iron and coal for making steel, a dense population supported by fertile soils and a climate suitable for crops, and access to markets, a "modern," industrial western society can develop. Where climate does not permit reliable abundant crop production, population remains low, industries can't be built, and technology must utilize what is available. Americans seeing a few Dené Indians in northwestern Canada living in a tent and eating fish, rabbits, and an occasional moose are likely to think the Dené are "primitive," lacking in technology, until the Americans try to live in such a cold, inhospitable land. Dené have an elaborate technology of hunting and fishing devices, clothing and shelter, and food processing, but it is carried out with materials available in their land. Dené are not primitive: Their technology and manner of living are different from Americans' because their land and its resources are different.

Another example of the falseness of supposing some peoples today are primitive can be seen in the case of the Mbuti and Efe "pygmies" of the Congo in central Africa. These people are short, a biological adaptation to moving in dense tropical forest. They are skilled in harvesting wild foods and animals in the forest, and live by trading what they produce from the forest for agricultural products and manufactured goods in Congo markets. In the forest, the Mbuti and Efe wear little clothing and occupy camps of lightly built leaf-covered homes, since the climate is hot and humid. No electric power lines have been built deep into the dense forest, so the people working there don't have television and other appliances, though they do enjoy battery-powered radios. Having no year-round settlements, they don't build big churches or schools. Are the Mbuti and Efe "primitive?" No, they are specialized *rural* producers exploiting the unusual resources of a difficult environment, the dense tropical rain forest, *that even today cannot be successfully farmed on a long-term basis.* Their minimal clothing and airy homes are more healthful than American styles would be in that climate. Were it not for the highly developed skills of the "pygmies" harvesting forest products, no humans could live in that environment.

In a nutshell, all humans living at any one time are equally evolved. That is, all societies have equally long histories of working out means of living in their environments. All humans have some traits that *biologists* call primitive because

> Differences in human societies today represent adaptations to different environments, as well as differing histories.

South India, 1930. Shaduf-type pump drawing water to irrigate fields. Labor is abundant, and there is no machinery requiring expensive fuel or technicians to maintain—this simple machine doesn't break down.

Photo credit: Milwaukee Public Museum.

these genetic traits have been retained from our ancestors of millions of years ago, and *all* humans in the world today have more recently generated traits marking our species *Homo sapiens sapiens*.

Cultural Relativism

You may have heard, "I can't accept anthropologists' ideas because they believe in cultural relativism." What is the problem here?

Rice paddies, Bali, 1930. Highly sophisticated irrigated terrace agriculture sustains a dense population.

Photo credit: Milwaukee Public Museum.

Franz Boas, the most influential leader of American anthropology in the early years of this century, campaigned tirelessly for human rights. At a time when American Indian children were being kidnapped from their homes, kept in boarding schools for years, and beaten if they spoke their own languages, Boas argued that American Indians had the human right to retain their ancestral languages and beliefs. In a country that segregated African Americans, mocked their way of speaking and said they had childlike brains, Boas supported African-American scholars including W. E. B. Du Bois and Zora Neale Hurston,

Angola, Africa, 1930. Making affordable metal tools in a village. The blacksmith is hammering out a knife while his assistant pumps a bellows keeping the coals hot for the forge.
Photo credit: Milwaukee Public Museum.

and tried to raise money for Black colleges. Boas insisted that cultural differences are related to differences in environment as well as historical opportunities and events. The technology and customs of a society are related to both its environment and its contacts, throughout its history, with other societies. "Cultural relativism" is the opposite of ethnocentrism: It acknowledges that other societies are, like our own, reasonable responses to the circumstances they must deal with.

Neither Boas nor other anthropologists would reject moral standards based on human rights and dignity. Indeed,

> *Cultural relativism* recognizes the effects of environmental challenges and historical events on societal values. *It does NOT mean we must accept practices that violate human rights.*

Boas was impressed by the universality of moral standards valuing the life of one's fellows, respect for others in one's group, and the obligation to care for spouse, children, and parents. Unfortunately, morality may not be extended past the boundaries of one's own group—killing in battle may be encouraged even as murder within the group is outlawed.

Anthropology does not attack the values held most deeply in American society. Cross-cultural comparison shows that valuing material possessions and privilege bought with money is rejected by some societies, and so it is by many Americans. Most Americans agree we can and should tolerate diverse opinions and behavior, as long as no one else's life, liberty, or pursuit of happiness is harmed. Cultural relativism says comparing cultures is like comparing apples and oranges: They share the basic characteristics of all fruit, and their differences are due to their evolved adaptation to different climates. Both apples and oranges are good fruit; if you prefer one to the other, it may be because you became accustomed to one as a child.

Confronting False Knowledge

Every chapter in this textbook, and whatever other readings your instructor has assigned, will contain information that contradicts popular "knowledge." Be alert for these contradictions to what is popularly assumed. Keep a notebook log as you read, listing anthropological knowledge that challenges stereotypes. You don't have to accept what we say; you do have to consider it. Write down what surprises you and why it strikes you as new or strange. What statements in

Anthropologists debunk false knowledge, though we seldom get billboard fame.
Photo credit: Milwaukee Public Museum.

your readings or lectures support the new information? What kind of additional information do you require to better understand the statement? Why does the author, or your instructor, accept the information? Scientific argument is *principled*, that is to say, scientists state the premises they accept as valid, the data (observations) they consider to be relevant to the question, and how strongly these data appear to support their conclusion—the likelihood (the probability) that they have sufficient observations to answer a "how" or "why" question. Scientists generally want more data, but time and money are never unlimited and scientists figure that, at a certain point, they have enough instances of a phenomenon occurring that they can see a pattern or critical features. Scientists continually test accepted explanations against new observations. You have a scientist's ability to set out the assumptions (premises) underlying an opinion, check the sources of information, evaluate how much data has been brought to the question, and how well the data support the conclusion. Use the scientific method to test popular notions and to test what you are given in this course.

Discuss your opinions with your instructor, read more from the library. You are a citizen responsible for your own life and those with whom you live. We believe anthropology is a liberating study, showing us the diversity and the common bonds of humans and thereby giving each of us more options and better judgment to choose wisely.

Humans as a Biological Species

To be human is to be a living creature—an organism, sharing the characteristics of earthly life with a multitude of other organisms. Our physical nature demands means to sustain life and limits our capabilities, although our large and complex brains enable us to stretch those limits. Because we are a species of organism on this earth, we must:

> Humans are *unique* animals because of our remarkable brains. We still share many bodily characteristics with other animals. Science discusses our physical nature, making no judgment on spiritual matters.

- breathe oxygen from the air. Clothing and buildings must permit a flow of air. We must guard against drowning in water.

- ingest nutrients. Our teeth and digestive system are adapted to process a particular range of plants and animals—we are *omnivores* (*omni-vore*, "everything-devour"). *Mal*nutrition ("bad" nutrition) can result from too few calories or from failure to ingest a necessary variety of vitamins, minerals, protein, fat and carbohydrate.

- drink liquid. Human settlements must be located reasonably close to a water source.

- sleep. Humans are diurnal (active in daylight), although people can adapt to being active at night provided they have the opportunity to sleep for about eight hours in every twenty-four hour day. Erratic sleeping opportunities or extended lack of sleep sicken humans.

- eliminate body wastes: carbon dioxide, urine, feces. Sanitary disposal of body wastes becomes a serious problem in densely populated areas.

- reproduce. An individual can be healthy although celibate, but if a social group is to last through generations, some men and women must copulate and nurture the offspring. Young humans are so helpless that long-term care of offspring is a necessary part of human reproduction.

- avoid extremes of heat and cold. Being mammals, our metabolism burns calories, or we sweat, to keep our body temperature close to an ideal. Our internal metabolism cannot cope with freezing or fiery heat.

Understanding human behavior requires recognizing how much is its response to these biological demands.

Evolution

Contemporary biological science embeds the concept that variation in populations allows certain organisms to survive and reproduce successfully in an envi-

---

Biological evolution says nothing about the origin of the universe and seldom discusses possible means of originating life. Biological evolution describes changes in populations of organisms through earth history.
Accepting scientific explanations derived from an evolutionary framework has no bearing on religious faith. Science is "atheistic" only because it asks religious leaders to deal with spiritual questions.

---

ronment for which other organisms may not be adapted. Over the course of time, as environments change through climate shifts, erosion or soil deposition, and land rising or sinking, some species of organisms will be stranded without sufficient necessities for life and will move or become extinct; other organisms will move in or a formerly unusual variant will become common. The variations that permit these shifts and changes may come about from gene mutations or from new combinations of genes. These shifts and changes are the reality of organic evolution.

The idea of changes in populations of organisms through time goes back thousands of years and is found in many religious philosophies, including the Judeo-Christian-Islamic tradition in the Book of Genesis. European colonization of portions of other continents challenged European biologists to explain an amazing amount of variation in organisms. Supposing a god sitting in a workshop turning out all these variations seemed to downgrade the god, to make him into an overworked sweatshop laborer. It makes sense, to many religious people, to believe that a *process* was instituted that would lead into a multiplicity of variations through time. If one believes that a spiritual creator instituted this process, one can be called a "theistic evolutionist" (*theos*, "god"); all the major religious denominations in America are comfortable with theistic evolution. Science by definition doesn't concern spiritual questions, so scientists are free to follow whatever faith they wish.

The eighteenth and nineteenth centuries were a period of great efforts, on the part of European thinkers, to systematize knowledge. In eighteenth-century France, the philosopher Diderot supervised the preparation of an illustrated encyclopedia of all the activities of his country, while in Scotland volumes were prepared under the name Encyclopedia Britannica. The Swedish naturalist Carl Linné devised a chart or table with categories like nested boxes, each with one or a few clear attributes by which an organism could be fitted into an appropriate relationship with others more or less similar. "Linnean taxonomy" remains the basis for assessing relationships between organisms (see chart "Classifications of Organisms").

Linnean Classification System illustrated by the human species:

Kingdom: Animalia (all mobile organisms with more than one cell)

Phylum: Chordata (organisms with central nerve cord and gill slits)

Subphylum: Vertebrata (organisms with backbones [including nerve cord])

Class: Mammalia (vertebrates of which the females secrete milk for the young)

Subclass: Eutheria (vertebrates of which the females carry the young in a uterus, attached to a placenta for delivering nourishment to the fetus)

Order: Primates (a number of basically similar placental mammals with flexible grasping hands and feet, relatively large brains)

Suborder: Anthropoidea (monkeys, apes, humans)

(The other major suborder is the Prosimii, comprising lemurs, lorises, and tarsiers)

Superfamily: Hominoidae ("humanlike:" apes and humans)

(The other superfamilies are Ceboidea [American monkeys] and Cercopithecoidea [Old World monkeys])

Family: Hominidae ("*human*," not just "human-like;" notice the second "o" ["-oid-"] has been dropped)

(The other families are Hylobatidae [gibbons, siamangs] and Pongidae [chimpanzee, *Pan*; gorilla, *Gorilla*; orangutan, *Pongo*])

Genus: Homo (humans; there is only one genus of humans today)

Species: Homo sapiens (humans; there is only one species of human today)

Subspecies: Homo sapiens sapiens (humans; only one subspecies today)

Any organism, living or fossil, can be fitted into an appropriate category in the Linnean system by identifying physical characteristics. The system becomes a shorthand summarizing distinguishing characteristics of organisms.

Note that the Linnean system is used worldwide but is by no means the only reasonable or useful system of classifying organisms. Linné highlighted the physical parts used in reproduction in drawing up many of his classes, in part because obviously these are essential if the species is to be perpetuated, in part because he wanted his system to be useful to farmers breeding better crops and livestock. Societies in other areas have their own "ethno-science" systems, in which a flightless bird such as the ostrich might be classed with mammals

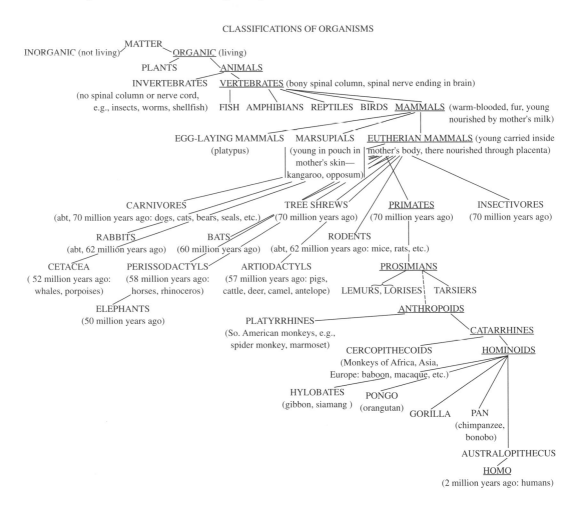

CLASSIFICATIONS OF ORGANISMS

because it runs on the ground and cares for its young, or wild pigs and farm-held pigs might be considered different species because they look and behave recognizably differently.

Why species are similar, orders quite different, or how they got that way did not enter into Linné's system. The introduction of "scientific agriculture" in eighteenth-century Europe, landlords experimenting with breeding as well as cultivation methods, keeping careful notes and comparing them with other gentlemen and farmers, heightened interest in the process of developing new varieties. Production of new breeds under the eyes of literate scientists, coupled with the great number of new species recorded on exploration voyages and often brought home as specimens, stimulated discussion of how variations appear and become populations. An English medical doctor, Erasmus Darwin, at the end of the eighteenth century wrote a very long poem speculating about processes of change in organisms. Half a century later, in 1859, his grandson Charles Darwin published a solidly researched book *On the Origin of Species* (note: *not* about the origin of life, only of new species or breeds). Charles Darwin realized that wild populations could be subject to selection for survival just as farmers select livestock they wish to breed: "Natural" selection would consist of availability of resources necessary for an organism's survival, and the organism's capacity for obtaining and utilizing those resources. Through time, better-adapted organisms would prevail and become the bulk of the population of their species until the environment changed, whereupon a variant better able to cope with the changed environment would in its turn become more common over generations. If no suitable variants existed, the species could go extinct.

"Darwinian evolution" means the principle of natural selection on organisms. It is not all there is to evolutionary biology; genetics is an important field unknown to Darwin, and ecology has become a complementary scientific field of study. In the century and a half since Darwin first published, biology has greatly expanded and refined its knowledge. Within the field, scientists may argue over the relevance or validity of data (are observations thorough? well described? or possibly confused or difficult to figure out?). Arguments spring up over whether interpretations fit the data. Overall, nevertheless, biology accepts in its general framework the Darwinian principle of natural selection and the broader concept that genetic variations in organisms produce, over time, different species more or less well adapted to their environments. A corollary to this concept is that very different species may have derived from one ancient ancestral population, and in theory, all organisms in the Animal or in the Plant Kingdom may be ultimately related.

> Medical research accepts evolutionary biology. Experimentation on nonhuman animals would be useless if our species were not ultimately genetically related to others. Experimentation on bacteria and viruses also uses principles of evolutionary biology to create vaccines and biotechnology.

Definition of Organic Evolution

Organic evolution is defined (by the eminent biologist Ernst Mayr) as "change in the *genetic* properties from generation to generation owing to differential reproduction."

Evolution does not happen to individuals, only to populations. An individual organism is conceived with a set of genes that will not change during the individual's life; there cannot be any change in the genetic properties of individual organisms. It is within the aggregate of individuals making up a population of organisms that evolution can appear as younger generations replace their parents. The population is a *gene pool:* Like a car pool, it is a group of individuals that share among themselves but exclude strangers. Each individual in the pool is in a sense a vehicle for his or her genes, ready to contribute that vehicle at an appropriate time to mates in the pool. Not every individual will actually ride in every other member's vehicle, but the *potential* of doing so exists.

Members of the population pull out sets of genes when they select mates from the group, and the offspring of the mating pair will combine the genes of two parents from the gene pool. "Differential reproduction" refers to differences in the number of surviving offspring produced by pairs of parents; some pairs have many healthy offspring and others may have only one, or their offspring may die young. The genes in the fruitful pair are reproduced many times and will be common in the younger generation's population gene pool. Any unique genes of the unsuccessful mates will disappear when the individual dies. Notice that we're not looking at an all-or-nothing replacement from generation to generation, but a shift in the proportion of the population having certain genes conducive to reproduction and survival in that group's environment.

An example: Erasmus Darwin had seven children, his son Robert had five, and Robert's son Charles had ten children of which three died young. Generation after generation the contribution of Darwin genes to the population continued. Herbert Spencer, whose version of evolution was popular in Charles Darwin's lifetime but is poor science, never married nor had children. *Differential reproduction* is illustrated by Spencer's failure to reproduce, leaving Darwins to dominate the later generations of the population. We can also see how *natural selection* might be at work here, for the Darwins held a strong commitment to marriage and nurturing children while Spencer showed antisocial qualities: He rejected a good woman who loved him because she wasn't beautiful enough for his taste, and he publicly advocated abandoning the poor to die.

Populations, then, are what evolve through differential reproduction of their members. Technically, the population is the *species,* defined by Ernst Mayr as "groups of actually or potentially interbreeding populations which are reproductively isolated from other such groups." The test for whether individual organisms belong in the same species is whether they can successfully breed. If they can't, they belong in separate species.

It looks simple, testing whether organisms can or cannot breed with another from a species. The test obviously can't tell us whether fossils come from one or more species because dead organisms can't breed, hence the many debates over to what species a fossil belonged. Organisms from closely related species may breed but produce nonfertile offspring, the most common example being the sterile mule produced by the mating of horse and donkey. Here, horse and donkey can conceive a viable offspring but that animal cannot reproduce itself, so it never contributes to an ongoing species population. Other animal populations such as herring gulls may look like they could produce fertile offspring across population groupings but will not mate with birds who differ slightly from themselves in markings. Thus the key words "reproductive isolation": populations that either are physically isolated from others or that isolate themselves by behavior. We should also note that some populations are called separate species even though they readily mate and produce fertile offspring—dogs, wolves, and coyotes are an example. In this instance, human concern to keep

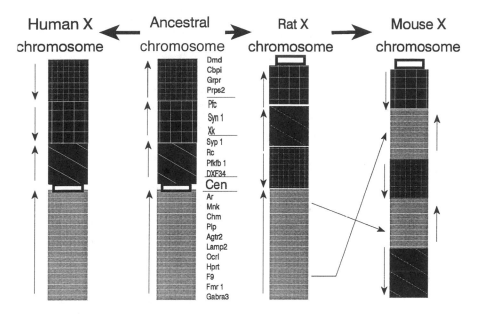

Human X chromosome	Ancestral chromosome	Rat X chromosome	Mouse X chromosome

Diagram of gene arrangements in X chromosomes from three different mammals and the probable ancestral prototype. Second from left, the early ancestral prototype, with the genetic names of several of the known genes listed to the right of the chromosome (by no means all of the thousands of genes on each of these species' X chromosomes are listed on this graph!). Vertical arrows show orientations as compared to the ancestral prototype sequence: genetic sections that have rearranged are shown as filled blocks, and where block patterns are the same, the same set of genes is present. On the left, the human X chromosome; on the right, the X chromosomes of rat and mouse, with the rat positioned closer to the ancestral prototype. The central region of the rat chromosome is a group of genes that have been inverted and moved from the terminal (top) end of the ancestral chromosome. The mouse X chromosome is most divergent from the ancestral prototype, with more inversions and transpositions than appear in the human and rat X chromosomes. Note that all ancestral genes are conserved and nearly all retain the same neighboring genes on these X chromosomes of three species of mammals; only the relative positions of certain segments differ between these species' X chromosomes. These X chromosome arrangements demonstrate Darwin's principle of "descent with modification," the foundation of evolutionary biology.

Credit: James Courtright, Marquette University

domesticated dogs separate from wild canines persuaded Linné to name three species for the canines.

Overall, understanding the species as "groups of actually or potentially interbreeding populations which are reproductively isolated from other such groups" focuses understanding on the ongoing dynamic of life, the generations-long view that helps us comprehend changes appearing as some mates produce many offspring, others none or few.

Genetics

Genes are sections of the strings of DNA within the nucleus of a cell. DNA stands for deoxyribonucleic acid (*Deoxyribo Nucleic Acid*), a compound of a sugar, phosphoric acid, and nitrogenous bases. Proteins accompany the DNA. Different bases may combine with the sugar and phosphate, producing different genes. Ribonucleic acid (RNA) is another compound in the cell nucleus and transmits chemical "messages" from DNA to the rest of the cell. The strings of DNA in cell nuclei are called *chromosomes* ("colored bodies," because they take up dye and so will stand out in a photograph). Each species has its normal number of chromosomes, 46 in humans, and these are paired. The thousands of genes (DNA sequences) carried in cell nuclei on the chromosomes include many that are repeated in other species, even throughout a Linnean Family, Order, or Phylum (implying evolutionary relationships), and a lesser number characteristic only of the particular species. A species thus can be identified by its distinctive *genetic codes.*

> Genes are chemical compounds inside cells in organisms. These chemical compounds affect the growth and health of organisms.

In sexually reproducing organisms, a very large percentage of both animals and plants, each parent contributes only one, not the pair, of each chromosome in his or her cell nuclei. That way, the offspring gets its pairs of chromosomes by putting together the single ones from the parents. Most of the genes on the new chromosome pairs will be duplicates, but there may be slight differences between particular genes (segments of DNA) between the parents' chromosomes. Variant genes are termed *alleles* ("allo-", "other"). When each parent's gene is a duplicate of the other, the new individual is said to be *homozygous* for that gene ("homo-" meaning "the same," "-zygous" from *zygote,* the fertilized egg). When the zygote contains alleles for a gene, i.e., a difference between the gene from one parent and from the other, the new individual is said to be *heterozygous* ("hetero-," "different"). Sometimes it is obvious that the offspring is different in some respect from one of its parents; often the *expression of the allele* is modified in the heterozygous organism by the expression of the other allele or by factors such as nutrition during the organism's growth, so that its heterozygous condition is "masked."

This can have dramatic consequences for humans, as you see in this letter to advice columnist Ann Landers:

> Dear Ann: Is it possible for two parents who have dark hair and blue eyes to have a light-haired, brown-eyed child?
>
> Let me start at the beginning. All my life I have been told that "Jake" is my real father. Jake and my mother divorced when I was about 7 years old. Jake has black hair and blue eyes. My mother has brown hair and blue-green eyes. I have naturally reddish-blond hair and hazel-brown eyes.
>
> My mother remarried very soon after the divorce to a man she has known since high school. "Bob" has red hair and brown eyes.

People who do not realize that Bob is my stepfather comment on how much I am getting to look like him and how lucky I am to have inherited those beautiful red highlights. . . .

Is Jake my real father? . . . Bob and I don't get along very well. If it turned out that he was my real father, I would die.

Ann Landers replied, " I checked with an expert on genetics who said that hazel-brown eyes are the result of pigment that can come from parents with any color eyes. Two light-eyed people can indeed have a hazel-brown-eyed child. It's more than likely that Jake is indeed your father, so relax" (Ann Landers 2/10/92, permission granted by Ann Landers and Creators' Syndicate).

In other words, the child inherited, for eye color allele, one for blue (from her father) and one for blue-green (indicating her mother is herself heterozygous for eye color). The child is heterozygous for eye color, neither parent's allele fully dominates expression, and the child shows the light-brown color indicating partial expression of both parents' alleles. Similarly, her true father's black hair masks his own heterozygosity for this gene, and coupled with the mother's heterozygosity for hair color, the child exhibits hair color superficially like that of the mother's second husband.

Heterozygosity can be advantageous when an organism inherits one allele that causes a dangerous condition but the other parent contributes a normal allele. Examples include hemophilia, the condition in which blood does not clot so that even a scratch can bleed endlessly until the sufferer dies. The allele that results in failure of blood to clot is on the "X" chromosome that also has the gene determining sex. Females inherit two X chromosomes, males inherit one from the mother (who has two, is homozygous for sex) and a differing, "Y" chromosome from the father (who has an X from his mother but a Y from his father, thus can contribute an X making a homozygous, female offspring or a Y making a heterozygous, male offspring). If a male receives from his mother an X chromosome with the hemophilia allele, there is no normal clotting allele on the paired, Y chromosome, and the boy manifests hemophilia. Girls are usually protected by receiving a normal clotting allele from their father, even if the mother carries and may pass on one hemophilia allele. Natural selection removed hemophiliac boys from the human population by their dying young from excessive bleeding. Medical technology today can save these boys, who may grow up and could pass on the hemophilia gene to daughters. With natural selection hindered, the possibility of an increase in the very rare condition of hemophilia in females is increased.

Another example of the advantage of heterozygosity is the case of sickle-cell anemia. The gene for this condition is expressed in a tendency for red blood cells to wither, becoming thin and curved (like sickles) instead of the healthy round full shape. If a person is homozygous for this gene, the person is likely to die from inadequate red blood cells. It happens that young children who are heterozygous for sickle-cell are better able to resist the virulent disease falciparum malaria, caused by a microscopic parasite living in blood. The malaria parasite seems to need nice round red blood cells to flourish. Heterozygous children are more likely to survive infection from the malaria parasite, and unlikely to develop serious sickle-cell anemia. Children who are homozygous for normal red blood cells easily die from falciparum malaria, children who are homozygous for sickle cell die from the anemia. Result? In tropical countries where falciparum malaria is common, a large proportion of the people are heterozygous for sickle cell. With both parents heterozygous, families are at risk for babies dying young from malaria (the babies who inherit a normal red blood cell allele from each heterozygous parent) or children dying from sickle-cell anemia (children inheriting the sickle-cell gene from each heterozygous parent), but some of their children, heterozygous like their parents, have a good chance to survive. There is a close correlation between regions with the falciparum parasite—tropical forest Africa, India, marshy areas of Greece and South Arabian oases—and regions with high proportion of people heterozygous for sickle cell.

Packed in the tiny head of the sperm and in the woman's ovum (egg), genes on their chromosomes are the basic chemical compounds regulating life. An individual's set of genes is the *genotype*. Between the amalgamation of sperm and egg that creates a fertilized zygote, and the visible creature that is born and grows up, many influences affect the expression of the genotype. What you see, in organisms, is their *phenotype* ("pheno-," "show"). The phenotype will, first, show incompletely expressed genes, especially when the genotype is heterozygous (as in the hazel-eyed woman who wrote to Ann Landers) as well as the expression of dominant or homozygous genes; and second, show the effects of nutrition, infections, healthful or unhealthy living conditions. Many Americans can see how poor nutrition, inadequate medical aid, and hard work imposed on children limited the growth of immigrant grandparents or great-grandparents, while a better-fed, easier childhood allowed their American-born offspring to grow taller—to achieve a phenotype that expressed the full genetic potential for stature.

> *Genotype:* the set of genes in an individual's cells.
> *Phenotype:* an individual's appearance.

Population Variability

The variations in populations that can help their survival or generate new species—as environments may change—arise from several causes:

- mutation
- structural changes on the chromosome
- genetic drift
- sexual mating.

Mutation is the only cause of really new genes. Especially in the process of meiosis, during which adults produce gametes—sperm or ovum—with only one of each pair of chromosomes (in order that the anticipated zygote will have the normal pairs), the chemical bases in the compounds we call genes may be altered. Nearly always the alteration is fatal, causing the embryo to die. Occasionally, the mutation is not fatal but does result in deformity in the phenotype. Rarely, the mutation results in a better-adapted organism, which then may survive and reproduce, adding the mutation to the species' gene pool. Mutations may occur in cells in an adult organism, from smoking tobacco, from exposure to radiation, or from taking some drugs. Since mutations do occur, especially during meiosis, in all species and under all conditions, some seem to be spontaneous—the transcription of DNA involves several steps—and we cannot prevent the possibility, only reduce the probability by avoiding exposure to known mutagenic agents.

Structural changes on the chromosome, generally called "crossing-over," is also most likely during meiosis as the chromosome pairs separate and float toward opposite sides of the cell. A segment of the DNA chain that is the chromosome may break off and fail to be reattached, or may attach to another section of the chromosome. Even though the genes themselves have not been altered, the sequence of genes on a chromosome string affects their expression.

Genetic drift refers to changes in gene pools resulting from removing some ancestral alleles from a population. The way this usually happens is that some individuals become separated from a larger parent population. The few form their own, new gene pool. Lacking the whole range of genotypes found in the original population, the new pool has less variability and some characteristics that in the original group would be uncommon may happen to be carried into the budded-off group. Let us suppose a parent population of a million people has only a few hundred blue-eyed individuals, a miniscule percentage. Suppose a boatload of ten adventurers happened to include one blue-eyed and one (heterozygous) hazel-eyed person: the boatload was shipwrecked on a large, lonely island, creating a new gene pool of ten individuals of which one-fifth had the allele for blue eyes. Genetic drift will make this allele more common in the new gene pool than it had been in the ancestral pool. *Note that genetic drift does NOT refer to chromosomes floating through the cell during meiosis;* it refers to *populations.* Genetic drift is particularly interesting to humans because so many of our populations were founded by small groups traveling away from earlier habitats.

Sexual mating is the everyday, ongoing source of variations in populations, individuals with unique genotypes being created constantly through the sexual union of two individuals. Gene pools are populations of variations. The many thousands of genes in humans, most with allele variants, give a practically infinite number of combinations. It is this that enables forensic anthropologists to determine the DNA of cells, say in bloodstains on a knife, and find whether it matches the DNA of a suspected murderer. The possibility of two individuals having exactly the same genotype is so astronomically low that courts generally accept DNA matches as proof of identity (defense lawyers, of course, may argue that the sample was tampered with or the lab tests poorly done).

Summary

Evolutionary biology includes the study of humans. Because we are physically animals, we must breathe oxygen from air, eat, drink, sleep, eliminate body wastes, and avoid extreme temperatures. Survival of our species requires that most adults mate to reproduce. Societies develop customs and technology to promote individual and group survival (generally speaking; war and oppression are practices that promote certain individuals' survival at the expense of others.)

Western science uses a systematic classification scheme, devised by the eighteenth-century Swedish naturalist Carl Linné, to organize knowledge about organisms. Through this system broad similarities between species are evident. In recent years, chemical analysis of cells confirms similarities. Biologists explain these similarities by the principle of evolutionary change through variations in organisms, some variations being more successful at surviving and reproducing in a particular environment than are others. Successful variants will be more numerous in that environment. If the environment changes, other variants may be more successful and may breed (through differential reproduction) into a population distinct enough to be termed a new species. This is Darwin's principle of natural selection.

Populations can be thought of as gene pools, the individuals in the population sharing their genes with one another when they mate and each contributes to the gene set of an offspring. Genes are chemical compounds, segments of long strings of DNA we call chromosomes. Humans have 46 chromosomes (23 pairs) in the nucleus of each cell in the body. An individual's set of genes is their genotype. The effects of these chemical compounds are modified by (1) paired genes, one from each parent, differing somewhat—that is, having alleles of a gene; and (2) poor conditions during the individual's growth. An individual's appearance—phenotype—reflects the interplay of genes and life experiences.

The variability within populations, so essential to adaptation to changing environments, comes basically from gene mutations: changes in the chemical compounds of DNA. Changes in the genotypes also occur during processes of cell division when segments of a DNA string (chromosome) may break apart and reconnect to other segments. Variations within populations are constantly produced by sexual mating, simply by each parent contributing its set of chromosomes into a new cell (zygote) that will combine genes of mother and father. Populations may change over generations if a few individuals leave the original group and start a new breeding group. Not all the genes in the larger, original group will happen to be taken into the new small group, and the new group will not produce the same range of individuals to be seen in the original population. This effect of dividing populations is called genetic drift.

RECOMMENDED READINGS

Desmond, Adrian and James Moore, *Darwin*. (New York: Time Warner Books, 1991).
   A marvelous biography full of drama.

Gould, Stephen Jay. This gifted writer, who is also a leading scientist, has published a series of books (*Ontogeny and Phylogeny*, 1977; *Mismeasure of Man; Time's Arrow;* others) and collected essays (beginning with *Ever Since Darwin*) on geology, biology and evolution. Look for Gould's latest.

Harrison, G. A., J. M. Tanner, D. R. Pilbeam, and P. T. Baker, *Human Biology*. Oxford: Oxford University Press. 1988 (third edition), Technical but authoritative.

If You are Interested in the Question of Religious Issues Related to Science

Godfrey, Laurie R., ed., *Scientists Confront Creationists*. New York: W. W. Norton Co. 1983. Chapters by careful scientists explaining misconceptions raised by some "scientific creationists."

Frye, Roland M., ed., *Is God a Creationist? Religious Arguments Against Creation-Science*. New York: Scribner's. 1984. Essays by theologians from each of the major American denominations.

4

The Primates

Primates. The highest, the Number One animals, the prime—said Linné when he named the animal kingdom Order containing humans. A bit of bias here in favor of ourselves. Within the Order Primates, four groups are recognized and ranked from oldest types ("lower") to most recently evolved ("higher"):

Most recent: Hominids (humans)

- Hominoids (humans and the living species of apes)

- Anthropoids (monkeys, apes)

Earliest types: Prosimians (lemurs, lorises, tarsiers)

Years ago of Appearance
Humans—2 million
Hominids—5 million
Apes, monkeys—35 million
Prosimians—65 million
(Mammals—180 million)
(Vertebrates—500 million)

This list is not a list of replacements through time, but a ranking of *living* species according to the age of the earliest fossils of their type. Prosimians resemble the earliest primates known through fossils, monkeys and apes resemble later fossils, and human fossils appear latest in the layers of rocks analyzed by geologists. Living prosimians as well as a variety of anthropoids may be seen in zoos.

The earliest primates evolved from populations of small mammals from which eventually evolved—besides primates—bats, colugos (also called "flying lemurs," although they are not actually lemurs), and tree shrews, a mouselike insect-eating animal. The ancestral populations had well-developed visual capacity and handlike front paws, which in bats and colugos developed skin between the fingers that acts as wings. Primates and tree shrews never developed this specialization, keeping the hand that in the anthropoid primates including humans is so essential for feeding.

Many of the characteristics of primates seem to be adaptations for living on the branches of trees in tropical forests. (That is, there was *natural selection* for animals that ran up into trees and ate food available on the branches. In the trees, there was less danger and less competition than on the ground.) The ancestral population had claws on the ends of its fingers and toes, as tree shrews still

living in trees: *arboreal* ("arbor": tree); living on the ground: *terrestrial* ("terra": earth)

do, but a mutation in early primates gave us flat nails instead of claws: We primates are better able to grasp and manipulate objects with our fingertips, no claws curving out hindering our grip. (Watch a cat trying to hold a ball, to see how claws interfere with grasping.) Early primates relied on vision, more than smell, to locate food, and because quick-moving insects as well as fruit were a good source of food, there was natural selection for eyes able to gauge distance, muscle structure able to grab small things fast, and brains able to coordinate eye and hand. Primate brains have a greater number of specialized stimulus-response areas than do many other animal brains, and we can

primates' eyes are side-by-side on the front of the head, giving overlapping vision fields (*stereoscopic* vision—like the two speakers in a stereo set giving overlapping sound fields). The overlap allows us to see in depth.

clearly see continuing natural selection for relatively large and also complex brains throughout the history of primates, culminating in the exceptionally large and complex brains of the last type of primate to appear, humans. Eye sockets in primates are completely backed with bone, protecting the brain better than the tubelike sockets of other animals.

Prosimians

Prosimians (Latin for "before [*pro-*] apes [-*simia*]") give us an idea of what primates looked like millions of years ago before monkeys and apes had evolved. All the prosimians live in the tropics, mostly in forests, and the greatest number live on the island of Madagascar where there were no monkeys or apes to compete with them for food and territory—nor humans, who did not colonize Madagascar until about four thousand years ago. This large island well off the east coast of Africa was a refuge for lemurs. Other prosimians—lorises, bush-babies or galagos, and tarsiers—live in Africa, India, and on islands in Indonesia, Sri Lanka and the Philippines. Zoos most commonly show lemurs, lorises and bush-babies. Some lemurs look rather like raccoons, bush-babies look rather like cuddly monkeys, and taken together, the prosimians on exhibit in a large zoo give us a picture of the range of species from which monkeys and apes could evolve.

For the study of human evolution, tarsiers are particularly important although less numerous now than lemurs, lorises, and bush-babies. Tarsiers look like small monkeys with big eyes, they sit erect and use their front paws as hands. These characteristics, plus anatomical details identified by researchers, make it likely that the earliest monkeys and apes were mutations from tarsier-type populations. The few surviving tarsier populations, in Indonesia and the Philippines, move about at night, behavior that protects them from competing directly with later-evolved, more intelligent primates. (In other words, tarsiers occupy an *ecological niche* different from that of simiiform primates: The tarsiers' niche is *nocturnal* [night-living] while other primates are *diurnal* [day-living].)

The concept of *ecological niche* helps explain how new species may develop and other species persist for millions of years. Environments may be thought of like large furnished rooms. A potted plant may occupy a sunny window ledge in the room: That is its *niche* where it has a space, air, and obtains its nutrients. That niche isn't enough for a cat, which needs a food dish, water, and a litter box, using more of the room for its niche. A mouse in the room has its niche in the woodwork, scurrying out at night (nocturnally) to take food. Cat and mouse occupy overlapping niches, a bad situation for the mouse which can itself become food in the cat's niche. Every species of organism is adapted to survive in a particular environment, its ecological niche. When an environment changes or organisms migrate to a new environment, they have an opportunity to move into a new ecological niche. A variant in the species population, perhaps a mutation, may be better adapted to survive and reproduce in that new niche than are most of the original population, and through differential reproduction and continuing natural selection a new species may develop. An example was seen recently in London when a mouse with genetic potential to grow heavy fur slipped into a supermarket cooler. Its unusual fur enabled the animal to survive in the cold. When the mouse mated, it passed on its gene for heavy fur to its offspring, who, like their parent, could take advantage of the abundance of food in the new niche. If city exterminators had not interfered, London would have had a new species of mouse living in market coolers.

> *ecological niche:* particular environment in which a species survives.

Anthropoidea

Both monkey and ape species appear in the fossil record around 35 million years ago, suggesting several lines of evolution from tarsier populations. There is a basic division between monkeys native to South America—the platyrrhines

> The term *Simiiformes* has been suggested in place of Anthropoidea, because there are mostly monkey and ape genera in the suborder. Linné used *Simia* ("apes"), but once it became clear humans belonged in the same suborder, the name Anthropoidea ("manlike") was preferred.

("flat-nosed")—and the monkeys, apes, and humans native to Africa and Eurasia—the catarrhini ("downward-nosed," referring to the opening of the nostrils). Platyrrhines include a variety of monkeys and also marmosets, smaller animals with claws rather than nails, the claws perhaps advantageous to these small primates in the trees, where larger primates are better served by grasping

Pair of lemurs (Africa)
Credit: Wisconsin Regional Primate
Center and Timothy Keith-Lucas

Tarsiers (Asia)
Credit: Wisconsin Regional Primate
Center and David Haring

Marmoset (South America)
Credit: Andrew J. Petto

hands with flat nails. Platyrrhine monkeys have long *prehensile* tails, tails they can wrap around branches to hold on as they swing along through the trees or hang from a branch as they pick fruit. Hands, too, are prehensile. Catarrhines have prehensile hands but either no tails (apes, humans) or tails good only to help balance, unable to grasp (African and Asian monkeys).

prehensile: grasping.

Catarrhine monkeys exhibit various specialized tooth forms that adapt species for particular diets. Apes and humans share a generalized dentition, making for a more omnivorous (*omni-*, "all"; *vore*, "eats": eats vegetables and meats) diet. The monkeys are of two basic types, the cercopithecids including such monkeys as the patas, mona, and diana monkeys, baboons, and rhesus and other macaques, and the leaf-eating colobus monkeys, including Asian langurs, which have segmented stomachs with a compartment where cellulose in leaves is broken down to make it digestible. Baboons and macaques are relatively large monkeys that spend much time on the ground. Monkeys are found throughout Africa and southern Asia to the major islands off it, and formerly in southern Europe, in tropical and sub-tropical forests and grasslands, with one species so far north in Japan that it endures snow in winter. Monkeys illustrate well how spread of organisms into new habitats leads to the evolution of new species as particular variants prove better adapted to one or another habitat. Gray langurs in India have found an ecological niche in Hindu temples, where they prosper because they remind worshippers of the Monkey King in the great epic, the Ramayana.

Apes comprise four living major types, the gibbons and siamang (*Hylobates*), the orangutan (*Pongo*), the gorilla (*Gorilla*), and chimpanzee (*Pan*). From the point of view of biologists, it is better to mark out three types: gibbons and siamangs; orangutans; and gorillas, chimpanzees and humans. That is to say, the similarities between gorillas, chimpanzees, and humans are so considerable that a proper biological classification puts the three together in a sub-family (*Hominidae*). Of the four ape genera, gibbons, siamangs (a large species of gibbon), and orangutans are found in Asia, and gorillas and chimpanzees in Africa, where it seems likely that humans also evolved. Gibbons and siamangs are the smallest apes; they have extremely long arms and prefer to move by swinging themselves along high tree branches, sometimes launching themselves from one branch to another like circus aerialists. Orangutans are approximately human size, and although their very long arms let them hold on and swing from branches, their weight requires them to take care, and they walk along tree limbs or climb using feet as well as hands. Chimpanzees and gorillas have long arms on which they lean as they walk on the ground, putting the backs of their hands down (curving the fingers up toward them), a practice termed "knuckle-walking." These apes do some swinging in trees, especially if they're climbing after fruit, but like the orangutan, their large size makes walking safer than flying grabs at branches. "Pygmy chimpanzees," or bonobos, are more arboreal than the common, larger chimpanzees. Roughly similar body size and the related strong tendency to walk more or less upright would logically class together, in the family *Hominidae* (or *Pongidae*), orangutans, the African apes and humans, in contrast to monkeys and gibbons, all smaller than the *Hominidae* and *Pongidae*.

Pair of patas monkeys (Africa)—smaller female on left, larger male on right show sexual dimorphism in this largely terrestrial primate.
Credit: Wisconsin Regional Primate Center and Anne Zeller

Pair of macaques (Taiwan)—another terrestrial species with marked sexual dimorphism (male on left, female on right).
Credit: Wisconsin Regional Primate Center and Andrew Petto

Gibbon with her child (Asia)—gibbons are more arboreal than the other apes and use their very long arms to swing along tree branches.

Credit: Wisconsin Regional Primate Center and Nancy Staley

Bonobo (Africa)—these "pygmy chimpanzees" are the apes most similar to humans. Male pictured here is playing with a straw. Behind him his companion Bonobo reaches for it.

Credit: Milwaukee County Zoo Photo/M. A. Nepper

Gorilla (Africa)—Female gorilla with her infant in her arm. She is knuckle-walking while carrying the infant. Notice that the infant has not yet developed the heavy bone structure of adult gorillas.

Credit: Milwaukee County Zoo Photo/M. A. Nepper

Chimpanzees, orangutans, and gibbons and siamangs are omnivores, feeding primarily on plants but eating insects and occasionally meat. Gorillas are vegetarians, eating quantities of leaves and bamboo shoots; their food is lower in nutrients than in fiber, necessitating their spending most of every day sitting and munching. Chimpanzee males have been observed ganging together to capture young monkeys or baby antelopes to eat, some of the apes yelling at and driving off the mother animal while others sneak in to seize the young. Chimpanzees have been observed using tools to obtain food, long flexible sticks to poke into termite mounds or holes in trees to pull out edible insects, and setting hard nuts on one stone and pounding with a second stone to crack the shell. Observers have seen chimpanzees hitting at objects with sticks and throwing stones at tourists. All the apes and monkeys communicate by means of dozens of distinct calls and noises, differing somewhat from one group to another even in the same species. Chimpanzees use several gestures identical to human gestures: hugging each other, kissing, extending the hand in friendship. Gorillas, chimpanzees, and orangutans build sleeping nests by weaving branches together and lining the nest with soft leaves. Young apes need to learn how to do this by watching their mothers. Nest-building, food-getting techniques, and vocabularies of calls indicate that apes, like humans, are highly dependent on the culture they learn from their parents.

Reproduction

Primates as a rule have one or two young per pregnancy, relatively long pregnancies, and young already well developed at birth (eyes open, fur well grown). Even though the babies can already see, primate mothers actively care for their young. Among animals in general, species with litters of helpless young requiring close care by the mother (such as dogs and cats) contrast with species in which the young can stand up and follow the mother soon after birth, requiring less maternal attention (such as cattle and deer). Primates don't fit neatly into either category, because particularly among the "higher" primates (monkeys, apes, and humans) mothers carry their babies, devoting more attention to them than is typical when the newborn is fully formed. Primates' *reproductive strategy* is to have few offspring per female but to maximize their survival chances through parental care. Humans show this reproductive strategy especially clearly, with the longest juvenile stage (around fourteen to eighteen years) and extraordinary adult investment in our young—"it takes a village to raise a child" is as true whether it is neighbors who help with children or the many dozens of paid adults who help American children in schools, clinics, sports teams, and agencies.

Humans are born more helpless than other infant primates, and take much longer to reach maturity. It is not that we just grow slowly; in fact, human brains grow *more* than other primates' do, human legs grow faster and become longer than other primates', while human jaws do grow more slowly and never reach the size (relative to body size) of other primates' jaws. Humans' long childhood of relatively slow growth maximizes our bodies' capacities to funnel nutrients into brain growth, and may also help the immune system resist disease by maximizing nutrients available to combat illness. Natural selection would have favored hominid children whose overall growth was slow while their brains grew large. What happens in humans contrasted to other primates is that we have prolonged, overall slow growth until at last in adolescence growth is accelerated. In human females, sexual maturity coincides with the end of growth; in males growth continues for a few more years resulting in larger size for human males than for females. Other primates show steadier as well as relatively faster juvenile growth. In human populations today, well-nourished children not only grow larger but also get into the final adolescent growth spurt, and sexual maturity, at an earlier age than children do in poor communities unable to feed them well. Impoverished diets produce smaller people who may not have completed growth until nearly twenty for women, the early twenties for men. This slower growth gives poor children the ability to maximize brain growth even if they don't achieve their genetic potential for height and weight.

Primate Social Behavior

Surveying the variety of primates, we can see adaptation to many niches in tropical forests, plus expansion into tropical grasslands resulting in more genera of primates, and finally, very recently in earth history, expansion of one genus, humans, into temperate and arctic zones. Social behavior is molded by the environment a species inhabits. Grassland species spend a good deal of time on the ground, trees being few and scattered, and therefore are more visible and more vulnerable to predators (hunting animals) than are primates living in trees. Grassland species therefore tend to stay in larger groups, where some animals will act as lookouts, calling loudly when a predator is sighted and giving the rest of the troop precious time to run for the nearest tree. More strongly arboreal species tend to show less organization. Size of group is related also to density of food, with larger groups where food is abundant (as when fig trees fruit), and smaller or even lone animals where food is scattered. The Asian forests where orangutans live provide only scattered food resources for these large primates, and each adult orang usually seeks its food alone.

Sexual dimorphism refers to species in which males and females differ, especially in size, in more than reproductive organs. Among ground-living primates, adult males generally are larger and heavier than adult females, and have larger canine teeth (fangs). Adult males frequently threaten predators approaching their troop, while females carry the young to a safer spot. Male gorillas, which can be twice the size of females, are famous for their chest-pounding threats that frighten off practically everybody. Male baboons bare their long fangs, several perhaps standing together as a living, snarling fence in front of their mates and offspring. In contrast, highly arboreal primates, including gibbons as well

sexual dimorphism: "di-" (or "bi-"): two, "morph": body, so: two types of bodies, according to sex.

as many monkeys and prosimians, show little or no dimorphism, and males are less likely to threaten while females retreat, although males have been observed trying to distract predators by jumping around on branches as females with young try to get away.

Sexual dimorphism is correlated with social relations in primates in that species that mate monogamously (pair for long periods) do not show dimorphism—males and females, instead, are the same size. Species where one or a few adult males breed with a group of females, a common pattern among primates, tend to have males larger than females. One big male with a "harem" of females breeding exclusively with their protector is rare, observed only with gorillas and one species of baboon. Chimpanzee troops have several adult males and females who mate and share a territory; a young adult female chimpanzee is likely to leave her parents' troop and join another to find mates. "Pygmy chimpanzees" (bonobos) are less sexually dimorphic than the common, larger, terrestial chimpanzees. Males and females spend more time in pairs and make love more frequently than common chimpanzees. The term "make love" seems appropriate because bonobo pairs remain close, embracing, looking at each other's face, leading into copulating face-to-face more often than other apes do. Many monkey troops are primarily groups of females who tolerate males joining them for mating and protection. It is significant that social patterns among primates seem to be less fixed, more adjusted to local circumstances and individuals' personalities than is seen among other mammals.

Monkeys and apes, like humans, often show interest in other adults' babies, and in many species females cooperate in child care, one adult watching a little one while its mother gets some food, one grooming another's infant or playing with juveniles. Infants hang on to their mothers' fur, and ape mothers use their arms to hold their babies. (A mother gorilla in a zoo saw a little human boy fall into the gorillas' enclosure, ran over, picked up the boy and carried him in her arms to the door where zookeepers could retrieve him.) There is, unhappily, an ugly side to primate interest in others' babies: Observers have seen males invade a troop, drive away its principal adult male, seize his offspring from their mothers' arms and kill them, apparently wanting the females to bear only the invaders' children. Jealous females have been observed hurting and even killing another mother's child. Primates' capacity for flexibility in behavior, for figuring out what to do instead of blindly acting from instinct, is a capacity for evil as well as good.

Summary

Primates evolved from an early mammal population that was ancestral also to tree shrews, bats, and "flying lemurs" (not a true lemur). The earliest primates were small, arboreal, omnivorous mammals (lived in trees, ate both plants and meat—in this case, insects). Each paw had five flexible fingers. Catching insects made for natural selection for eyes in the front of the head with overlapping vision fields giving depth perception, for quick movements, and for intelligence to react quickly to prey's erratic motions.

Prosimians, the first major types of primates, spread throughout the tropics, primarily in forests but extending into grasslands where more new species and eventually genera evolved adapting to many ecological niches. The principal types of prosimians are lemurs, surviving on the large island of Madagascar in the Indian Ocean off East Africa; lorises, found over much of Africa and surviving by feeding at night when monkey competitors and hunting animals are mostly sleeping; and tarsiers, also nocturnal (night-living), living in forests of Indonesia and the Philippines. Tarsiers are more like simians than are the lemurs and lorises, and presumably are descended from an ancestral population from which monkeys and apes (and humans) have also descended.

Monkeys and apes (simians) first appeared about 35 million years ago, or some 30 million years after prosimians. With prosimians already throughout the tropics in a great number of ecological niches, simians competed with the older types of primates primarily by using greater intelligence to take over food and safe sleeping places. Thus today's prosimians exist by feeding at night when their competitors aren't active, or in the case of lemurs, because of being on a large island that became separated from Africa before simians evolved and is too far from the coast for simians to swim or float over to on branches. Monkeys and apes include species, such as colobus monkeys, that have evolved specialized feeding capacities enabling them to live in particular ecological niches such as leafy trees without fruit. The majority of simian species, and humans, remain omnivores, eating mostly fruit and green plants but occasionally insects or smaller animals. In addition to the many arboreal monkeys and the gibbons, there are a number of monkey and ape genera that spend most of their waking hours on the ground, although sleeping in trees for protection. Ground-living (terrestrial) primates are bigger than related arboreal species and show more sexual dimorphism (one sex, usually males, larger than the other). Where males are larger than females, they often aggressively confront predators while the females carrying young run to trees for safety. The majority of primates live in groups of females and young, some species with one or a few males as their

DILBERT reprinted by permission of United Feature Syndicate, Inc.

mates, other species tolerating many males in the group. There are also primate species where males and females pair off in lasting monogamous relationships.

Apes evolved about the same time as monkeys but are larger than monkeys and lack tails. Of existing apes, gibbons and the closely related, somewhat larger siamangs live in Asian forests where they swing through the trees and feed hanging by an arm from a branch. Orangutans also live in Asian forests, are larger than gibbons, and walk along wide tree branches, holding on to upper branches for balance. Adult orangs are solitary except when they wish to mate, although the females keep their juveniles with them for years until fully grown. Chimpanzees and gorillas live in Africa, the chimpanzees in groups of adults of both sexes and young, the gorillas in female groups attended by one adult male. (Other males keep a distance until they can attract females or replace a group's male.) The African apes are physically and genetically closer to humans than are the Asian apes, and chimpanzees most resemble humans in behavior.

RECOMMENDED READING

Jolly, Alison, *The Evolution of Primate Behavior,* Second edition. New York: Macmillan, 1985. Jolly surveys prosimians, monkeys, and apes, discussing how human behavior seems to have evolved. Her sensitivity to moral questions raises this book above ordinary reporting.

Development of the Genus Homo.

About five million years ago, a genus appeared in Africa that differed from ancestral ape populations in habitually standing and walking upright. This new genus is termed *Australopithecus*. From it evolved, over about three million years, our own genus *Homo*. *Australopithecus* and *Homo* together are the *hominids*.

Australopithecus looked somewhat like a pygmy chimpanzee, except that its legs were longer, its arms shorter. Because human and chimpanzee genes are almost identical, and the pygmy chimpanzee (bonobo) especially similar to humans in its genes and biochemistry, it is reasonable to suppose that the early *Australopithecus* resembled bonobos in much of their behavior as well. *Australopithecus* fossils from around four million years ago were still well adapted to moving in trees (arboreal) in spite of the pelvis and legs being strongly modified for upright walking and running. Brains of *Australopithecus* were the size of chimpanzee brains, about 400 cubic centimeters (cc.); human brains are three times this size. The major noticeable differences between African apes and humans today is in brain size and habitual posture, but when ancestral populations diverged about five million years ago, the difference was principally in posture.

Assessing the difference between apes and *Australopithecus* around four million years ago, we should keep in mind that it is characteristic of tarsiers, monkeys and apes to hold the body upright. Simians sit upright to eat, using their hands to bring food to their mouths, mother simians often use an arm to hold an infant, and all simians have been observed to occasionally walk or run upright on hind legs at least for a few steps. Natural selection among anthropoid primates for intel-

bipedal: "two [bi-] legs [ped]"
(4-legged: quadrupedal)

Australopithecus afarensis. Male and female reconstructions from skeletons and estimates of similarity to other hominids and apes.

Credit: Courtesy Department of Library Services American Museum of Natural History

ligent use of the hands favored erect posture and a tendency toward occasional bipedal movement, especially when carrying something (food, an infant, or—among African apes—stones or sticks to throw). *Australopithecines* derived from a mutation that shortened the pelvis, lengthened the legs, and modified the angle of insertion of femur (thigh bone) into pelvis (hip joint). As you can observe from people who have been paralyzed from a very young age, without

Famous fossils: News stories dramatizing discoveries help researchers gain funds, but obscure the real day-to-day drudgery of science. "Lucy," nicknamed after a Beatles song, is a set of australopithecine bones making up about two-thirds of a complete skeleton, perhaps from one individual. Found in Ethiopia (East Africa), "Lucy" is the best example of an australopithecine. Dozens of less-complete fossils are also vital to understanding hominid evolution but not so appealing to the public.

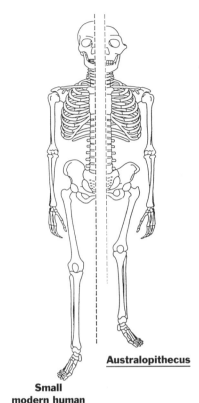

Comparison of skeletons of a small adult human (a Pygmy from Congo), left, and Australopithecus afarensis *of nearly four million years ago, right. Both individuals weighed about 60 pounds; the human was four feet tall and the* Australopithecus *about three and one-half feet tall. Note the human has a larger cranium (brain case), smaller jaw, larger pelvis, and longer leg.* Australopithecus *has relatively longer arms because it has shorter legs; note also the thickness of its femur (upper leg bone, in thigh), actually thicker in midshaft than the human's femur.*

Credit: From "How Big Were Early Hominids?", by Henry McHenry, *Evolutionary Anthropology* 1 (1):15–20 © 1992 Henry McHenry. Reprinted by permission of Wiley-Liss, Inc., a subsidiary of John Wiley & Sons, Inc.

Australopithecus

**Small
modern human
(Pygmy, from Congo)**

exercise the legs never develop the length and musculature usual in humans. The mutation oriented australopithecines to easily walk bipedally, and exercise in this mode developed the longer legs and musculature. Habitually standing upright, australopithecines' heads balanced on top of their spines instead of hanging at an angle from the neck as in four-legged (quadrupedal) animals and apes. We can tell this because in the hominids, the foramen magnum ("large hole") into which the top of the spine is inserted is in the middle of the base of the skull, whereas in other animals it is in the back or, in apes, at the angle between back and base.

A remarkable find at the site of Laetoli in Tanzania (East Africa), near Olduvai Gorge, by archaeologist Mary Leakey revealed footprints of three australopithecines preserved in powdery volcanic ash. The imprints prove that these australopithecines, one about four and one-half feet tall, another a bit shorter than four feet, had feet like ours and walked much as we do, though apparently not able to stride taking long steps.

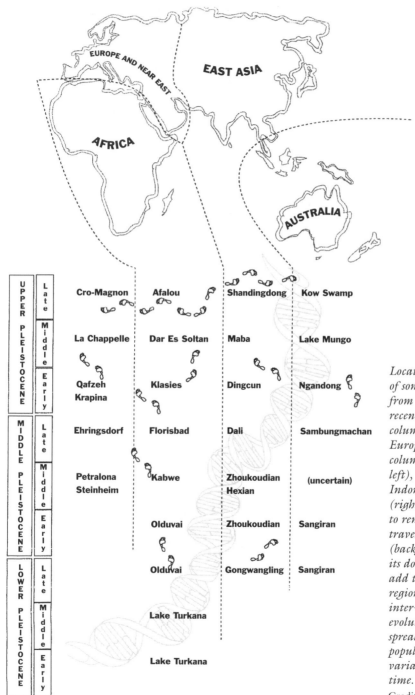

Locations, in time and space, of some Homo *fossils. Time, from older (lower) to more recent (upper) on left; columns place fossils in Europe/Near East (left-hand column), Africa (middle left), Asia (middle right), or Indonesia and Australia (right-hand). Footprints are to remind you that humans traveled, carrying their genes (background figure, DNA in its double-helix structure) to add to populations in other regions. Through occasional inter-regional mating, evolutionary innovations were spread throughout human populations, while regional variations persisted through time.*

Credit: Carl Rank from information by Milford Wolpoff.

By two million years ago, larger hominids had evolved in Africa, alongside a continuation of the smaller, lightly built, "gracile" (slender) australopithecines. Some of the larger species retained many australopithecine features including brains not much increased from ape size—about 450 cc. in the gracile australopithecine and 500 cc. in the "robust" species (since brain size roughly correlates with body size in mammals, the size of gracile and robust australopithecine brains is relatively the same). Robust australopithecines probably ate more plant foods, gracile australopithecines a more omnivorous diet, the size and diet differences between the genera corresponding to the differences between gorillas and chimpanzees. It is likely that there was sexual dimorphism among australopithecines, the general condition in relatively large, terrestrial primates.

In addition to species of australopithecines, by two million years ago there lived in East Africa populations of larger hominids that were more fully bipedal and terrestrial and were evolving larger brains: *Homo*. Fossils of *Homo* found in Olduvai Gorge, dating from just under two million years ago, were labeled *Homo habilis* by Mary Leakey's paleontologist husband Louis Leakey. Their son Richard Leakey later found hominid fossils of about the same age at the site of Koobi Fora near Lake Turkana, Kenya, in East Africa. *Homo habilis* skulls contained brains averaging 650 cc. Stone chopping tools and crude knives have been discovered in East Africa dating to two and a half million years ago. Natural selection for an ecological-behavioral niche where use of tools contributed to a healthy diet may have favored evolution of *Homo* with less climbing and more walking on the ground, plus more attention to the possibilities of tool use and use of the hands manipulating objects. Meanwhile, both gracile and robust species of australopithecines lived throughout Africa for another million years. (And it seems possible, judging from bones at Olduvai, that *Homo habilis* may have hunted australopithecines.) We can't rule out the possibility that australopithecines may have made stone tools, it just seems sensible to suppose that, given the genus and the earliest tools evidenced at around the same period, it was the newly evolved genus, *Homo*, that began the practice of making stone tools.

> On the television show *Friends* the romantic character, Ross, is a museum curator. In a 1996 episode, Ross is about to make out with Rachel when the phone interrupts. Ross: "*Australopithecus* isn't supposed to be in that display. No, no, *Homo habilis* was erect. *Australopithecus* was never fully erect."

Homo Erectus

Popular science stories and textbooks like to show "the evolution of humans" as a single line of fossils, one apparently replacing another. In fact, until about thirty thousand years ago—*very* recent indeed from the long view of millions of years of primate evolution—there were more than one species or subspecies of hominids. The present situation of only one genus, one species, one subspecies of hominid is peculiar and unique.

Because there are not many fossils of *Homo habilis*, and none of one complete individual, no one can state exactly how many species or subspecies of the earliest *Homo* were living around two million years ago. So far, all the earliest hominid fossils, from australopithecines to *Homo habilis*, come from Africa, especially East and South Africa where dry, open country exposes fossil beds. Judging from the variety of australopithecine species and subspecies, known from a greater number of fossils, there were probably several distinct populations of early *Homo* in Africa, competing successfully with australopithecines for food and safe sleeping places. The advantage gained by having brains one and a half times larger than those of australopithecines allowed variations in early *Homo* populations, their survival assisted by figuring out how to make and use tools and very probably by improved group strategies for obtaining resources and protecting the troop. Without cities, markets, or wars to attract or force people to travel long distances, early *Homo* populations would have a greater degree of reproductive isolation than historic humans, thus more speciation (evolution of new subspecies and species).

Around one and a half million years ago, the earliest *Homo* populations had evolved into what is generally termed *Homo erectus*. (Some paleoanthropologists simplify the history by using the term *Homo sapiens* for these as well as

Homo erectus group, male and female. Reconstructions from skeletons and estimates of probable hair and skin color, with butchering activity deduced from stone tools and animal bones found in associated sites.
Credit: Courtesy Department of Library Services American Museum of Natural History

later *Homo,* noting that there are no really substantial differences or breaks in time between the *erectus* and the *sapiens* species into which this earlier species evolved.) The genus *Homo* had, during the Pleistocene, subspecies reflecting its greatly expanded range of Africa and throughout tropical and temperate Asia into what are now islands of Indonesia. *Homo erectus* brains were around 1,000 cc., overlapping the brain size range of humans today. Their bodies and limbs were heavier than modern humans, with correspondingly heavy muscle development and thick, ridged bones to support their weight and withstand the stress of the pull of the muscles. *Homo erectus* skulls were low and long front-to-back, in contrast to modern humans' high rounded skulls. Above the eye sockets and across the back of the skulls are projecting thickenings of the bone where the powerful jaw and neck muscles attached; such a ridge is called a torus, hence *Homo erectus* is noted for large prominent supraorbital ("above eye") and occipital ("back of head") toruses.

Note that the African apes evolved a more robust (gorilla) and a lighter (chimpanzee) pair of genera; *Australopithecus* evolved robust and gracile genera; it took about half a million years for a gracile species of *Homo,* our own species *Homo sapiens,* to evolve after the *Homo erectus* type appeared. This picture suggests that the hominid way of life could be successfully pursued both by powerfully built and by lighter populations. The heavier built would require more food and, like gorillas, might have been adapted to environments with an abundance of foods, especially edible plants; larger bodies mean larger digestive system accommodating more slow-digesting fibrous food. The gracile type gets by with less food although seeking highly nutritious food (which would make it favor meat). The gracile types could colonize environments with too little year-round food to support robust populations, while conversely the large hominids could live on less-nutritious plants where highly nutritious food is scarce. The ranges of gracile and robust populations could overlap, as seems evidenced by fossils of both types of australopithecines in some regions of Africa.

Homo erectus made stone tools, the cruder Oldowan and more specific Acheulian forms (see Chapter 7, Prehistory). They ate meat as well as plants. Whether they used fire to cook is debated: some researchers have claimed evidence of campfires in a site with a fossil robust australopithecine, which of course could have been the victim of *Homo habilis* who walked away with their own bodies intact. Much stronger, and later, evidence comes from Zhoukoudian cave near Beijing, China (Beijing was formerly spelled "Peking"). Half-a-million-year-old layers in the cave contain fire-blackened hearths, charred animal bones, and fossil hominids classified as late *Homo erectus.* The strong evidence for first human use of fire comes at the time when *Homo sapiens* is evolving out of *Homo erectus* populations. Zhoukoudian *erectus* skulls have smaller teeth, no fangs, and larger brains compared to earlier *erectus* skulls from Java and Africa. Could the use of fire for tenderizing food have allowed survival of mutant *Homo* with smaller jaw and teeth, individuals who might not have survived in an era where food had to be chewed raw? And did lighter jaws and teeth facilitate development of human language with its precise pronunciations of thousands of words? These remain questions because the mouth and throat parts critical for human speech are made of soft tissue and weren't preserved; nor do the skulls tell us whether the speech areas inside the soft-tissue brain were increasing. Anatomists have linked the vocal tract with characteristics of bones of the upper body, and this evidence suggests that at least early *Homo erectus* did not have the speech abilities of *Homo sapiens*.

Fire hearths at Zhoukoudian were important for warmth. Beijing is in the northern half of China. Cold winters would have been dangerous for hominids without clothing and fire—or fur. A mutation has occurred that caused hominids to no longer grow fur, but no one knows when this happened, whether australopithecines had chimpanzee-like fur or only the fine hair of humans, whether *Homo erectus* was furry. Nor do we know whether being virtually hairless is advantageous or merely a condition associated on a chromosome with another mutation that conferred a real advantage. Even if *erectus* had fur, fire's warmth would have been appreciated by the people in the cave, listening to the bitter winds roaring out of the steppes far to the north. Fires would have protected the people, too, for humans are the only creatures that can overcome the instinctive fear of fire.

Homo Sapiens

Around 300,000 years ago, *Homo sapiens* was replacing *Homo erectus*. Some of the *sapiens* fossils from this period are not very different from late *erectus*, prompting disagreement among researchers about which label to give to certain specimens. There is also the more important unanswered question: Was natural selection favoring *sapiens*-type hominids so that our type was evolving in parallel among a number of late *erectus* populations? Or did *sapiens* evolve in one area of Africa and migrate to Europe and Asia, either interbreeding with *erectus* in Asia or driving them to extinction? There seems no way of deciding whether the variations in archaic (early) *sapiens* represent interbreeding or parallel evolution. Furthermore, this is *not* an either/or choice, because parallel evolution permits adventuresome individuals to travel and try mating with people in foreign territories. Picture to yourself a late-*erectus* young lady, bored to tears by the nerds in her parents' band, eyeing a strange-talking, odd-looking but lively fellow who strode up to the campfire one day, from who knows where . . .

> The Piltdown Hoax: In 1911, a skull like that of modern humans with an apelike jaw was said to have been found in an English gravel pit. It was claimed these proved that intelligent humans evolved in England. Not until 1953 did a researcher look closely at these "fossils" and see file marks and modern brown stain. Wishful thinking had blinded some English anatomists to a practical joke.

THE FAR SIDE   By GARY LARSON

"Mom! The kids at school say we're a family of Nerdenthals! ... Is that true?"

Another ancient race of hominids: the nerds?

Basic differences between *Homo erectus* and *Homo sapiens* include the full modern capacity for long strides and other gaits in *sapiens;* a higher and rounder skull without the thick torus over the eyes and in the back; larger brain (1100–1500 cc.); smaller teeth in a reduced jaw that retains a thickening along the lower edge of the lower jaw for muscle attachment, thereby making a chin (in other hominids the whole lower jaw is thick and appears rounded); and lighter build, with less robust upper-body musculature correlating with thinner, less ridged bones. Humans' lower body musculature, supporting our bipedal standing, walking, and running, is relatively more powerfully developed.

Homo sapiens looks rather like an adolescent *Homo erectus,* relatively slender, the head with that rounded shape seen in young children (and cute cartoon characters). Mutations affecting rate of growth in humans, affecting the timing during growth of the development of particular bodily features (and of behavior capacities), and affecting achievement of sexual maturity may have resulted in the various differences between earlier and anatomically modern humans.

The markedly larger cranium portion of the modern skull and of the brain beneath it may be due to a genetic delay in sexual maturity, allowing more time for growth of the brain and consequently a larger brain when the individual finally achieves adulthood. The very large brain could better invent tools and cooperative labor to compensate for lesser physical strength, lessening natural selection for powerful upper-body and jaw musculature. Add to the small light childlike jaw a childlike eagerness to try out words, sounds, word games, and puzzles, and *sapiens'* capacity for developing modern culture is clearly enhanced.

Another unusual characteristic of humans is that adult females ovulate every month unless pregnant or nursing a baby. (The baby must suckle every couple of hours to suppress ovulation.) Most female mammals ovulate only during part of the year, and many show outward signs of being ready to conceive (that is, in estrus or "heat"): reddening and swelling of the area around the vulva, becoming somewhat nervous and excitable. Males of these species are aroused by females in estrus but remain uninterested in sex when the females are not in this state. Humans, in contrast, know no season for love or lust. Human females can conceive during several days every month, and since there are no outward signs readily perceived, human males are unaware of when these days occur. Human females' breasts are more enlarged than those of other primates, and human males' penises are larger than those of ape males. With upright posture and no fur, these human secondary sexual characters are prominent. Compared to other primates, human adults are more consistently and easily sexually aroused. The tendency is elaborated in humans' cultures into songs, drama, symbols, played with to enhance the emotional charge of many customs that bond members of the community.

Races of Homo Sapiens in the Pleistocene

There was more genetic diversity in *Homo* during the million years of the Pleistocene, the geologic era ending about 10,000 years ago, than there has been in the succeeding Holocene, the modern geologic era beginning 10,000 years ago. What Americans call "racial" differences between human populations are superficial, contrasted with differences between Pleistocene populations or within contemporary ape genera. Biological races are defined as populations that might evolve into separate species—but this is highly unlikely to happen with widely traveling modern humans. Pleistocene humans were less numerous than historic humans, lacked ships, and were affected by sea-level changes alternately opening and drowning land passages. (During the epochs of massive glaciation, so much water was frozen in the immense continental glaciers that sea level fell as much as 350 feet.) In the late Pleistocene, from about 100,000 to 30,000 years ago, there were at least two human races, *Homo sapiens sapiens* and *Homo sapiens neanderthalensis*. (Whether these are *sub*species of the single species *Homo sapiens,* or two species of the genus *Homo* is debated. Recent examination of a limited DNA sample from the original Neanderthal skeleton, showed sequences different from any known present human or ape genome. Such difference may indicate the Neanderthal population separated half a million years ago from the African *Homo erectus* population ancestral to *Homo sapiens sapiens.* On the other side of the debate there are archaeologists' observations that no *cultural* difference appears until about 40,000 years ago. If Neanderthals were a distinct species, more than a geographically based race, how is it they made tools so similar to those of the early *sapiens sapiens* societies?)

Neanderthalensis was first recognized as a distinct race in 1856, when a fossil was discovered in a cave in a valley near Düsseldorf, Germany. Local people liked to stroll in the pretty valley that a town poet called *das Neander thal,* "the Neander vale," after a Greek river because its ordinary German name didn't fit his poetry. The fossil was clearly human but its bones were exceptionally thick, and it had supraorbital and occipital toruses unlike any modern humans. Charles Darwin's book on evolution and natural selection, published in 1859 while anatomists were still debating over the German fossil, stimulated the hypothesis that the specimen represented an extinct species of humans. Its extraordinary muscular development, reflected by the heavy bones, led biologists to suppose that natural selection came to favor the development of intelligence over the brute strength they saw in the ancient Neanderthal fossil. ("Thal" is spelled "tal" in contemporary German.) The notion that Neanderthal was an ape-man brute was fostered around 1870 by a French anatomist who claimed that a squat ugly Neanderthal was the ancestor of the Prussian Germans fighting his country in the Franco-Prussian War; the French, he insisted, were descended from graceful, large-brained "Cro-Magnon" (*Homo sapiens sapiens*) fossils found in a French valley.

It turned out that both Neanderthals and the modern-type humans found in the French cave had the same large cranial capacity. So far as we can tell, lacking the soft parts of the brain itself, the two populations can have been equally intelligent. Neanderthals resembled *Homo erectus* in powerful musculature and thick, ridged bones to support it. *Homo sapiens sapiens* have lighter skeletons and musculature. The skulls of Neanderthals appear lower and longer, with supraorbital and occipital toruses, in accordance with the heavy neck and jaw muscles. *Homo sapiens sapiens* skulls are high and round because jaw and neck muscles are light, only slightly stressing the skull they pull on. Intelligence is likely to have been comparable because *Homo sapiens sapiens* as well as Neanderthals made the same general types of stone tools for thousands of years.

Neanderthals had broad shoulders, relatively short arms and legs, robust torsos, and short but strong fingers. The most pronounced "classic" specimens of Neanderthal type are found in Europe and Western Asia, living during several stages of late Pleistocene glaciations. Neanderthals' heavy, short-limbed bodies would have been well adapted to a cold climate, conserving body heat by reducing skin surface area relative to body weight. *Homo sapiens sapiens'* more slender build is better adapted to warm climates, the longer limbs and torso

Homo sapiens neanderthalensis, male and female. Reconstructions from skeletons and estimates of probable hair and skin color; the male is shown using a stone blade to whittle a wooden spear, the female is using a stone scraper to cleanse and soften a hide.
Credit: Courtesy Department of Library Services American Museum of Natural History.

providing more skin surface for the cooling evaporation of perspiration. The earliest *Homo sapiens sapiens* appear in Africa. Neanderthals and *Homo sapiens sapiens* thus seem to be what biologists term geographic races, populations adapted to differing environments.

Most researchers date the earliest *Homo sapiens sapiens,* in Africa, to around 120,000 years ago. This happens to be the time of the last interglacial period, when ice sheets melted to the polar ice caps, sea level rose with the influx of meltwater to even higher than today, and subtropical vegetation and animals extended farther north than at present (hippopotamuses in northern Europe!). "Anatomically modern humans" spread into the eastern Mediterranean area, appearing in Israel, along with Neanderthals, in Qafzeh cave at 90,000 years ago.

Glaciations and bordering cold tundra in northern Eurasia recurred beginning around 118,000 years ago. The relatively short interglacial era (126,000–118,000 years ago) followed by the relatively rapid return of colder climate may have discouraged migrations of *Homo sapiens sapiens* northward. Anatomically modern humans don't show up in Western Europe until about 35,000 years ago, coexisting with "classic" Neanderthals, although only for a few thousand years. It is significant that *Homo sapiens sapiens* comes into Western Europe with a warmer climate period (an "interstadial" rather than interglacial, because there was less glacial melting in this "stage" ["-stad-":stage] than had occurred at 126,000 years ago). Cold glacial periods recurred up to 18,000 years ago, but once settled in temperate latitudes, *Homo sapiens sapiens* seems to have figured out how to cope with cold by means of tailored fur clothing, lined tents, or iglu-style homes.

Asia seems to show more continuity between earlier *Homo* and *Homo sapiens sapiens,* or at least not the apparent relatively abrupt replacement of Neanderthals by *sapiens sapiens* that is seen in Western Europe. Another perspective is to note that only in Western Eurasia was there a markedly distinct "classic" Neanderthal, while in Africa and Asia greater diversity of *Homo sapiens* shows shifts rather than abrupt changes in populations. Anthropologist Christy Turner challenges even that perspective in arguing that Southeast Asia may have been the locale of the evolutionary emergence of modern *Homo sapiens sapiens* about 50,000 years ago, a time when sea levels were at their lowest and the new race could have migrated widely, possibly using bamboo boats to cross some straits. Turner notes that people using boats could have traveled faster than people on foot, and might have spread diseases to regions where the archaic humans lacked the Southeast Asians' immunity, in this way reducing resistance to the travelers' colonization. (Turner's model for this scenario is the devastation suffered by American Indian populations from diseases brought by European invaders whose forebears had survived those diseases' first impact in Europe.) The fact that Australia was colonized by humans at least 40,000 years ago fits Turner's hypothesis that boats facilitated the worldwide spread of humans. During the maximum cold period, low sea level let Siberia and Alaska join as one land mass; humans could have migrated from Asia overland into America, perhaps along coastal plains now underneath today's higher sea level.

> Christy Turner reminds us that Southeast Asia is not in a far corner of the globe, as it appears on Mercator projection maps, but central between Europe, Northeast Asia, southern Africa, and Australia (around 6000 air miles from any of these).

Did Neanderthals and archaic *Homo sapiens* in Asia become extinct? As with early *Homo sapiens* and late *Homo erectus,* both observed human behavior and some physical evidence suggest interbreeding. Gene alleles from the existing populations could be carried in the new interbreeding populations without showing in the phenotypes of most heterozygous individuals, occasionally then appearing incompletely expressed in a few members of the mixed population. In regions of Europe where many sites of "classic" Neanderthals occur, one can see some people with relatively low and long heads, well muscled, compactly built—reminiscent of Neanderthals who may have been among their very distant ancestors.

Anatomically Modern Humans

Homo sapiens sapiens' light, slender anatomy is advantageous, compared to archaic *Homo sapiens* and Neanderthals, in two ways: (1) it requires fewer calories to keep it active because less energy is burned carrying its weight, and (2) its greater skin surface, contrasted to thick-bodied, short-limbed Neanderthals, cools more efficiently in hot climates. The second advantage would have been significant in the evolution of anatomically modern humans in Africa and the adjacent Near East, while discouraging their expansion north into the cold lands occupied by heat-conserving Neanderthals. The first advantage—needing fewer calories to keep going because not so many are consumed in carrying one's own weight as one moves—would have been selected for if populations were experiencing food shortages. During the Late Pleistocene, the great glaciations not only closed off vast regions of northern Eurasia and mountain zones but also disrupted rainfall patterns so that portions of Africa and southwestern Asia became arid, reducing vegetation and animals available for human food. Under these conditions, the slender modern humans would burn fewer calories on long treks to find food. If they could invent more efficient tools, they would also burn fewer calories processing food. Thus adverse climate in warmer regions selected for populations efficient in energy consumption and motivated to experiment with technology to substitute for energy-wasting brute muscular strength. When the glaciation trend waned about 50,000 years ago, the fluctuating but overall warming curve favored the northward migration of anatomically modern humans, now with technology considerably more sophisticated than European Neanderthals were using.

Excavations in the Near East (Israel, Lebanon) have uncovered 15,000 years of changes in artifacts (tools and other crafted objects) bridging the Middle Paleolithic (Mousterian) and Upper Paleolithic (Aurignacian) cultures. Anatomically modern human societies there (and probably in adjacent northeastern Africa) were refining techniques of chipping stone to readily produce quantities of thin, sharp blades rather than the thicker Mousterian flakes that used more flint but cut less well. These anatomically modern people created techniques to cut, shape and polish bone and antler to make new kinds of tools. No doubt they also improved woodworking (wood wasn't preserved in the sites), and with their new techniques fashioned beads, pendants, and little figurines—ornaments in stone, shell, and mammoth-tusk ivory never before seen. Aurignacian blades and pointed, smoothed bone tools would have been well suited to sewing clothing and tents. We don't know whether Neanderthals might have had enough body hair to help them keep warm; we do know that anatomically modern humans must have clothing to survive in cold climates. When, around 35,000 years ago, anatomically modern people with their varied and attractive Aurignacian technology expanded north and into Europe, the "classic" Neanderthals of Western Europe learned some of these techniques, producing for several thousand years a much-modified Mousterian incorporating Aurignacian inventions. In the end, by 30,000 years ago, both the Neanderthal race and its Mousterian culture were no longer to be seen.

Meat procurement by hominids shifted from the pattern common in all hunting animals of picking off the infirm, young, and old prey, to a unique human concentration on healthy adult animals. Such animals are prime for meat, and for bone and horn to make artifacts from. They are also most difficult to overcome, alert, fast, and dangerous if cornered. Hunters needed to plan strategy carefully to stalk, ambush or trap, and dispatch prime game. Interestingly, Western European Neanderthals as well as anatomically modern humans harvested prime adult game (i.e., Neanderthals seem to have had the intelligence to hunt as do anatomically modern humans).

Neanderthals' Mousterian tools could have scraped and softened hides but do not seem suited to sewing tailored clothing. Upper Paleolithic, anatomically modern humans required fewer calories for mere survival. They further reduced calorie needs by conserving body heat with sewn clothing and tents, gained prime meat from their hunting skills, invented fishing, no doubt improved harvesting and processing of plant foods, and from the combination of these factors obtained time to manufacture ornaments and organize social events. The general evolutionary trend in primates toward larger, more complex brains coupled with hands capable of fine manipulations culminated in hominid development of *Homo sapiens sapiens:* us.

Summary

Hominids separated from the same ancestral population as chimpanzees and gorillas around five million years ago, in Africa. The earliest hominids were *Australopithecus,* bipedal creatures about four feet tall, with brains not much larger than those of apes. About two million years ago, there evolved a new genus, *Homo,* and stone tools were first made. After a few hundred thousand years, *Homo erectus* was the recognizable hominid, with brains twice the size of apes' brains and the custom of making several distinct types of stone tools (and no doubt tools of perishable materials, too) to process food, hides, and wood. Use of fire, a dramatic innovation dared only by humans, appears 500,000 years ago. Cooking food over fire rendered many foods more edible, especially to young children and the elderly, contributing to population survival and lessening natural selection for powerful jaws. *Homo erectus* spread throughout Asia and into Europe, as well as through Africa.

Homo sapiens evolved about 300,000 years ago. By 120,000 years ago, two subspecies of *Homo sapiens* had developed: in Africa and the adjacent eastern Mediterranean lands, anatomically modern *Homo sapiens sapiens,* and in western Eurasia, the more robust, cold-adapted *Homo sapiens neanderthalensis.* A period of warmer climate around 35,000 years ago encouraged anatomically modern humans, who by then had invented a greater variety of efficient tools and also beads and carved figurines, to expand northward in Eurasia. At first Neanderthals coexisted with anatomically modern immigrants, copying some of their tool types, but by 30,000 years ago the Neanderthal race was submerged in the anatomically modern human populations. For the last 30,000 years, only modern humans have existed, inhabiting every continent and living by means of a variety of tools, shelters, clothing, and social relationships.

RECOMMENDED READING

Walker, Alan. and Pat Shipman. *The Wisdom of the Bones: In Search of Human Origins.* New York: Alfred A. Knopf, 1996. Walker recounts his study of the nearly complete skeleton of a teen-age *Homo erectus* boy, found in Africa. Every question raised about features of the fossil opened up further questions, making Walker's work a detective story involving a variety of experts. The style is lively, as if you were beside the anthropologist as he is alternately puzzled and excited.

6

Variation in Homo Sapiens

Americans are socialized to immediately identify people in "racial" categories: Black, White, Hispanic, Asian, American Indian, Pacific Islander. "Race" identification is made on one or a few traits identifiable even on fully clothed people. "Race" traits are binary (either/or)—"white" skin or not; families speak Spanish or not; "slant" eyes or not; light brown skin but no "African" features. Children of parents from different "races" are classified into the lower-status "race." "Race" powerfully affects everyone who lives in the United States.

> Race: reproductively isolated population evolving into a new species. *Not* applicable to contemporary human populations!

Anthropologists ever since Franz Boas have been explaining to Americans that American "racial" categories are social constructs poorly connected to biological facts. There have been no true (biological) races within the human species for the past 30,000 years, and there are none now. Nevertheless, since 1964, U.S. law has banned discrimination based on alleged "race," U.S. Census forms still ask for "race" identification, supposedly to help discover patterns of persisting discrimination. "Race" in America is what "class" is in Europe or "caste" in India, a means of maintaining social distinctions of wealth and power through automatically assigning people to their forebears' status. Because the United States was officially founded on the principle of inalienable human rights to life, liberty, and the pursuit of happiness, what is actually a system of social *class* categories is masked by calling the categories "races." Slavery was finally made unconstitutional after 1863, but the notion conveniently persisted that certain populations are biologically bred to hard labor, others to management and power.

It would be funny, were the anecdotes not so often cruel, to describe some of the nonsense imposed on Americans in the name of race. An anthropologist

"Bi-racial" twin brothers. The boys' parents have both European and African ancestry: one twin happened to get the African gene allele for more melanin in the skin, the other the European allele for less melanin. Note how closely similar the twins' features are—can you ignore the difference in skin color?
CREDIT: Rex USA/The Sun

with some African ancestry is married to a psychologist with only European ancestry; their daughter is called "Black" in America but when she visits Brazil, she was called "morena" and told she is not "Black" (*preta* in Brazil)—as she says, "When I got on the plane I was Black but when I got off the plane I was no longer Black!" Another American family with one parent of part African descent, the other entirely European, visited two schools in a city attempting to create "racial balance" in its schools. At one school—in a Black neighborhood—the parents were asked to check off "White" on the "race" question on the enrollment form; at the other school—in a White neighborhood—the parents were asked to check off "Black." At each school, the secretary making the request was looking directly at the two attractive brown-skinned children standing beside their parents. Tragic stories can be told, too. Sylvester Long, popularly known as Chief Buffalo Child Long Lance, was a strikingly handsome, athletic, highly intelligent man born in 1890 to a family in North Carolina that appeared Black. Unlike his parents, two brothers, and sister, Sylvester manifested genes from two American Indian great-grandmothers. His father's employer suggested the boy claim he was American Indian and take advantage of free schooling available to Indians. The schooling was much inferior to that available to Whites but better than poor Blacks like the Longs could obtain. Sylvester became a successful journalist and occasional actor but at the price of always concealing his Black ancestry; he never dared visit his family, broke off an engagement rather than risk revealing his secret, and finally, exhausted by a life of evading discrimination, shot himself.

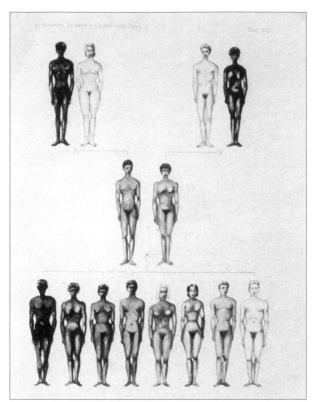

First and second generation offspring of African-European matings. The first generation children are genotypically heterozygous for skin color, hair form, and body shape, phenotypically showing blending (neither parent's alleles dominant). The children of this heterozygous couple may inherit only African alleles, only European alleles, or be heterozygous; alleles are passed on independently so that an individual may inherit one grandparent's skin-color allele and another grandparent's hair-form allele or body-shape alleles. The chart illustrates a hypothetical but possible family. Note that before the U.S. Civil War, if either of the Africans in the parental generation was held in slavery, all *the children and all the grandchildren would probably have been slaves, their free Euro-American grandparents disregarded by American society. Incidentally, this chart exhibits "Mendelian sorting" of alleles: differences between first and second generation offspring of mixed matings, first charted by Darwin's contemporary, the Austrian scientist Johann Gregor Mendel, in his research with pea plants.*

CREDIT: R. Biasutti, *Le Razze e I Popoli della Terra*, 1967, tav. IX

Major Human Populations

Human populations, like other organisms, show the effect of large natural barriers separating breeding groups. Europeans, Northeast Asians, Southeast Asians, Africans, American Indians, Australians, and Polynesians are distinguishable populations. Each of these major populations can be pictured through "typical" individuals *BUT the populations grade into one another across continents and on the edges of natural barriers.*

Conventionally, *Homo sapiens sapiens* has been divided into three or five "races": Caucasoid or European, named from supposedly most typical examples being found in the Caucasus Mountains of Russia; Mongoloid or (East) Asian, named from the Mongols of Central Asia; Negroids, named from their skin color (*negro*, "black"). To these three are sometimes added American Indians (otherwise included among Mongoloids) and Australoids (Australia and New Guinea). Negroids, in Africa, Australoids, and American Indians each have a continent surrounded by water to keep them relatively reproductively isolated.

Caucasoids and Mongoloids share a wide continent with the world's highest mountains, the Himalayas, in the middle separating them. Biologists use the term "geographic races" for such breeding populations associated with territories that are separated by geographic features.

Caucasoids are distinguished by reduced melanin, giving them the lightest skin. Plus, a minority of Caucasoids inherit mutations producing blue eyes and blond or red hair. Mongoloids tend to have slightly more melanin than Caucasoids, black straight hair, brown eyes. A subtype in northern Asia exhibits a fold on the inner side (near the nose) of the eyelids, narrowing the amount of eye exposed. This is an adaptation protecting against cold and bright glaring snow; northern Europeans are likely to have a similar mutation with the fold appearing on the outer sides of the eyelid, away from the nose. Negroids have more melanin than the other populations and tightly curling hair. Both are adaptations to the tropics: Melanin protects against sunburn, and the tight curls allow more air circulation and evaporation than long straight hair does. It is not surprising that Australoids, in the tropics of Australia and New Guinea, also have dark skin, curly hair, and broad noses, although otherwise differing from Africans. American Indians, Southeast Asians, and Pacific Islanders north and east of New Guinea and the adjacent western Pacific, share Mongoloid characteristics minus the cold adaptations. "Pygmies" or "Negritos" are dark, small-stature populations in tropical forests of Africa, Malaysia, and the Philippines. They are not genetically close and represent parallel evolutions selecting for small stature, perhaps because the lack of sunlight in these dense forests reduces the vitamin D needed for calcium metabolism, thereby favoring individuals with light small bones requiring less calcium. Dark-skinned populations tend to have broad noses because both high melanin and broad nasal passages help maintain health in humid tropics, so both have been favored through natural selection. Conversely, high narrow noses protect health in dry or cold climates and therefore have been selected for in deserts and in cold regions. In this case, there is no correlation with skin color.

Causes of differences between major human breeding populations include mutations, chromosome structure changes, and genetic drift, all of these subject to natural selection. Populations differ in the *proportion* of alleles. For example, a greater proportion of Europeans have the A blood antigen allele than have the B allele, while the proportions are reversed for East Asians. No sizable populations are exclusively one or the other, indicating that nowhere has there been strong natural selection for one or the other allele. Besides A and B blood antigens there are additional alleles, making all major human populations *polymorphic* for a blood antigen gene. (Keep in mind that *individuals* within the populations have only one pair of alleles, either two of the same [homozygous] or two different alleles [heterozygous]. Lumping the individuals in a population lets us say the *population* is polymorphic.) For practically all the genes so far tested, major populations are polymorphic, reflecting both a lack of strong natural selection pressure on most human alleles, and interbreeding between populations.

> polymorphic: "many" (poly-) "bodies" (-morph)

Where natural selection has affected the gene make-up of populations, resistance to disease has in several cases been demonstrated. Best known is the higher resistance to falciparum malaria shown by persons heterozygous for

Garifuna ("Black Caribs") on St. Vincent Island are descended from marriages of local Carib and Arawak Indians with Africans brought in as slaves. On the island, gene tests indicate equal ancestry from Indian and African. In 1797, rebel Garifuna were exiled to Honduras where malaria had become endemic. Here, Garifuna with the African allele protecting against malaria survived while those who happened to inherit the Indian allele more often died. Mainland Garifuna test more "African" than their Island cousins due to natural selection by malaria.

the sickle-cell red blood cell (with selection against homozygous normal red-blood-cell and against homozygous sickle-cell persons). Similarly, persons with blood antigen O, mainly found in South American Indian populations, seem less resistant to virus diseases (hence the high mortality when invaded by Europeans). It may be that the low proportion of O in Europeans is the result of natural selection, generations ago, against O-type people in Europe through early death from virus diseases while the more resistant A-types recovered from these diseases and reproduced. Note—again!—that all major human populations are very polymorphic, a situation that maximizes the chance that some of their members will survive the attacks of new diseases.

Genetic Drift

Humans' willingness to seek a better life in a new place has spun off little colonies countless times over thousands of years. Each colony has held a portion of the total gene pool of its parent population. Given a limited portion of the total original gene pool, plus the selective effects of a new environment, colonies would come to differ from the parent population in lacking some genes, in having relatively more of some and fewer of other genes compared to the parent population and, in time, in possessing new genetic material resulting from mutations and chromosome structural changes. Strictly speaking, "genetic drift" refers only to the chance differences due to the colony happening to have some but not all of the parental gene pool. This throw-of-the-dice kind of chance—even if a colony were deliberately made up of people with a certain appearance, their phenotypes would mask recessive or partially expressed genes unseen by the choosers—has been a strong factor in creating the differences seen in human populations.

A clear example of genetic drift has been observed in a remarkable natural experiment, the Pitcairn Islanders. In 1787, the British navy ship H.M.S. *Bounty* sailed to Tahiti in the Pacific. Its commander, Captain Bligh, was ordered to take on board at Tahiti a shipment of breadfruit trees, native to Polynesia, and convey them halfway around the world to the West Indies, where they would be planted to provide cheap food for the slaves working on British sugar plantations. Once in Tahiti, it took several months for hundreds of bread-fruit saplings to be potted and secured on the ship. While a few crewmen were busy at this task, others were free to lounge on the beach and become friends with local people. When the Bounty was ready to resume its months-long sea journey, the Englishmen hated to leave their tropical paradise. A few days out, junior officer Fletcher Christian, a young man who had some brushes with the law already in England, organized a mutiny.[1] Captain Bligh and a few loyal men were put off in a lifeboat, which they rowed over 3000 miles to land. Christian sailed the *Bounty* back to Tahiti, left ashore those Englishmen who wanted to stay, and picked up twelve Tahitian women, six men, and one woman's baby girl. Eight English seamen remained with Christian. To hide from the British navy that would be out to arrest and execute the mutineers, the *Bounty* then sailed to an uninhabited, isolated island called Pitcairn, hundreds of miles from any other island. The mutineers carried everything useful off the ship to the high, cliff-encircled island and scuttled the *Bounty* so it wouldn't betray their hide-out.

Within ten years, all but one of the fifteen men were dead. The Tahitian men were killed when they rebelled against the Englishmen's insistence they should be slaves. Most of the Englishmen were killed in quarrels (home-brew-fueled brawls). Several of the Englishmen had fathered children before they died; other children were fathered by the one surviving man, seaman John Adams. All the children, of course, had Tahitian mothers. Over several generations, the population on Pitcairn grew to make a distinct population, manifesting both British and Tahitian genes. Nine Englishmen and twelve Tahitian women obviously were a very small, random sample of the parent populations of Britain and Tahiti, so many traits seen in the large parent populations are not present on Pitcairn. On the island, there was limited choice of mates and a likelihood that cousins would marry, distributing the founders' genes throughout the colony. The "founder effect" of a high percentage of the colony possessing a gene not at all common in the parent populations was observed in the high incidence of decayed and lost teeth among Pitcairn people. This was due to a gene carried by John Adams, who, according to the log of the *Bounty,* had frequent toothaches and had lost teeth to decay already in his twenties. Adams' allele for poor resistance to tooth decay is maladaptive (not adaptive) but not fatal, allowing people inheriting it to grow up and reproduce. Natural selection would not have *favored* that gene causing pain and loss of chewing power in adults, but because they could still eat and reproduce, neither was there selection *against* the defect. A great many traits distinctive of one or another population are probably due to chance rather than natural selection.

---

[1] *Mutiny on the Bounty* has twice been made into a movie, the first starring Charles Laughton as Bligh, the second starring Marlon Brando, both based on the popular history by Nordhoff and Hall.

Adaptation

Human populations exhibit adaptations to environments both genetically and phenotypically (i.e., individual *plasticity*, the ability to respond to stress or to maximizing factors such as excellent nutrition). Several genetic adaptations have been mentioned already: variations in skin melanin content associated with differences in sunlight ultraviolet radiation; broad or high, narrow noses correlated with humid versus dry or cold air; eyelid fold where cold and bright snow can damage eyes; slender people maximizing skin surface where heat must be dissipated, and stocky people where body heat must be conserved against cold. Phenotypical responses are also well known: tanning when skin is exposed to sunlight, short people maturing late when food for children is generally inadequate, and marked increases in stature and body weight when offspring of a stunted population receive abundant and nutritious food. Research by Franz Boas early in the twentieth century demonstrated that not only height and weight, but also the relative width of the head are affected by childhood nutrition and health conditions: The longer an immigrant family had lived in the United States, the wider its U.S.-born children's heads were compared to the heads of parents reared in poverty abroad. Boas's research persuaded members of Congress that immigrants were not inferior but disadvantaged, and influenced continuation of liberal immigration policies.

One adaptation requiring both genetic and phenotypic contributions is adjustment to living at high altitudes. The higher one goes, the less oxygen pressure in the air, so people at high altitudes are better off with large lungs able to pull in plenty of the low-oxygen air with every breath. Sure enough, there has been natural selection for large lungs/broad chest in Tibet and the Altiplano of the Andes of South America (Peru and Bolivia), where for thousands of years people have lived at 12,000 or more feet above sea level (3500 meters or more). Full aerobic capacity at high altitudes results when the child of a high-altitude population grows up at the high altitude. If the child grows up near sea level and then as an adult moves to the high plateau, he or she will not have the full aerobic capacity of others who never left the plateau. People from lower altitudes who visit the high plateaus experience headaches, loss of appetite, weakness, and rapid heartbeat due to the decreased amount of oxygen in the red blood cells. They feel okay after a day or few days, but tests show that they can't match the workload capacity of those who are native to the high altitude.

Heat and cold tolerance similarly are greatest in individuals who grow up in the conditions of high heat or considerable cold, while persons who move to such conditions can acclimate after a few days without achieving the full tolerance capacity of the natives. There has been some natural selection for tolerance of cold in the Arctic and in places like the Central Desert of Australia, where nights are close to freezing although days are warm. Inuit in the Arctic have the best blood flow to hands and feet of any population tested, a capacity that keeps the hands and feet warm, protecting against frostbite. Central Desert Australian aborigines are accustomed to sleeping near a fire in a light shelter, a custom that allows their skin on the side away from the fire to cool to a degree that sets foreigners to shivering; whether these Australians' ability to sleep without feeling discomfort is due to natural selection for tolerance, to habit since early childhood, or to a combination of genotype and habit has not yet been determined.

Ethnicity and "Race"

Geographic races may be associated with languages and customs, simply because breeding populations are made up of persons living with others among whom they will find mates. Sharing a language and customs is common between mates, and the language and customs are likely to be learned by the couple's children. There is, however, no physical connection between genotype, language, and customs: If not handicapped, a human child learns the language and customs of the home in which it lives, regardless of its biological ancestry. Within any human breeding population (geographical race), the range of intelligence, strength, beauty, kindness, musical talent, sense of humor, willingness to work hard, mathematical ability, and so on, is much wider than any averaged differences between populations.

The U. S. Census categories mix up biological traits ("White," "Black," both referring to allele for skin color), language spoken ("Hispanic"), and geographical races (American Indian, Pacific Islander, Asian). "Hispanics" may be European, or European, African or Asian immigrants to Latin America, or American Indian, or descended from two or more of these geographical races. None of the census categories is an ethnic group, that is, derived from a nation with distinct language and customs; instead, each of the census categories is comprised of many ethnic groups. Television news daily teaches us that some of the most bitter prejudice is raised against people nearly identical to one another. In every war, neighbors turn upon one another. Shakespeare's tragic play *Romeo and Juliet* pictures the fatal enmity between two closely similar wealthy families. Real life gives us many similar stories, for example the prejudice between German Lutherans and Norwegian Lutherans in a small Wisconsin town, where high school sweethearts, he of German and she of Norwegian descent, had to elope to find an unprejudiced minister to marry them, and even the couple's grandchildren were ostracized because they were "tainted" by the other faction's "blood."

Millions of Americans, as millions on other continents, have parents or earlier ancestors from more than one geographical race. The census forms don't give these people a suitable category ("Other" seems strange, when "Mixed" would be the honest answer). In effect, millions of Americans are pushed to deny some of their ancestors when choosing a category to mark. Growing up in America, people are confused over the significance of the few visible signs so emphasized in our society. An African American anthropologist expected to be hailed as a brother when he went to a West African village as participant observer, and he was deeply hurt when the villagers saw him as "American," very different from themselves (he didn't speak their language; he was rich by their standards; his clothes were different . . .). An American Indian anthropologist resents the assumption she will work exclusively with American Indians—"Why shouldn't I go to New Guinea? No one thought Margaret Mead should only study other White Americans!" For both these anthropologists, the extended formal education through which they earned Ph.D. degrees was far more significant for their lives than the allele for skin color they happened to manifest.

Summary

"Race" is a social category in America. No contemporary human populations are reproductively isolated, so none are evolving into new species. Major geographical barriers lessen interbreeding between regions on opposite sides of the barrier, allowing each large region to maintain a breeding population differing in some traits from populations in other regions. (These breeding populations are called geographic races.) What Americans term "races" include three geographic races, American Indian, Asian, and Pacific Islander, but the "Hispanic" designation refers to a language, not a geographic population, and "White" and "Black" refer to alleles for skin color. None of these "race" designations allows for the phenotypic variations due to ancestry from more than one geographic race.

Major human geographic races include Western Eurasian or "Caucasoid," Eastern Asian or "Mongoloid," African or "Negroid," American Indian, and Australoid. Three of these geographic races occupy continents surrounded by ocean, and the first two, occupying the very broad Eurasian continent, are separated by the Himalayan mountain chain.

Some of the distinguishing traits of geographic races represent natural selection for adaptation to their environments: dark skin and broad nose for humid tropics, light skin for northern regions with less sunlight, high narrow noses for dry air, epicanthic (eyelid) fold for cold regions with bright snow. Blood types differ, Type A may represent natural selection for better immunity to virus diseases. Other distinguishing traits may simply be "neutral" mutations that happened to occur and be passed on within a breeding population.

There is no fixed relationship between geographic race and the ability to speak a particular language, perform well in academic subjects, train successfully for sports, or any other cultural practice. Within each geographic race there is a wide range of talents and intelligence. The one human species to which we all belong covers the earth, every region's population exhibiting some minor distinguishing traits grading into adjacent populations.

RECOMMENDED READING

Harrison, G. A., J. M. Tanner, D. R. Pilbeam, P. T. Baker. *Human Biology,* 3d Ed. Oxford: Oxford University Press, 1988.

C·H·A·P·T·E·R

7

Prehistory

PART 1 THE PALEOLITHIC

Nearly all of human existence passed before writing was invented. That means that nearly all we know of humans over two million years comes from information obtained from the kind of evidence a detective uses: objects and the circumstances in which they are found. The very long period before the relatively recent creation of written documents of history is termed "prehistory." Archaeologists discover and identify evidence of human lives in the past, prehistoric and also historic, and interpret the evidence through cross-cultural comparisons with other sites from the past and with historic and contemporary societies.

How the Archaeologist Works

How does the archaeologist know where to dig? Either local people have reported noticing artifacts on the ground—or in some regions, they have seen ruins—or the archaeologist has surveyed an area, walking over sections looking for artifacts. Frequently, in recent years, the survey has been conducted to meet government requirements to protect our cultural her-

> *artifacts* (Latin *artes*, "skills," + *factum*, "made,"): things that have been made, not natural objects

itage: Before road or building construction can destroy historic or prehistoric remains, the area to be affected must be surveyed by a competent archaeologist, and, if significant remains are present, the construction should be rerouted if possible, and if not, the remains recorded and salvaged.

When a site is to be excavated, the first step is to record thoroughly the appearance of the site before it is disturbed. This is done with photographs and a contour map on which visible remains are marked. The contour map is keyed to a geological benchmark or other permanent marker so that the exact location of the excavation can be determined again.

Next, a grid is laid out, using a surveyor's transit or theodolite, with steel pins or wooden stakes put into the ground at regular intervals, usually a meter (approximately one yard) apart. Location of each key point—pin or stake—is marked on the master map prepared for the site. Everything discovered, artifacts and alterations of the natural environment, is measured by triangulation from one of the key points or directly by use of the transit, and the exact find spot recorded on the master map. The information is also recorded in the archaeologist's notebook. Frequently now, a personal computer is brought into the field and data processed through programs created for archaeologists.

Excavation normally is done with small hand tools, often a cut-down and sharpened mason's trowel, so that the excavators are close to the work and can instantly stop when they feel the trowel touching an object or they notice discoloration in the soil. The artifact or soil stain is then delicately uncovered and its exact location and appearance recorded before it is moved. Photographs and scale drawings as well as notebook and map notations are means of recording the information on the discovery and its association.

Sometimes archaeologists use sensing instruments to assist their judgment on the probable location of buried evidence, and they may hire earth-moving machinery to remove the top layer of soil (if it has been churned up by plowing or is the result of recent flood silting). Machinery is only used preliminary to the hand excavation.

Everything uncovered during excavation is placed in bags labeled with the grid location and find-spot measurements. Laboratory workers, on the site or back at the archaeologist's headquarters, clean the artifacts sufficiently to analyze them and write a catalog number indelibly on the artifact. The catalog number identifies the artifact with its excavation record.

As the excavation proceeds, the archaeologist is alert to recognize patterns of association. Discolored soil often is the effect of decayed timber from ancient structures, or of pits dug into the ground to store food or dispose of trash. Bits of ash, charcoal, and reddened soil indicate fires, perhaps cooking hearths. These discolorations frequently can be seen to form patterns outlining houses and activity areas where the ancient people processed food, manufactured tools, or carried out religious rituals. The artifacts associated with these patterned discolorations are clues to the activities carried out.

Most sites have been occupied again and again, or over a long time span. (That's why they may be threatened with destruction, people today finding the locality as suitable for occupation as the people of the past did.) Repeated occupation tends to form layers (*strata* [plural; the singular is *stratum*: both are Latin]). The oldest layer, or stratum, will usually be the lowest down, and the one above it will be later in time. This is called the Law of Superposition, a fancy way of pointing out that the first thing laid down has to be on the bottom, and things laid down next will be on top of the previously placed thing. The most recent stratum will usually be on top. By recording the *stratigraphy,* or sequence of strata (layers), the archaeologist can discover which occupation is most recent, which are older, and in what order of age. Noting the association of artifacts and features such as soil stains and hearths within a stratum, and their separation from strata above or below, the archaeologist can date the artifacts and features within the sequence of occupations at the site. By sending charcoal (from wood) or other organic material within a stratum to a radiocarbon dating laboratory (run by physicists), the archaeologist gets an estimate of age, in years before the present, of when that organic matter lived. Very likely, the occupants of the site who left that particular layer of evidence lived at the same time as the plant burned into charcoal and radiocarbon dated. That *association* with dated organic matter then dates the stratum.

> stratigraphy: layers (of soil or rock)

Excavation is only part of an archaeological project. Weeks in the field are followed by months in the laboratory, closely examining the artifacts for evidence of use and manufacturing process, examining the maps and scale drawings for patterns perhaps not obvious in the field, comparing artifacts and patterns to those of other sites to discover economic and possible political relationships of the ancient people, and collaborating with experts in animal, plant, and climate history to determine the ecology of the site in the past.

How do you become an archaeologist? If you want to earn your living at it, you need at least an M.A. degree in anthropology, preferably a Ph.D., specializing in archaeology. If you're interested but not *that* much, there are avocational archaeologists' groups in every state and province. They collaborate with professional archaeologists, notify members of opportunities to volunteer for digs or for laboratory work, and arrange lectures. Read *Archaeology* magazine (published by the Archaeological Institute of America) for lists of addresses to contact, or inquire from your instructor or your state or province museum. Archaeology is one science that anyone can participate in, from kindergarteners to senior citizens, provided they follow the directions of the professional dig supervisor.

Archaeologists know a few things about humans in the past simply by knowing they were humans, members of our genus, *Homo.* We are certain that they reproduced by the unions of adult males and females, that the adult females nursed the babies, because *Homo* is a mammalian genus. We know that the young required years of adult care because we have bones of ancient young *Homo* that indicate the relatively slow growth rate and prolonged juvenile stage typical of humans. We can be pretty certain that all *Homo* lived in social groups, because nearly all primates are gregarious mammals, and the extended juvenile stage would be dangerous—nonadaptive, likely to be selected against in evolution—unless the juveniles had several adults around to protect them. Our interpretation of prehistoric human life begins with the expectation that evidence derives from social groups.

V. Gordon Childe, an Australian-born British archaeologist who was a leader in archaeological interpretation from the 1920s until his death in 1957, remarked that what the archaeologist finds can be thought of as fossilized social

How the Archaeologist Works

Excavation of a fur traders' post, Canada. In 1768, a Scots immigrant businessman in Montreal, Canada, teamed with a French-Canadian voyageur *(backwoods trader) to build a set of log cabins on the Saskatchewan River in central western Canada, at a camping location popular with Indian travelers. The post was abandoned a few years later, the cabins burned down, and gradually all was covered with soil. Because the trading post was independent of the competing Hudson's Bay Company, it was not well documented. The independent traders lived with Indian wives and children, so the post contained both European and American Indian artifacts of the frontier period.*

A. Aerial view of the site on the high bank of the river. Trees have grown over the site. In the center, left of the truck, trees were cleared and rectangular excavation pits opened along the grid laid out on the site by the archaeologists.

B. The crew: left to right, two local workmen; the archaeologist; her child; Reinhard Lehne, lab technician (in charge of conserving artifacts); David Wilcox, graduate student in archaeology; Colin Watson, crew foreman experienced in archaeological excavation; local workman.

C. Mapping the site before excavation. Archaeologist uses transit to determine fixed points for a contour map. (Site is under trees.)

D. *Preparing the site map on a plane table with alidade: marking in a benchmark in adjacent field.*

E. *Early in the excavation. A rectangular grid, matching one marked on the contour map, has been laid out on the site with small wooden stakes and string. Enough trees have been cleared to permit excavation. Workman in foreground has uncovered roof logs from a burned cabin; note paper bags by his shoulder, to hold artifacts found in his square that day. Archaeologist is working in square on right. Field foreman Watson has measured in a discovered feature and is recording its exact placement in his notebook. A second workman is excavating by scraping with a trowel. Behind Watson and in lower right corner are metal mesh screens for sifting excavated soil, to be sure no small artifacts or fragments of bone or plants are missed.*

F. *Close-up of workman using trowel.*

G. *Roof logs fallen from a burned cabin, left in place* (in situ) *as remainder of grid square is excavated. In middle of side of pit can be seen a pair of horizontal lines, light above and dark below: these are* strata *(layers) resulting from charcoal from burned cabin (dark layer) and (light layer above it) burned clay chinking from between cabin logs. The charred dark stratum marks the surface in 1768. Dark oval in right center at corner of pit is soil filled in a rodent burrow. Note the archaeologists' orientation arrow for the photo, pointing north, and numbers and letter identifying the grid square for the site map.*

H. *Strata in an excavation trench wall: light layer from burned clay chinking has charcoal layers above and below it in this section. This fur trade post proved to be a simple site with only the one occupation, marked by the set of narrow strata from the burning of the cabins. Note the orientation arrow pointing north and identifying label with site code (FhNa-19, in official Canadian site records), date and excavator's initials (top right corner), name of site ("Finlay," after the Montreal merchant who built it), grid number (78R16) and trench face ("west wall"). Plastic sheets protect earlier excavated sections from rain.*

I. *In another section of the site, recorded as FhNa-3 and called "Francois" after Finlay's voyageur partner, a U-shape (center, in trench wall) filled with decomposing loose leaves and stones marks a vandals' pit. Treasure hunters had dug into the site years before. Archaeologists learn to distinguish such modern vandals' pits from older features of a site.*

J. Excavated fireplace from trader's cabin. A puddled clay hearth extends as an apron beyond the base of the rock chimney. One charred log remains on the hearth (above point of orientation arrow), with burned logs from cabin wall and roof in lower right. A small rectangular label and nail to left of hearth log marks where a fragment of a china teacup was recovered. Plastic sheeting on right protects trench wall.

K. Wilcox excavates trash dump showing up as a long narrow oval stained dark against the undisturbed natural light soil. The traders' discarded artifacts and butchered animal bones remain in the square under excavation but have been recorded and removed from the excavated squares above. An excavator's trowel is lying in lower left.

L. A small storage cellar (rounded dark stains in middle of photo) originally under the floor of a trader's cabin. Some light-colored burned chinking from the walls fell into the little cellar (darker stain around lighter circle outlined in charcoal) when the cabin burned. Burned cabin logs are in upper part of excavation square.

M. *Indian artifacts beside traders' cabin: center left, beside identification label, pieces (sherds) of a small Indian-made clay pot, perhaps a child's pot. Above it, upper middle left, a tinkler (used today on dance costumes to create tinkling sound) made by rolling piece of sheet metal into cone. Tinklers were popular trade items. Note identification label includes exact position of artifacts ("1.4´ N[orth of grid square line]" and "1.1´ b[elow] d[atum point marking surface before excavation]").*

N. *After the excavation season: analyzing artifacts in the laboratory. A hand lens is being used to determine structure of artifact found in a trader's trash pit.*

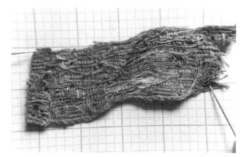

O. *The artifact under examination: a fragment of European linen interwoven with strips of shiny brass to look like gold, used for epaulets on eighteenth-century European military officers' coats. Fur traders gave officers' decorated coats to Indian leaders, hoping to win them as customers. Artifacts such as this fragment, the tinkler and the little clay pot help us picture the human beings who lived their cultures in the sites archaeologists study.*

Credit: Alice Beck Kehoe and Saskatchewan Power Corporation

behavior. Behavior itself is ephemeral, it disappears as it is performed, but it frequently leaves a residue. Objects and changes in the environment result from human actions, so the actions or behavior can be inferred from their residue of objects and environmental changes. The archaeologist works as a historical scientist from the *principle of actualism:* We observe actions and their effects in the present and match what we find preserved from the past to these present-day observations, inferring that the effects preserved from the past proceeded from the same causes as similar effects today. We can't really *prove* that any particular evidence from the past was the result of an action that causes similar effects today, but if we don't *assume* causes and effects today probably operated also in past time, there would be no historical sciences.

> What if we don't accept the principle of actualism? Science-fiction writers have written tales of creatures from other galaxies who manufactured fossils and stone tools and placed them in the situations in which archaeologists find them, supposedly in order to cover up an extraterrestrial cause of life on earth. Adherents of some religions want to believe God or saints worked miracles in the past, so that the past is different from our own experience. You may believe, or speculate, as you please—but you can't consider yourself to be thinking as a scientist unless you limit your explanations of phenomena to actions similar to those observed today. Anything outside the physical universe we can observe is outside science; that's part of the definition of science.

Archaeologists look for artifacts and associated marks in the surroundings. *Artifacts* are anything that has been made, anything that is not a natural item. Usually we think of artifacts as objects, but technically any human alteration of the environment is an artifact of human action. Most of the artifacts studied by archaeologists were made of stone, bone, or pottery clay; everything else made in ancient times is likely to have decayed away. Sometimes unusual circumstances such as peat bogs or extremely dry deserts preserve normally perishable artifacts such as cloth because the extreme conditions kill bacteria and other organisms that consume matter. Artifacts are fossilized human behavior in that they are the material aspect of actions, for example a stone knife is the "fossilized" part of a person's action of cutting something, and a sherd (broken piece) of pottery is the preserved part of the action of cooking, serving, or storing food.

To obtain the maximum information on the ancient action, archaeologists collaborate with other scientists. Chemists analyze traces of food on sherds, or microscopic traces of blood on stone knife blades to identify what animals were butchered. Soil scientists determine the conditions that probably caused the characteristics of the soil in which artifacts were lying and, with geologists, they advise the archaeologist on how natural conditions affected the preservation of artifacts. Archaeologists themselves use high-powered microscopes to see tiny scratches on the working edges of artifacts. Then, they experiment by whittling wood, cutting bone, and so on with similar artifacts the archaeologists themselves have made. They examine the differing kinds of scratches left by the experimental actions, then infer that the ancient evidence comes from such actions. In this way, the functions of artifacts can be inferred from their working edges.

Artifacts simply as objects, unanalyzed, have little scientific value: it is their association with other artifacts and surroundings that give us most of our information. When well-meaning collectors ask archaeologists what they can tell them about the "arrowheads" in a shoebox (or—gasp!—glued into a frame in the shape of an "Indian chief"), the answer has to be, "Not much." An artifact torn from its association is called an "orphan" by archaeologists, an object without the relations that give it meaning. It's critically important not to disturb a find until an experienced professional archaeologist has been able to record the full association (by photographs, mapping, and notes) and examine exactly how the artifact lies in the ground, the color and characteristics of the soil, what else lies near it, and how near. By such painstaking recording of associations, the archaeologist Mary Leakey and her husband Louis Leakey, who was an expert on fossil hominids, were able to identify the *Homo habilis* camp site in Olduvai Gorge, in Tanzania in East Africa. The *pattern of association* of the stone artifacts with broken game animal bones and a crude pile of stones led the Leakeys to infer a small group of humans sitting together, eating meat and marrow from bones, perhaps huddling beside the piled stones to sleep out of the wind blowing from the nearby lake. The association of these artifacts below a layer of volcanic ash permitted the Leakeys to date the camp as older than 1,700,000 years, since the ash had been dated in a physics laboratory to that age. Part of the Leakeys' interpretation came from their knowledge that the early humans were surely gregarious mammals, therefore the accumulation of game animal bones and stone artifacts is likely to represent a social group, not a solitary creature eating alone day after day.

Interpreting Early Hominids

The Beginnings of Culture, or, Will the First Humans Please Stand Up?
Benjamin Franklin thought that toolmaking set humans apart from other animals. The twentieth-century American anthropologist Leslie White said it was humans' use of symbols. When did characteristically human behavior first appear?

Anthropologists have tested these claims of human uniqueness by observing nonhuman primates, other mammals, and birds. Jane Goodall watched chimpanzees fish honey-sweet termites out of their hills by peeling a twig smooth, then poking it into the termites' holes and pulling it out laden with the insects. Particularly significant was Goodall's observation that the chimpanzees prepared the "fishing rod" *before* finding a termite hill: They knew it was the season for the insects to be ripe with a sweet taste; they found a suitable-size twig, broke it off and made it smooth, then went off looking for a termite hill. Clearly, the chimpanzees *thought* about their project and had a mental picture of a termite-fishing rod. Goodall also observed Egyptian vultures use rocks to crack open food, and we have known for centuries that sea otters crack shellfish open by hitting them with rocks. These animals use tools, and, in the case of the chimpanzees fishing for termites, the animals are making the tools, not just picking up a handy rock. Chimpanzees and gorillas regularly make nestlike beds of twigs and leaves in crotches of trees. Little toddler apes have been observed closely watching their mothers making the bed for the night, then trying to imitate them. The little ones' first attempts are too loose and bumpy for sleeping in, but in time the skill is mastered and the young ape no longer sleeps with the mother in her nest bed. A bed is as much an artifact as a termite-fishing rod or a stone knife.

Many animals show some capacity to think. Simply learning to recognize predators involves distinguishing certain characteristics of the dangerous species and generalizing from predators actually sensed to a conceptual category "DANGEROUS BEINGS." Animals that learn quickly and reliably to react defensively when the distinguishing characteristic is sensed are likely to survive and reproduce, those that don't pay attention or can't generalize are likely to die without offspring, so there has been natural selection for intelligence for millions of years. Mammals, with their relatively large brains, are particularly capable of processing variations in information signals.

The most striking of all the observations and experiments to determine the uniqueness of humans involve teaching apes to communicate with humans or to use tools. One experimenter demonstrated stone tool making to a captive orangutan and showed it how the stone knife could cut a string suspending food. The orang had no difficulty chipping a sharp edge on a piece of flint and using it to cut the suspended food down. More controversial have been the various experiments teaching versions of human languages to apes. Most of the experiments have used chimpanzees, although Francine Patterson claims to have taught a gorilla, Koko, hundreds of sign-language words. An early experiment, in the 1930s, was with a baby chimpanzee, Vicki, cared for like a human baby by a young married couple, both psychologists. Vicki played with neighborhood children but couldn't produce English words, even when her "parents" withheld food or drink to force her to ask for them. Another married psychologist couple, Allen and Beatrice Gardner, tried a generation later to improve on the Vicki experiment by teaching their young female chimpanzee, Washoe, to use her hands for sign language. The Gardners realized that chimpanzees' mouth structure will not permit them to make the sounds required for human languages, while chimpanzees' hands are similar enough to humans' to imitate sign language. Washoe seemed to learn several hundred signs in American Sign Language (used by deaf people—what you see when lectures or videos are interpreted for the deaf). She seemed able to create new sequences of signs to communicate her own ideas, for example putting together signs for her trainer, Roger, and for "dirty" to express how she felt about Roger when he refused to take her out to play. Critics of the Gardners' work and similar experiments have charged that eager humans read messages into the chimpanzees' hand motions, that what the apes do is no more than monkey see, monkey do, imitating the trainers without real understanding. To get around that possibility, other experiments have invented symbol languages with plastic shapes and colors standing for words. Their apes have learned to place the plastic symbols in grammatical sentences to obtain food or playtime, and like Washoe these apes have occasionally set up an original communication that makes sense. Is that by chance? It's surprisingly difficult to tell for sure. One complicating aspect of the experiments is that apes are strong and potentially dangerous animals. Once they are out of babyhood, they must be chained or confined in the laboratories, and that is apt to anger them. Ideally, free-living apes like those Jane Goodall observes could be induced to learn sign language, resolving the question of whether the captive apes really have demonstrated capacity for human language, or are forced to go through tricks.

If experiments disagree on apes' capacity for human cultural behavior, how much more challenging it is for archaeologists to pinpoint the time when human culture began! Do we say it was two million years ago when the first of the genus *Homo* appears? Do we insist that the use of human language is the critical factor, and, if so, how can we recognize it in archaeological material? Are the crude stone tools at Olduvai Gorge the sign of Franklin's Man the Toolmaker? What if australopithecines used rocks they picked up, animal bones such as jawbones and teeth, and horns as tools? Raymond Dart, the anthropologist who first identified the genus *Australopithecus*, suggested these hominids had an "osteodontokeratic culture" (*osteo*: bones, *donto*: teeth, *keratic*: horn). What if australopithecines made tools out of wood, like the chimpanzees' termite-fishing rods? What if female australopithecines made carrying slings for their babies? These wooden, hide, or fiber artifacts would all have decayed away.

The Paleolithic: From Earliest Homo to the end of the Ice Age

Background.   Using stones for hammers and breaking them to make sharp edges to use as knives is simple. Stones would be what early hominids would be likely to use for tools. Humans all over the world use stones; some human societies used stone artifacts and not metal even in the historic period. It seems obvious to people familiar with complex industrial technology that there would have been a universal stage of human development in which hominids used stone but had not invented technology for smelting metal. Both Classical Roman and Chinese writers wrote of a Stone Age preceding the discovery of metallurgy. In the eighteenth century, philosophers laid out a logical human progress from an animal-like Stage of Savagery, when stones and wooden clubs were the only weapons; through a Stage of Barbarism, when animals were domesticated and crafts of carpentry and weaving invented; to a Stage of Agriculture, when farming, markets, and metallurgy were developed. The philosophers, Europeans all, claimed their Western European nations, and only they, represented the highest stage of human progress, the Age of Commerce. Europeans, they said, were "polished" by their cultivation of knowledge, the arts, and refined manners, a far cry from distant "rude" tribes, distant in the past or distant in remote lands. Cultural differences were measured from the European upperclass ideal, with non-western nations equated with ancient peoples in the supposed earlier stages of progress. This claimed "universal history" was put together in philosophers' studies from popular travel books, missionaries' stories, import-export merchants' memoirs, and accounts from Classical Greek, Roman, and Arab authors. The philosophers neither conducted thorough examination of historical documents nor fieldwork outside Europe. Their "universal histories" were *models* of what *could* have been, based on the assumption—now rejected by evolutionary biologists and by historians—that organic life progresses from simple to complex unless held back at some stage.

As European overseas colonizations expanded, many citizens were disturbed at the ruthless wars of conquest against nations whose only crime seemed to be occupancy of lands and resources of value to Europe. Political philosophers were ready to answer these qualms. John Locke, an Englishman employed by a prominent aristocrat, was appointed Secretary to the Board of Trade when his patron's party came to power in 1689. Locke wrote two *Treatises on Government* that claimed nonWestern nations were undeveloped because, he asserted, their inhabitants did not hold private title to land as European law provided, and did not buy and sell land for money. Failing to achieve a political economy similar to Europe's, these overseas nations had failed, in his estimation, to fulfill the basis for a moral society and therefore, he argued, it was right and just for Europeans to conquer them and impose European governance. "Stone Age" people lacked European technology and that indicated, in his reasoning, they lacked self-discipline, the work ethic, morality. Locke's intellectual brilliance obscured the ax he was grinding for his employers, the Board of Trade and, later, the proprietors of Carolina colony.

Writers less subtle than Locke blatantly equated American Indians, Africans, and Australians with the Stage of Savagery that they equated with early hominids. One of Benjamin Franklin's contemporaries, in a piece of pure racist propaganda, declared American Indians to be "Men-Brutes of the Forest" who don't farm, "except a very inconsiderable quantity that some of their Women plant. . . . They do not provide for To-Morrow." Franklin knew, from serving on treaty negotiations, that Indians had well-organized governments and considerable investments in agriculture and trade. (The Pilgrims and the Jamestown colonists survived only through the generosity of Indian neighbors providing thousands of bushels of corn from their storehouses.) Franklin respected the Indian nations bordering his colony, but the stereotype of the savage living from day to day like an animal was more popular than the truth. Biased descriptions of nonwestern peoples at the frontier of European conquests were used to picture the philosophers' Stage of Savagery. Nineteenth-century archaeologists naively continued the false equation of geographically distant peoples with humans in remote times, illustrating books on cultural evolution with sketches of American Indians, Africans, Pacific Islanders, and Asians.

> CAUTION! *False knowledge:* the notion that non-western peoples are the same as early stages of human history

Conventional Stages of Human Cultural History.   In 1865, one of Charles Darwin's associates divided human existence into periods he labeled "Paleolithic" ("Ancient Stone"), evidenced by chipped stone artifacts and little else; "Neolithic" ("New Stone"), evidenced in sites with polished stone artifacts assumed to be closer in time to the "polished nations" of modern Europe; "Bronze Age," when copper or bronze artifacts appear, and "Iron Age." Copper is more often found in pure, easily worked nuggets than is iron, so it was assumed that copper was the first metal to be worked and then melted and mixed with tin or arsenic to make the harder alloy, bronze. The Iron Age depended on more difficult technology than the preceding ages, and it continues into the present, with iron and its alloy, steel, still being common artifact material. Now, notice that we have four Ages labeled by principal tool raw material and the philosophers had four Stages of cultural development. Combine these, and they had a Paleolithic Stage of Savagery, a Neolithic Stage of Barbarism, a Bronze Age of Agricultural Civilizations, and an Iron Age of Commerce. The principal artifact material discovered in a site came to be used as an *index* to a presumed general stage of cultural development just as, in geology and paleontology, fossils such as certain dinosaurs identified different time periods in the history of the earth.

Conventions die hard—they are, after all, part of our popular culture—and we still have the nineteenth-century labels "Paleolithic" and "Neolithic," to which was soon added "Mesolithic" to complete our magic number three. The cultural tradition shared by speakers of the Indo-European languages (e.g., English, French, German, Spanish) teaches that it is desirable, or proper, to structure utterances into three parts (beginning, middle, end; noun, verb, object; youth, adulthood, old age; Heaven, earth, and Hell; fairies grant three wishes . . .). The Paleolithic is conventionally subdivided into three stages, Lower, Middle, and Upper. Back in 1877, the American anthropologist Lewis Henry Morgan wrote in his *Ancient Society* of three stages each divided into three, a Lower, Middle, and Upper Stage of Savagery, ditto of Barbarism, and of Civilization. The book was quite popular. Fitting archaeological data into any of these conventional, magical three parts is like the Greek mythical character Procrustes fitting every visitor to his bed by lopping off their feet or head, or stretching them to breaking. Classification is an essential component of scientific analysis, but it must be drawn from working with data, not from a preconceived logical scheme or thoughtless slipping into a very old popular cultural pattern.

The Paleolithic. What we label "Paleolithic" was a long, long period of time, 99% of the span of existence of our genus, *Homo*.

Remember the timelines your sixth-grade teacher drew?

— YEARS AGO —

2,000,000	**1,000,000**	**10,000**
P A L E O L I T H I C		NEOLITHIC

There is no way we can tell what sounds our very ancient ancestors made, what ideas they had of themselves and the world about them, what they may have made out of wood, leather, plant fibers. Did they make nestlike beds for themselves like chimpanzees and gorillas? Did they skin game animals and soften their hides for bedding, like some historic peoples? Was there a "home base" to which they planned to return after scattering to seek food, or did they move around together? Did they regularly share food, as is the norm in the human societies we know directly, or did all but the littlest children find their own food, eating together if there was a large amount of food at one place but not planning to provide for others? We don't even know whether, in the most ancient sites, the association of stone artifacts and game animal bones with butchering marks represents human hunting or only scavenging of kills made by other animals. About all we can say is that for the first million and a half years of the existence of our genus, *Homo,* our ancestors lived in small groups of women with their young children and probably some men, fathers to some of the children. The men no doubt usually assisted the women in protecting the children—natural selection would have favored such groups—and may have shared food with them. Both men and women would have learned to recognize a variety of raw materials suitable for bedding and tools, and would have collected these materials, often carrying them some distance from their source to use in a new camp. It is highly likely that each adult made his or her own stone tools, and used bone splinters and wooden sticks also as tools. If rock overhangs and similar natural shelters were handy, Paleolithic people would have taken advantage of them, but generally, early humans would have had to camp in the open. Possibly they made huts of bark strips, leaves, or thatch—such perishable shelters leave too little trace for archaeological discovery after a million or so years. (They didn't live inside caves. Caves are dark and damp.)

that Australopithecines traveled in small groups is evidenced at Laetoli in Tanzania, where Mary Leakey found footprints of several hominids together.

The greatest invention in the history of humankind was made in the Paleolithic: control of fire. This invention had a tremendous effect upon our development. Controlling fire enabled humans to live in cold regions, opening up huge areas of the globe to human expansion. Controlling fire gave humans an advantage over every other animal, for there *is* one behavior that distinguishes humans from all other creatures, and that is technology to control fire. Around a blazing campfire, humans were safe from hunting animals. Fire enabled people to render a great variety of foods edible, and took the stress of chewing raw foods off our teeth and jaws, allowing survival of the light, easily moved jaw needed for human speech. In time, fire made possible the smelting of metals and the combustion engine. Fire probably had a psychological effect, too: Humans knew they had tamed one of the terrifying forces of nature. As so many myths around the world tell it, for humans to control fire was a godlike act. By half a million years ago, this great leap in human capacity had spread throughout most of the human world; evidence for it has been found from China to England.

Lower Paleolithic. The Lower Paleolithic—in deep deposits of human occupation of places such as Olduvai, the lower strata—covers almost all of the existence of our genus, *Homo.* Beginning somewhat over two million years ago, the Lower Paleolithic's earliest component is called the *Oldowan,* after Olduvai in Africa. Crude stone choppers, sharp-edged flakes, and what Louis Leakey frankly termed bashing stones are the common artifacts. *Homo habilis* and *Homo erectus* bones are associated with these artifacts in some sites. (Australopithecines have not been definitely linked with the manufacture of stone artifacts.) Oldowan artifacts are chipped only enough to get the needed working edge, but as the Leakeys pointed out, the artifacts are not made simply by picking up a rock; the hominids knew and selected the types of rock that can be chipped to a sharp edge. Stone artifacts chipped on both sides are termed *Acheulian,* after sites around the city of St. Acheul in France where the significance of these artifacts was first recognized by the pioneer nineteenth-century archaeologist Jacques Boucher de Perthes. Best known of Acheulian-type artifacts are the hand axes, really butcher knives chipped out of hand-size nodules of flint. Acheulians made smaller knives on stone flakes and used round stones for hammers. A few sites with unusual preservation conditions still contain wooden poles with whittled, fire-hardened points, possibly spears.

A major difference between Oldowan and Acheulian sites is that some Acheulian artifacts are finished into symmetrical, pleasing shapes, whereas Oldowan sites have only artifacts roughly chipped just to get a working edge. It may well be that activities at "Oldowan" sites required only the cruder artifacts, and those at some of the "Acheulian" sites utilized more carefully finished tools; both Oldowan and Acheulian artifacts have been discovered associated with remains of *Homo erectus.* The aesthetic sense, the sense of balance and pattern displayed in many Acheulian artifacts, leads linguist Mary LeCron Foster to suggest that human speech, with its strong patterning and reliance on abstraction, may have evolved in the Lower Paleolithic. Foster notes some very basic similarities shared by a great variety of known languages, tendencies for lip movements to mimic the sense of the word (you open your lips to say "open," close them to say "close"), and postulates such mimicking by makers of Acheulian artifacts creating human speech. In the later Lower Paleolithic, by half a million years ago—when control of fire became generally known—humans began moving into colder regions from our tropical and subtropical homelands. Adapting to a greater variety of habitats spurred both physical and cultural change. After a couple hundred thousand years, early *Homo sapiens* appeared.

Middle Paleolithic.   Around one hundred thousand years ago, the Lower Paleolithic is said to have been succeeded by the Middle Paleolithic. "Middle Paleolithic" is identified by types of artifacts termed *Mousterian,* from the French rock-shelter Le Moustier where they were recognized over a century ago. Mousterian artifacts continue the trend begun in the Acheulian toward more carefully and completely finished tools, with butt ends shaped and smoothed to fit comfortably in the hand or possibly in wooden handles. Tools for different purposes were becoming more standardized. Many were manufactured by a technique

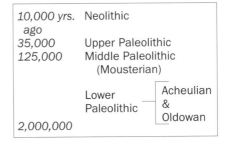

called Levalloisian (again, after a French site) by which flint nodules were chipped into a turtle-shell shape ("tortoise core," *core* referring to the core of the stone nodule), then blows struck skillfully along the edge of the flattened upper surface so that rounded flakes are knocked off. Levalloisian flakes were standardized by the preparation of the nodule, thereby more quickly and efficiently finished into knives or scrapers. (You might say that Middle Paleolithic people invented the basic idea that eventually became mass production and the assembly line.) Considerable continuity in many regions between later Acheulian and succeeding Mousterian stone artifact production and types parallels the basic continuity in evolutionary development between later *Homo erectus* and early *Homo sapiens.*

Where hominid bones have been associated with Mousterian artifacts, the bones are those of Neanderthals (*Homo sapiens neanderthalensis*). Most Mousterian sites have no human bones, and it is highly possible that particularly in Africa, early *Homo sapiens sapiens* made Mousterian artifacts. The most startling innovation in the Middle Paleolithic is the practice of burying deceased humans. At Shanidar Cave (a large chamberlike rock shelter) in northern Iraq, the body of a Neanderthal man killed by falling rock, probably from an earthquake, was covered up with additional rocks. Analysis of soil settled on top of this burial revealed pollen from a variety of flowering plants clustered on the grave, like a bouquet of flowers. Several of the plants are used for medicinal purposes by the Kurdish people of the region today, although whether the Neanderthals knew the curative powers of these herbs cannot be determined. Another intriguing aspect of that burial is that the man had only one arm but was nevertheless respected by his companions. An earlier rockfall at Shanidar had killed a young man recovering from a spear jabbed in his ribs; he, too, was properly buried by the survivors. Other Neanderthals in Western Asia cherished a child so much that when it died, they placed wild goat horns around its grave, like a little fence. Artifacts were sometimes placed in graves with Neanderthals, as if to be used in an afterlife (well, maybe just because they were his or her possessions and "belonged" with the deceased). No other animal buries its dead companions as humans do. Like the use of fire, the custom of burying the dead distinguishes *Homo sapiens*.

Neanderthals lived during one of the most severe phases of Pleistocene glaciation. "Classic" Neanderthals, the extremely robust, muscular, long-headed men and women like the skeleton originally recognized in the Neander Valley in Germany in 1856, occupied the cold lands south of the immense ice sheets. In Africa and the subtropical Near East, anatomically modern *Homo sapiens sapiens* were contemporary with the Neanderthals. By about 45,000 years ago, *Homo sapiens sapiens* seems to have been expanding northward, fanning out from the eastern Mediterranean region. The last Neanderthals in Europe are dated at 32,000 years ago. Already, Upper Paleolithic artifact types

(1) FLINT CORE A nodule of flint from an outcrop has been struck to knock off long narrow blades. Note the white weathered cortex surrounding the core.

(2) ACHEULIAN STONE FLAKE TOOLS
from Barbas, an Acheulian workshop site. The
base of each artifact has been thinned, possibly
to fit into a handle; the bases of the two upper
artifacts are narrowed to a tang.
Upper left, *side-scraper. The working edge is*
along the middle right side edge, used to scrape
hides or plant material.
Lower left, *another side-scraper, the working*
edge again on the middle right side edge.
Upper right, *knife, made on a thin flake. The*
working edge is the long left side edge.
Lower right, *another knife. The working edge*
is the diagonal upper right sloping edge.

(3) MOUSTERIAN (LEFT) AND UPPER PALEOLITHIC STONE FLAKE TOOLS
Left, *a Mousterian "point." The upper side of the tip is wide-angled and used for*
scraping, the left edge is acute-angled and used as a knife. The base has been chipped at
each end to make a tang to fit into a handle.
Middle, *mid-section of a Magdalenian blade, used as a knife. The left side is the working*
edge and the lower edge is slightly blunted.
Right, *Magdalenian end-scraper. The working edge is along the entire top side, used for*
scraping, and the lower end is chipped into a tang to fit into a handle.

were common in Europe and the Near East. Did invading *Homo sapiens sapiens* massacre the Neanderthals and take over their territories? No evidence of mass slaughters has come to light. Archaeologists have noticed that in some pleasant little rock shelters, there are a series of occupation strata, alternating Mousterian and early Upper Paleolithic artifact types. From this, we deduce that the *Homo sapiens sapiens* gradually moved into new territories, alternating at favored campsites with native Neanderthal families and very possibly intermarrying. In time, only *Homo sapiens sapiens* remains are found, associated with Upper Paleolithic artifacts. Mousterian artifacts went out of style, and *Homo sapiens sapiens* genes dominated in the populations. At least one experienced paleoanthropologist, the late Carleton Coon, was sure he could see traces of Neanderthal traits in some European populations today. Coon sagely remarked that in his worldwide travels, he observed little prejudice in *Homo sapiens sapiens* when it comes to mating (*marriage* is another story!) with other *Homo sapiens*. Not likely, said Coon, that humans in the early Upper Paleolithic were that much fussier about whom they slept with than their modern descendants. And nine months later . . .

Upper Paleolithic. Upper Paleolithic artifacts are more regionally distinctive than those of earlier periods. Pioneer archaeologists named the sequence in France after sites where the styles were first identified: Aurignacian (Aurignac Rockshelter), Solutrean (an open site at Solutré), Magdalenian (La Madeleine Rockshelter). Then excavation at other sites revealed another style, the Gravettian, approximately contemporary with late Aurignacian and Solutrean but more common in central Europe; and a Chatelperronian style that parallels the Aurignacian but shows more continuity with French Mousterian. In parts of Asia, stone tools don't show much refinement over time, probably because people were using tropical woods and bamboo rather than stone for cutting implements. Elsewhere in Eurasia and in Africa are a proliferation of style distinctions, and by the late Pleistocene, Upper Paleolithic people had explored all the way into America, producing more new styles on this continent.

Art blossomed in the Upper Paleolithic. In parts of Europe, people went deep into caves, lighting their way with torches or stone lamps with a wick floating in grease, to paint realistic animals on the cave walls. Why they would paint where few could ever enjoy the art is a puzzle: we assume the painting was part of religious rituals, held in dark, silent caves to heighten the aura of spirituality. Did they paint also on easily visible rockshelter walls? A few traces of paint protected by accumulations of soil testify to the likelihood that time and storms destroyed Paleolithic painting except that deep in caves. Upper Paleolithic artists sculpted, too. Spear throwers with carved animals or animal heads on the end, little female figurines, and carved phalluses were common, although books generally neglect mentioning the phalluses. Figurines and phalluses might have been love charms, or tokens of feminine and masculine roles. Upper Paleolithic artists occasionally modeled animals in clay. They carved mammoth-tusk ivory into figurines and beads, and pierced shells and animal teeth to string on neck-laces or sew as ornaments on clothing. They may have embroidered clothing with the fine bone needles invented in this period.

Not only were Upper Paleolithic peoples anatomically modern, their ways of life were also not so far different from those of historic peoples. Size of so-cial groups seems more varied in the Upper Paleolithic than earlier, some sites apparently holding several families each with its own cooking fire, others ev-idencing occasional larger gatherings. Housing for Upper Paleolithic peo-ples included tents, with linings to cut the draft, and huts. On the Russian Plain where mammoths were often encountered, the huge bones of these ex-tinct elephants were collected and used as frames for huts. Archaeologists have excavated some structures built of mammoth bones interlocked to make a herringbone-patterned wall. In France, rectangular pavements of cobblestones late in the Upper Paleolithic may indicate foundations for log cabins. Upper Paleolithic hunters drove herds of game into corrals to slaughter for hide cloth-ing and meat, and some tantalizing lines on reindeer and horses painted on cave walls raise the possibility that a few of these may have been harnessed as pack or sled animals. Fishing technology was another development in the Upper Paleolithic. Plant harvesting must have been carried on, but that leaves less trace for the archaeologist, except in the form of implements that may have been made to chop or shell plant foods or shred fiber (for making mats and baskets?).

The end of the Pleistocene geological epoch, 10,000 years ago (8000 B.C.), is said to mark the end of the Paleolithic. The date isn't quite as arbitrary as it may seem. A Swedish geologist surmised, a century ago, that the thin bands, alternating light and dark silt, making up the stratigraphy in old lake beds in his coun-try had resulted from the annual deposit of summer melt-

> B.P., "years ago" vs. B.C.: western culture counts time from the birth of Jesus, 2000 years before now. B.C., "Before Christ," are dates plus 2000 years "Before Present."

Doonesbury

BY GARRY TRUDEAU

waters from glaciers, followed each winter by cold-weather soil formation. Painstakingly counting the layers, called varves, from top to bottom of the deposits, the geologist counted a total of about 10,000 years from first melting of the Scandinavian final Pleistocene glaciers to eventual drying up, in the historic era, of the lakes so formed. "The end of the Pleistocene" was several thousand years of climate fluctuations, each centuries long—overlying, as it were, the basic warming trend that in fact would not reach its climax until 5,000 years ago (3000 B.C.). Warming climate away from the equator affected the equatorial zone, too, changing global wind patterns that in turn changed rainfall patterns.

Around 10,000 years ago, these worldwide shifts in climates had caused vegetation changes that in turn induced animal population changes. Some of the huge beasts flourishing on the rich Pleistocene grasslands could no longer find enough forage to remain healthy, and their species became extinct. None of us will ever see a live mammoth, a mastodon, or, thank goodness, a saber-toothed tiger ambling by our picnic. Other species survived by natural selection favoring smaller individuals. You can still see bison, but they've half the size of their Pleistocene ancestors. Still other species survived on one continent but not others. Camels disappeared from North America although they've survived in South America (as llamas and guanacos) and in Asia. Horses disappeared from the Americas, surviving in Eurasia and finally returning to the Americas on European ships after historic colonization began. Since, by the late Pleistocene, active hunting of large game animals was an important source of food and raw materials (hides, bones) for most humans, the climate changes necessitated adjustments in human strategies for the good life. These adjustments are reflected in the archaeological record of the post-Pleistocene epoch, that period which we are still in, the Holocene.

Conventional usage puts a Mesolithic period or stage between the Paleolithic—correlated with the Pliocene and Pleistocene geological epochs—and the farming Neolithic cultures in the Holocene. "Mesolithic" would be the several thousand years of fluctuating climate between the last continental glaciation and climates more like today. Humans in this Mesolithic period would be adapting their technology and social patterns to changes in their resources such as the extinction of the truly big game of the late Pleistocene. In Europe, there were several thousand years between the disappearance of many customary Upper Paleolithic game animals and the appearance of agricultural villages. During this Mesolithic period, Europeans adapted their economies to the Holocene environmental conditions. After agricultural villages came in, many of the Mesolithic societies continued to hunt, fish, and gather native foods, in many areas becoming specialized producers trading with the villagers for grain. Other regions of the world seem to show a more direct development of farming, early in the Holocene, from late Pleistocene Upper Paleolithic societies. Even in Europe, the degree to which the Mesolithic was an intervening *period* rather than specialized economies is debated. For speakers of Indo-European languages such as English, the neatness of a three-part set, Old (Paleo-), Middle (Meso-), and New (Neo-), drew archaeologists to extend the threefold division beyond its original region of discovery.

Summary, Part I: Archaeology, The Lower Paleolithic

Archaeology is the study of human societies of the past. Archaeologists do not do research on dinosaurs, fossil bones, or geology. The practice of archaeology involes:

1. discovering sites of human activity in the past. Most sites are reported by local people or discovered through construction work. Archaeologists also carry out surveys, checking historical records and satellite photos and systematically walking across an area, to discover the past human occupations of an area.

2. mapping the contour of a site; laying out a grid with small stakes; working within the mapped squares with hand tools, particularly cut-down sharpened masons' trowels; recording the exact location of every artifact and soil feature; sifting the excavated dirt to catch the smallest items; and cataloging everything removed with its exact location to preserve information on *context*—its relationships.

3. laboratory examination of all the excavated material, the features, and the records, often with the assistance of local people and of specialists in soil science, biology, geology, physics, and chemistry.

4. comparing information from the site with anthropological and historical information, to interpret the fragmentary evidence by means of similarities to the known effects of human activities. Because archaeological excavation destroys a site, archaeologists today focus on *preserving* sites, excavating only where construction or natural forces will destroy the site, or excavating only a limited portion of a site.

The Paleolithic or Old Stone Age covers nearly all the two million years of the existence of our genus *Homo*. Exactly when our early hominid ancestors could be termed "human" is a question of which behavior is distinctively human—making tools? using language structurally resembling historic languages? controlling fire? burying the dead? Complicating an answer is the problem that most of the evidence of human activities, for example speech or tools of perishable materials, will not be preserved for the archaeologist to discover. Apes and even a few other animals and birds are capable of making simple tools or structures and of communicating through wordlike sounds or signs, so there does not seem to be a hard-and-fast line between humans and all other creatures, unless it is the control of fire.

The Lower Paleolithic begins somewhat over two million years ago, marked by the use of chipped stone tools. The crudest stone tools are called Oldowan, after those found by the Leakeys in Olduvai Gorge in Tanzania, Africa. About a million and a half years ago, *Homo erectus* spent more effort chipping *biface* stone tools (*biface*, "two faces [sides]"), conforming to a mental pattern of the artifact rather than just trying to get a sharp or heavy edge. These more carefully manufactured stone tools are termed Acheulian. Cruder Oldowan-type stone tools continued to be made as well, and some regions probably used perishable hardwood or sharp bamboo tools rather than Acheulian-type stone tools.

The Middle Paleolithic or Mousterian, about 125,000–35,000 years ago, is the period of *Homo sapiens sapiens* and Neanderthals. People had realized that time and effort spent in shaping a piece of flint before knocking off a flake would increase overall efficiency, saving raw material and time in the long run. Mousterian-style stone tools are generally made from such prepared stone cores. The first deliberate burials of humans by their social groups occurred during the Middle Paleolithic

The Upper Paleolithic, about 35,000–10,000 years ago, sees the last of the Neanderthals and has instead anatomically modern humans, *Homo sapiens sapiens*. A great variety of stone tools were made, many exhibiting virtuoso skill in chipping stone, and different regions of the world show distinctive styles, each given a name by archaeologists. Humans migrated into the Americas during the Upper Paleolithic period. Recognizable art appears for the first time in the Upper Paleolithic, in the form of paintings, carvings, and clay sculpture.

Ikoma woman, Tanzania (Africa), 1928, grinding grain on a stone slab (metate).

Photo credit: Milwaukee Public Museum.

Dwellings constructed in open areas included tents with inner linings, like Plains Indian tipis, or in Russia, frames of interlocked mammoth bones over which hides were probably stretched. Herd animals were driven into corrals to be slaughtered, and fishing technology developed.

It is conventional to end the Paleolithic cultural period with the end of the Pleistocene geological epoch, 10,000 years ago (8000 B.C.). Earth's climatic shift from glacier-building, in the Pleistocene, to more or less modern climates in the Holocene stimulated human adjustments to the loss of mammoths and other game that became extinct and to changes in seasonal climates affecting vegetation. In Europe, several thousand years of human societies hunting modern species of game, fishing, and gathering native plants are termed the Mesolithic period. Some Mesolithic societies became specialized producers of native foods, trading with agricultural villagers, when agriculture came into Europe about 7000 B.C. Other areas of the world had more continuity between late Upper Paleolithic and early farming societies.

PART II: THE NEOLITHIC

Marked terminal-Pleistocene cultural changes in Eurasia are labeled "Neolithic." That term, meaning "New Stone [Age]," was applied because pioneering archaeologists of the nineteenth century believed that new techniques for working stone had been invented, specifically that metamorphosed rocks such as granite could now be pecked and polished into ax heads. Later discoveries showed that pecking and polishing stone was occasionally done in the Upper Paleolithic (that's how the stone figurines were made). The technique does become more common in the Holocene, and so ax heads made by this technique begin to predominate over those made by chipping. The shift to more pecking and grinding of metamorphosed stone went with an apparent major shift in food resources, to seeds and grain that needed to be ground or pounded into edible form. Some societies processed grain by placing it in a hollowed log or a bowl-shaped stone mortar and pounding it with log or stone pestles. Others ground it on millstone-like slabs of stone (called querns in Britain and *metates* in Hispanic America). Log mortars decayed away; milling stones remain to testify to the new Holocene reliance on grains.

The term "Neolithic," today, really means societies relying on cultivated food resources but without urban states. Neolithic is the equivalent of the Early Agriculture Stage of nineteenth-century evolutionists. Gordon Childe thought that reliance on cultivated resources, especially domesticates, was so radical a change in the social relations of people who had been hunter-gatherers that we should see the change as a "Neolithic Revolution," a political as well as economic change much greater than that from the American Revolution. The term "Neolithic" is not as a rule applied to prehistoric American societies in spite of the basic similarities in resource base and in time between many of them and Neolithic cultures in Eurasia. Pecked and ground stone ax-heads and milling

> Neolithic refers to societies with farming villages but no cities.

stones characterize early American farming cultures, too, but American archaeologists prefer to emphasize that these early farming cultures were the ancient, or archaic, forerunners of historic American Indian nations. For American cultures of Neolithic type, "Archaic" is the more usual term.

Conventional prehistory says the Neolithic first appeared in the Near East (Turkey, Syria, Lebanon, Israel, Jordan), where wheat and barley grow naturally. As the Pleistocene climate shifted into the Holocene, human communities in this zone of rainy, mild winters and dry, hot summers began to harvest quantities of wild wheat each year. Bushels of the grain were stored in covered pits in villages of round houses, some built on stone foundations. Permanent homes like this are a new invention in the Neolithic, so far as the archaeological record can tell. Parties of hunters, or perhaps families, went out hunting gazelle and wild sheep and goats, camping overnight in rockshelters. Probably carrying dried cooked grain to eat while traveling, hunting parties efficiently corralled herds and brought home abundant meat.

Populations increased, and people began to labor in the grain fields to increase the harvests. They would have burned off stubble to return nutrients to the soil and sown some of the grain they had harvested. Grain that had clung to the stalk until threshed was more likely to be sown than that which had blown off as soon as ripe, before people got

> Agricultural economist Ester Boserup argued that population increase stimulates more intensive farming, to provide food for a greater number of people.

to harvest it. Whether or not people were deliberately breeding wheat with a greater take-home yield, sowing some of their harvest led to a new, domesticated variety of wheat in which the grain waited, as it were, to be reaped instead of scattering in the wind.

Lentils and peas were also cultivated in the early Neolithic in the Near East, furnishing vegetable protein and fixing nitrogen in fields if planted after wheat had depleted it. Sheep, or goats, or both (these related wild species are so similar that it is extremely difficult to tell which was butchered in early Neolithic sites) were herded under human control as early as 11,000 years ago in Iraq near Shanidar Cave, about the same time that wheat and barley were apparently first cultivated. No one was making pottery yet in the earliest Neolithic villages, but in Israel, clay plaster was smoothed around the inside of storage pits (and also modeled over deceased villagers' skulls to give us remarkable likenesses of their living faces). In Iraq, shepherds were modeling little animal figurines from clay, much as had been done in the Gravettian of the Upper Paleolithic, a few thousand years before.

Skeletons of Early Neolithic people show general good health, with few indications of stressful periods of food scarcity or illness. Prosperity is reflected also in the long-distance trade that carried decorative shells far inland from the Mediterranean Sea and transported volcanic glass called obsidian hundreds of miles south and east from its outcrops in eastern Turkey. Obsidian, which looks like thick dark-colored bottle glass, can be easily flaked into thin, extremely sharp knife blades, even into razor blades, and was in great demand. Higher-yield seeds, domesticated animals, and agricultural inventions must have passed from community to community along the trade routes marked for the archaeologist by thousands and thousands of obsidian blades. Obsidian from an island in the Mediterranean off Greece proves that at the end of the Pleistocene, boats had been developed that were good enough to paddle out to the island and to transport back blocks of obsidian. Long-distance transport of flint particularly suited for flaking had been carried on in the Upper Paleolithic, possibly by canoes on rivers (sites with the desirable flint are strung along river valleys in central Europe), so the Neolithic obsidian trade is not so much new as an intensification of a late Paleolithic practice.

Outside the "Fertile Crescent" (a crescent-shaped area on the map, from the Greek border through the Near and Middle East [Iran and Iraq] and into Egypt), Neolithic farming seems to appear later. Or are we ignoring the cultivation of alternative crops and animals, native to other zones? A controversial hypothesis advanced by the late Eric Higgs, a British archaeologist, argues that the concentrations of hundreds of bones from herd game in Upper Paleolithic sites is evidence for the kind of semidomestication practiced by the historic Reindeer Saami (popularly called Lapps) in northern Scandinavia. Saami drive reindeer herds into corrals to slaughter as many as they need for meat and hides, and keep a few tied up in their camps, milking the does and using gelded males to pull sleds. For most of the year, the reindeer move freely, though Saami try to protect them from wolves (nowadays sometimes using helicopters to patrol). Saami consider the reindeer domesticated because when they corral herds, they mark the ears of the calves with their family brands, enabling the families to identify each year animals they claim to own. Under the conditions of northern Scandinavia, nothing would be gained by Saami shepherding reindeer year round. Higgs pointed out that late Pleistocene Europe was similar to Scandinavia in harboring many herds of reindeer, therefore it is reasonable to hypothesize that Upper Paleolithic Europeans may have managed reindeer as do the historic Saami. The archaeological sites with piles of hundreds of reindeer bones resemble corrals used as slaughtering places, and it would follow that if the Saami are said to have domestic reindeer, then we should say the same of the Upper Paleolithic reindeer slaughterers. Cave paintings that seem, to some archaeologists, to depict corralling herds, and the few that seem to show pack straps around reindeer and halters on horses, support Higgs's hypothesis.

Higgs's basic point is that domesticated animals and plants represent intense symbiosis (mutual dependence: Greek *sym:* together, *biosis:* living, "living together"). Those Upper Paleolithic hunters and present-day Reindeer Saami who depend upon reindeer live intimately with the herds, and the herd populations are affected by the humans' patrolling, corralling, and culling. Agriculture—people depending on a few, selected, high-yield species they cultivate, and those species dependent on their cultivators—wasn't invented overnight. It must have developed over generations, initially as people discovered, and shared with trading contacts, ways to assist desired plants and animals to grow well, or to gain greater amounts in the harvest. Characteristics of docility in animals and stability in plants at ripening time would have been selected for, regardless of whether the people consciously favored them. From the point of view of a domesticated plant or animal, the *people* who cultivate or care for it are the domesticated ones, the creatures who have been selected for their willingness to labor in behalf of the privileged plant or animal! That's symbiosis, each of the interacting pair smugly happy because the other lives "for" it.

Near Eastern Neolithic farming had been blocked in expansion northward by cold winters and rainy summers, climate detrimental to the growth and ripening of wild wheat. After centuries of farming at the northern border along the mountainous Balkan zone of southeastern Europe, by around 5500 B.C. knowledge of how to manage crops in the temperate zone had developed sufficiently to support colonies of farmers out along the central European river valleys. It took about as long for Neolithic farmers to expand through Europe as—6,000 years later—it would take for European invaders to expand throughout the Americas. Did the Neolithic colonizers fight the Mesolithic inhabitants of Europe? No evidence of battles has been discovered. Did the Mesolithic inhabitants welcome the farmers? There is considerable evidence of increased trade, including, along the Atlantic coast, intensified production of fish that probably was dried and exchanged for grain in adjacent farming communities. Grain, remember, is the basis for beer; maybe villagers brewed beer and traded jars of beer for the fish. (Archaeologist Robert Braidwood quite seriously suggested that thirst for beer was a motive for early farming. Would you labor in the fields just to get porridge or griddlecakes?)

Farming villages in Europe were radically different from preceding communities, not only because the men and women cleared woodlands to plant imported crops (wheat, barley, lentils, peas) and to pasture sheep and cattle, now domesticated, but additionally because the farmers built substantial thatched timber houses similar to those still traditional in much of Europe. One end of the rectangular home was finished into a sleeping and living room for the family, the other end was the stable for cattle. Keeping the cattle under the same roof used the animals' heat in the building during the winter. A work area often separated the family and stable sections of the long house. Pigs and sheep were penned next to the houses. About a dozen houses made up a village. With the fields around the village, crops rotated to preserve soil fertility, shepherds watching the flocks, pedlars retailing news along with ornaments and small tools, women spinning and weaving and men carpentering, the villages of the Danubians, as the Neolithic colonizers of Europe are called (they spread through and out from the Danube River Valley) looked much like historic European peasant communities.

Eastern Asia, too, had an expansion of Neolithic farming villages from around 5000 B.C. Central China farmers grew a variety of millet and raised pigs; they lived in timber-framed, adobe-plastered thatched homes, often round, sometimes rectangular, but never the long house-and-stable combination of Europe. Wheat found in minor amounts in Chinese Neolithic villages indicates some long-distance trade across the central Asian steppes (plains) with Neolithic towns in Iran. Southern Chinese and Indochinese grew rice, a wet tropics crop, and kept domesticated water buffaloes as well as pigs. To the west, India developed farming from an expansion through Afghanistan of the Near/Middle Eastern system based on wheat, with native zebu cattle domesticated in India.

Farming seems to have been invented independently in the Americas about 7000 B.C. American Indians domesticated maize (corn) and squash in Mexico, gradually breeding maize with larger cobs and larger kernels that by 2000 B.C. was supporting numerous permanent villages and the beginning of urban towns. In Peru, beans were domesticated at 7000 B.C., and by around 5000 B.C. chili peppers, potatoes, quinoa (a native grain), and guinea pigs were raised for food as they are today by Andes mountain villagers. In the tropical lowlands of eastern South America, manioc, a tuber (dried and ground, it is called tapioca), has been farmed for several thousand years. Tropical root and tuber crops such as manioc grow without extensive field clearance. They can be kept in the ground until needed rather than requiring harvesting at a certain season and then storage. Because these crops leave little preserved evidence, the history of tropical forest agriculture is a challenge to archaeologists. North America challenges archaeologists in a different way, because local plants were cultivated in the Midwest (small-seed grains now seen as weeds, and wild rice) and California (cacti, acorn oaks, seed-bearing grasses). In Eastern North America, deer populations and, on the Plains, bison populations were bolstered by Indians burning off forest to increase pasture for their favored game. European invaders couldn't see that these practices, and the cultivation of native plants, can be alternative forms of agriculture. Archaeologists debate whether to apply the term "agriculture" when there seems to have been no radical "Neolithic Revolution" change from Archaic hunting and plant harvesting. One clue implying agriculture is the cultivation, by 5,000 years ago, of maize and squash in North America, far north of the natural homeland of these plants in Mexico. Both these plants appear to have been minor crops for over 3,000 years, then around A.D. 900, Eastern, Midwestern, and Southwestern Indian societies start intensively raising maize as their principal food, clearing and hoeing fields. New, hardy, high-yield varieties of maize may have been the stimulus to such agriculture. Maize as a minor crop during the preceding 3,000 years indicates familiarity with agricultural practices. Turkeys and muscovy ducks were kept for food in late prehistoric Mexico, turkeys in North American agricultural communities, and, on the Plains, two types of dog were bred, a large strong animal as a beast of burden (carrying packs and pulling loads tied to a pair of poles yoked to its shoulders) and a smaller dog fattened for feasts.

Agriculture in humid tropical Africa and Pacific Islands, like that in lowland eastern South America, is generally difficult to discover archaeologically. In New Guinea after 7000 B.C., villagers were draining swampy ground by digging ditches and planting the root crops taro and yams in the ridged fields they created. Buried ridges and ditches can be identified archaeologically, demonstrating how early agriculture was on this large island. When Africans began raising yams is, so far at least, poorly known. Some archaeologists speculate tropical root crops may have been cultivated, though leaving no preserved evidence, for many thousands of years; others demand hard proof. Cattle herding was the basis of the East African economy as early as five thousand years ago. Farming is clearly evidenced in sub-Saharan Africa about 2,000 years ago, when Bantu-speaking nations expanded through much of the continent, carrying with them iron metallurgy, their cattle, and crops including sorghum and millet, all needing cleared fields and thus altering the natural environment.

The one continent on which Neolithic agriculture has not been recognized is Australia. Whether Australians really didn't raise crops, or whether we haven't learned to read traces of native Australian food crops from the archaeological record, can't easily be determined. We do know that some Australians constructed fish farms in the late prehistoric period. Australian Aborigines believe that their activities are necessary to sustain the plants and animals they harvest. European observers rejected the claim because the activities included prayers and ceremonies, but the pragmatic part of their work, requiring detailed, sophisticated knowledge of the biology and ecology of their food sources, does affect the food populations. Technically, it isn't agriculture, because fields are not cleared and planted, but Higgs's point about intensive symbiosis between human communities and their food resources applies to Australian practices, too.

The Urban Revolution

Agriculture changes the relation of people to natural resources. It was very common for people to assist favored plants to flourish, to increase the harvest, and to promote populations of grazing game herds by burning off the countryside in order to favor grasses and discourage woody plants. These forms of *cultivation* very likely were practiced in the Upper Paleolithic in most tropical and temperate zones, as Higgs hypothesized, and became the basis for *domestication*, selecting for genetic characteristics that made plants and animals easier for people to handle or caused them to yield more food, wool, or other product. Being genetically determined, domestication characteristics would be passed on generation after generation in the selected population, creating a new variety or species. *Agriculture* refers to a society's eco-

> *cultivation:* assisting plants to grow (weeding, watering, transplanting to better location). *domestication:* selecting for genetically changed plant or animal population, to make it more useful for human needs. *agriculture:* economy based on large-scale cultivation. (*Ager:* Latin for "field.")

nomic base, when preferred resources are cultivated on the larger scale of fields, not just a few plants. Agricultural societies allocate substantial time and labor to the cultivation of fields, and failure of cultivated crops means famine.

There is a major difference between an economy based on adaptation to natural resources, however assisted by cultivation, and an economy based on large-scale cultivation of a few selected crops. Plants and animals native to a region are adapted to its normal range of temperature, humidity, winds, storms, predators, and diseases. They may suffer in extremes of the range, be vulnerable to predators or diseases, but enough of their ancestors perpetuated the species through occasional bad years to build a population able to roll with the punches. Crops and animals imported from distant regions are much more likely to die under foreign conditions. They may do well for a few years, then be killed by an unseasonable temperature or a disease epidemic. Communities expecting to gain most of their food from the imported crop may starve: They spent their days laboring to raise the crop in fields they cleared, and when it freezes or dies from drought or hail or blight, there are too few wild areas left uncleared to provide native foods, or it's too late in the season to harvest wild foods. Agriculture is risky.

Why should people gamble on an agricultural crop when their ancestors lived comfortably harvesting local natural resources? Hunter-gatherers know the variety of their resources intimately, they schedule an annual round from harvest to harvest, storing some to tide them over the leanest months. Anthropologists who have lived with hunter-gatherers report that they are usu-

Jaipur, India, 1928, a walled city where caravans of draft animals carried goods between markets. This scene resembles early Mesopotamian cities.
Photo credit: Milwaukee Public Museum.

ally well nourished, though not fat, and show strong confidence that they will obtain food as expected. In some regions of low natural resources, such as deserts or northern forests, people may anticipate some weeks of belt tightening toward the end of the coldest or driest season, but no worse than farmers often face when waiting for the earliest crops to ripen. Agriculture doesn't provide a more secure source of food, it provides a greater amount of food per acre. It provides this in return for hard labor, more hours, and more exhausting work than gathering wild foods entails. Agriculture is the means to feed large numbers of people living permanently in one place.

Permanent settlements appeared in the early Holocene in many regions, perhaps as an adaptation to increasing human populations. Inventions in food procurement and processing, clothing, and shelter allowed ever more people to survive and reproduce. By around 10,000 years ago, it made sense for communities to establish a settlement with cultivated fields and pastures around it, dividing regions between the communities to maximize the utilization of resource potential. There would still be plenty of less desirable land to support firewood and game for hunting. Families could be large, partly because more hands meant more capacity to clear and cultivate fields, partly because women no longer had to carry babies and household gear from camp to camp, necessitating spacing births far enough apart that the older child could walk the required miles before the mother had a new baby to carry. Even if custom still urged four years or so between babies, to protect the mothers' health, the occasional slip-up could be accommodated, and over centuries, a slight increase in number of births per woman can result in substantial population growth.

As Holocene communities grew, those in locations where trade routes crossed or travelers were likely to seek accommodation grew larger than less conveniently situated ones. Artisans in the larger villages produced enough items to regularly exchange for others' surplus food production, a practice that seems to have begun in the Upper Paleolithic but was much increased in the Neolithic. It is likely that the more there was occupational specialization, the more people looked to leaders to oversee the various jobs and manage the distribution of both tasks and production. Fairs and markets had to be organized, disputes adjudicated. Managers built larger homes and storehouses so they could entertain foreign traders and the managers of other villages, and distribute necessities to the handicapped. Managers' skills were taught to their children, differentiating their children from those of ordinary villagers. An upper class developed, distinguished from the working class by its education for leadership. Upper-class people married persons of their class from other towns, consolidating regional leadership networks and maintaining class distinction. This narrative of how societies may have changed over the centuries after the "Neolithic Revolution," culminating in what Childe called the "Urban Revolution," sounds like a simple story. Much of the description is generalized from ethnographic observation of historic and contemporary societies of various sizes and economies. Archaeologists can't provide detailed histories of social behavior, so we must hypothesize from comparisons to known societies. Actual histories were diverse, region from region, but overall, the trend described is supported by data from excavated settlements in regional sequences covering several thousand years.

The paragraph above is a broad generalization, and it ignores a very critical point: *Cultural evolution did not result in all human societies becoming alike.* Once *Homo sapiens sapiens* had reached practically all the habitable regions of the world, in the late Pleistocene, adaptation to great environmental diversity coupled with diverse historical experiences of trade, epidemics, wars, and so on, created the great variety of present-day societies. Nineteenth-century theorists who believed our species had followed a single line of cultural evolutionary development from simple to complex societies, from hunting-gathering to urban agricultural-commercial economics, failed to realize that the great evolutionary principle of adaptation *must* produce diversity. Ecological conditions differ from place to place, therefore adaptations must be different. People who live in camps harvesting wild foods, or on small farms producing nearly all their own necessities, are not undeveloped, unevolved, or retarded; they represent successful, perhaps the best possible, adaptation to their environments, given their historical opportunities. We tell the story of how *some* hunter-gatherers switched to agriculture, how *some* agricultural villages grew into cities with markets, courts of law, temples. It's a favorite story for all of us who are citizens of primarily urban, industrial nations. It would be an alien story for Inuit in the Arctic, who relish the story of how *their* forebears invented clever technology to survive, in small communities, in some of the harshest country on earth. It would be a story about fools for a Mbuti or Efe in the forest in the Congo, laughing at how the big people in the towns outside the forest work like slaves day after day amid dirt and noise, while their own small, slender people enjoy the beauty of the tree-shaded land so generously giving them food and shelter. Focusing on narrating cultural development from Upper Paleolithic through Neolithic agriculture to urban states is really ethnocentric. Still, urban states are as much a part of the total human story as the descriptions of Arctic and tropical forest cultures.

V. Gordon Childe listed ten criteria that the archaeologist could look for to recognize a city, contrasted with a village. These were not meant to be a list of essential features of urban society, only a list of what could appear in the archaeological record.

1. settlements of city size. (They should be markedly larger than other settlements in the region, but Childe avoided putting any figures down.)
2. indications that the society was organized on the basis of territory rather than only by kin groups. Archaeologists might look for administrative buildings, symbols of territory and their rulers (for example, banners and crowns), fortresses or markers at defensible approaches to the territory.

3. capital wealth (i.e., wealth that can be invested), from taxes or tribute.

4. monumental public works (government buildings, temples, rulers' palaces, roads, irrigation systems). These would have required capital wealth, so become evidence for it.

5. class-stratified society. Differences in home size and furnishings, in graves, and in costumes seen in art all can indicate class stratification.

6. full-time craft specialists. Workshop areas with quantities of mass-produced or luxury manufactures indicate craft specialists. These in turn indicate markets.

7. long-distance trade in luxuries—another sign of class stratification.

8. representational art including human portraiture. We can't explain why smaller, more democratic societies generally seem not to have been interested in portraits. The archaeological record shows that the custom of painting or sculpting likenesses of actual individuals appears when class-stratified societies glorify their rulers. They also begin to personify their deities, not a coincidence because the rulers and deities are apt to be shown together.

9. writing. If the society did not carve inscriptions on stone, writing may not appear in the archaeological record. Some form of record-keeping is essential to manage urban states.

10. true science. By this, Childe meant a system of measurement, engineering, astronomy sufficient to construct a calendar, and mathematics necessary to manipulate the engineering system.

Archaeological sites with these evidences of urban societies are dated to the fifth millennium B.C. (5000–4000 B.C.) in Mesopotamia (Iran and Iraq). They are later everywhere else: third millennium B.C. (3000–2000 B.C.) in India and Egypt—both in direct trade contact with Mesopotamia; second millennium B.C. in the eastern Mediterranean and Greece, China, Mexico, and Peru; first millennium B.C. in Europe and North Africa; first millennium A.D. in sub-Saharan Africa and North America. To Gordon Childe, organizing cities was a radical innovation in societal form, deserving to be termed an Urban Revolution. Childe thus recognized two revolutionary societal reorganizations in human history, the Neolithic and the Urban "revolutions."

American archaeologists tend to explain the development of cities and urban states as the more or less inevitable outcome of population growth. Land suitable for farming is finite, and once the countryside is full of villages and fields, population increase has to be handled either by out-migration and colonization or by increased density in settlements. Both happen. Some people push past the frontiers, draining swamps, cutting forests, terracing mountainsides, building irrigation canals in deserts, becoming nomadic herders on steppes, sailing to islands, conquering other nations. Other people become goods manufacturers instead of seeking farmland, depending on surplus from agriculture to be exchanged for their products. Centrally located settlements grow into towns; optimally located towns grow into cities. Class stratification, bureaucracy, markets, and taxation are all social adaptations to large, dense populations.

Archaeologists in other parts of the world are more likely to explain the development of cities as simply the result of increase in trade. They note that Mesopotamia (Iran and Iraq) lies between the two great rivers Tigris and Euphrates, rising on the mountainous border of the Near East and flowing southeastward into the Persian Gulf leading into the Indian Ocean. Mesopotamian plains could produce an abundance of wheat and other crops but lacked stone suitable for cutting implements and timber for building. The rivers' headwaters are near major obsidian outcrops and in superb timberland (the Bible's famous "cedars of Lebanon"). Towns grew easily on the plains along these rivers, fed from the fields that could be irrigated from the rivers if necessary, and were busy importing, redistributing, and manufacturing. Leaders could accumulate capital wealth and invest it in palaces, impressive temples to the deities that favored them, grand plazas, fortresses. They could subsidize priests, artists, engineers, merchants, ship captains, soldiers. On the Mesopotamian plain, agriculture was less risky than in many other regions, and there were fewer alternative natural resources to support communities.

Once a number of cities had developed in Mesopotamia, they spurred development of cities in the more remote regions into which they traded. Egypt and India, both highly accessible by sea from the Persian Gulf, were the principal targets for Mesopotamian merchants. The overland route through the steppes to China, or the even more time-consuming sea route around Southeast Asia, discouraged much trade between Mesopotamia and China, though there was some. Urban states developed later in China, without much evidence of distant trade. Mexico and Peru are generally held to have developed urban states independently, but there is a tantalizing correlation between the rise of the Chinese states, the subsequent turmoil created, and the appearance of the earliest cities in Mexico and western South America. Agriculture and large populations were already in place in Latin America, and Polynesians were colonizing the Pacific Ocean islands, so there is a possibility that there were occasional contacts across the oceans. Foreign explorers and merchants at times might have catalyzed state developments in the regions they brought into trade with their homelands. (A catalyzing agent is a trigger, the last element that shifts a ready-to-change solution into its potential other condition.) The prospect of substantial profits from trade may have been the spur emboldening leaders or groups to commit themselves to construction and societal organization on a scale not yet attempted in their region.

A perspective emphasizing trade gives more weight to human decisions and less to an environmental determinism that makes people seem mechanically driven. It returns us to the question of strategies for prosperity. If prospects for wealth and power alliances appear, someone may seize the initiative. The actual very distant trade may prove impractical to sustain, but the moves toward consolidating the organization to achieve it have been made, and the ruling group can reach toward more practical objectives. Meanwhile, out on the far borders of territories, people may see little prospect of gain from involvement in an expanding state and may prefer to remain independent, minimizing risk (and the possibility of becoming dependent on the state) by harvesting a variety of foods, both cultivated and wild, and manufacturing nearly all their artifacts from local resources. These communities are not "backward" or "primitive," they judge it wiser to be free than to end up exploited laborers in a state that reserves ease and luxury for the aristocracy. Time and again, states overrun border communities, but that is history.

Once written documents are created recording events in a state, prehistory ends. Completely developed writing appears 5,000 years ago, that is, 3000 B.C., in Mesopotamia. Shortly afterward, a quite different style of writing appeared in Egypt. A few centuries later, writing—so far not deciphered—was used in India. It was another thousand or so years, late in the second millennium B.C. (1400–1200 B.C.), that writing was developed in China, the Near East, and Greece. In the middle of the first millennium B.C., ideographic writing was created in Mexico, and alphabetic writing systems in the eastern Mediterranean. Northern Europe did not create its writing systems until the middle of the first millennium A.D., as part of the spread of Christianity after the breakup of the Roman empire. Polynesians had a script by this time, also. The Peruvian kingdoms and the second millennium A.D. empire of Tawantinsuyu, ruled by the Inca, seem to have been managed entirely by means of accountants recording censuses, taxes, and other governmental data on abacus systems using sets of knots on colored strings. African states similarly had means of record-keeping, while valuing oral transmission of histories committed to the trained memories of officials and bards.

Invention of writing systems capable of putting down any fact or thought was a tremendous achievement of human minds, yet the dates we can give for these inventions, the dates for the beginnings of histories, obscure the variety of memory aids people have used. Notches on Upper Paleolithic bone artifacts sometimes were placed in regular sets. Perhaps they recorded days per phase of the moon for a calendar, or they may be tally marks. Historic American Indian women are known to have kept tallies of the number of hides tanned on the bone handle of a hide scraper, or to have made a notch for the birth of each child on a favorite awl. Priests of the Midewiwin religious society of the Ojibwe Indians around the Great Lakes made birch-bark scrolls on which they drew series of pictograph symbols to help them remember the details of rituals. Mesopotamians made little clay tokens for possessions such as sheep that might be consigned to a trader to sell, then modified tokens into pictograph form on clay tables, eventually simplifying the pictographs into cuneiform (*cunei:* "wedges") symbols that finally became phonetic. This evolution of writing from owners' tallies shipped in sealed clay envelopes along with goods consignments, to true writing transcribing religious myths and political histories as well as complex financial transactions—not to mention ordinary citizens' personal news and inquiries—took well over a thousand years in Mesopotamia. Egyptians may have been stimulated to perfect their writing system by their trading contacts with Mesopotamia, but Egyptian hieroglyphics don't resemble Mesopotamian cuneiform at all. The long, indigenous use of picture symbols in every part of the world, including Australia, coupled with the close association of true writing systems with urban states, indicate that it was the governmental functions of states that forced the creation of writing systems.

Most of the people in most states never learned to write or read because they were not expected to be active in government; only participatory democracies value universal literacy. Small societies manage political and economic affairs through face-to-face relationships, so they don't need writing. Nonliterate societies may train certain people to remember accurately histories and rituals, making these specialists living books. There is a tendency for literacy to promote formal ordered knowledge such as classification systems, formal logic, law codes, and also holy books believed to be the exact revealed Word of God; but ordered knowledge can be constructed and transmitted orally, so nonliterate societies aren't radically different from those with books.

We can conclude this chapter with the note that written documents can be as difficult to interpret for a factual history as the archaeological record. The subfield of historical archaeology—studying the sites and artifacts of historically documented societies—has revealed how much information is absent in documents and must be gained through other archaeological methods. Archaeology may demonstrate that claims in documents are deliberately false, or a version of events little better than myth. Prehistory is no longer all that archaeologists work on; archaeology is a set of methods to illuminate the human past, from the remote beginning of our species two million years ago, right into the twentieth century.

Summary, Part II: Neolithic and Urban Revolutions

Neolithic refers to settled agricultural communities. These are evident in a number of regions of Eurasia, Africa, the Americas, and New Guinea early in the Holocene epoch, by 7000 B.C., and the foundations of agricultural practices must have been observed and experimented with in the late Pleistocene epoch Upper Paleolithic. Grains (wheat, barley, millet, maize) were sown and cultivated, along with lentils, peas, beans, and similar protein-rich seed plants, in the temperate climates of Eurasia, North Africa, and Latin America, and yams in tropical New Guinea and possibly Africa. Producing food by clearing and hoeing fields and planting desired food staples, rather than harvesting only naturally occurring foods, supported larger populations than hunting and gathering usually would. In many regions, populations gradually became denser, living in permanent houses in towns with regular markets, temples, and officials to collect taxes and administer public affairs. Class stratification appears, with both wars of conquest and peaceful trade extending relations among political groups. Eventually, formal systems of record-keeping, including various types of writing, were instituted in the early cities.

This story of "the rise of civilization" is only one version of human history. Many societies resisted enslaving most of their people to hard labor in fields or manufacturing workshops. These societies continued harvesting naturally occurring foods, often becoming specialized producers regularly trading with agricultural communities on their borders. Seasonally shifting bands of hunter-gatherers could plant small fields or manage livestock. There are also parts of the inhabited world where climate conditions make agriculture impossible; peoples such as the Inuit of the Arctic and the Mbuti and Efe of the Central African tropical forest were inventing technology to improve their harvests of the animals and plants in these more challenging regions.

Archaeologist Gordon Childe was correct in pointing out the revolutionary impact of, first, agriculture and then the development of densely populated cities upon human social relationships. These Neolithic and urban "revolutions" occurred in each of the continents and major islands except, it seems, Australia, and no one region was markedly ahead of the others, although the geographic position of Mesopotamia in Western Asia may have facilitated its development into several city-states somewhat earlier than happened elsewhere. *History*, in the narrow sense of written documents recording political and economic events, "begins" in the many regions of Eurasia, the Americas, Africa, and the Pacific when relatively large, occupationally specialized, class-stratified societies developed formal systems of record-keeping to manage their affairs.

The "rise of civilizations" is only one of the narratives of human history. Contemporary societies that depend upon their sophisticated knowledge and skills to harvest naturally occurring food resources are as "advanced" in their histories as any college student in a high-rise apartment microwaving frozen pizza. Agriculture and cities are impossible or too costly even today in large areas of the world. Thus the Neolithic and urban "revolutions" were as historically located as the American Revolution, not universal happenings or resulting from genetically superior people, but rather adaptations to complex changes in particular regions where increasing the food supply through agricultural practices have been practical.

RECOMMENDED READING

Renfrew, Colin and Paul Bahn. *Archaeology: Theories, Methods, and Practice*. New York: Thames and Hudson. 1996. Note that the material discussed in this chapter is referenced in this text.

Fagan, Brian M. *People of the Earth: An Introduction to World Prehistory*. (Latest edition.) Glenview IL: Scott, Foresman.

Bruhns, Karen Olsen *Ancient South America*. Cambridge: Cambridge University Press. 1994.

Fagan, Brian M. *Ancient North America*. New York: Thames and Hudson, 1995.
Each of these books is profusely illustrated and clearly written for the general college stu-
dent. The authors are experienced archaeologists with a gift for writing.
Case Studies in Archaeology (Harcourt Brace), edited by Jeffrey Quilter. Books in this
series can be used to supplement this textbook, or as sources for term papers or pro-
jects.
Khok Phanom Di (Thailand), Charles Higham and Rachanie Thosarat, 1994.
The Ceren Site (Central America Maya), Payson D. Sheets, 1992.

Special Topics

Eugene Linden, *Apes, Men, and Language* (Penguin Books, 1974), is a lively and
thoughtful account of the controversies over the projects to teach apes to communicate in human languages. Linden discusses the question of how to define
"human."
W. C. McGrew, *Chimpanzee Material Culture: Implications for Human Evolution*
(Cambridge University Press, 1993), discusses ape tool use from the perspective of
"What is 'human'?" See also "Stone-Tool Bone-Surface Modification by Monkeys,"
G. C. Westergaard and S. J. Suomi, *Current Anthropology* 35(4):468–470 (1994),
for a recent discussion with bibliography.

8

Analyzing Societies: Communicating

Multimedia communication is basic to human cultures. All human societies use spoken language, gestures and body language, visual and aural symbols, and space to convey meaning. All known societies have complex languages capable of communicating abstract philosophical concepts as well as pragmatic knowledge. One marked difference between humans and apes occurs when infants are about six months old: Human infants intently watch people speaking and begin attempting to imitate speech, while ape infants' babble diminishes. Capacity for elaborated, fine-tuned language is in our genes and is a distinctive human characteristic.

Before we examine language, let us look at American anthropologist Ralph Linton's clarification of the place of objects in cultures. Linton suggested every object has, obviously, a *form*. Objects also have *uses*, utility. Then Linton pointed out that objects have *social functions* that may be quite other than the obvious use: For example, an old-fashioned balance scale may *function* today as a symbol for justice, though it can still be used for weighing. Finally, Linton directed our attention to the social *meaning* an object may carry: The balance scale functioning as a symbol for justice means equality before the law—wealth or political power are not supposed to overbalance justice. To give a more exotic example, aluminum cans have the familiar *form* in Papua New Guinea, and the familiar *use* of preserving food, *functioning* in meal preparation and *meaning,* in New Guinea, a luxury food for high-status people. Once emptied, they have a second *use* in rituals and dances, flattened and cut to shine in headdresses and as part of fancy pendants. Here they *function* to mark partici-

> *form:* directly observed
> *meaning:* associations society ascribes to the object or behavior
> *use:* object or behavior in relation to external [natural or social] environment
> *function:* object or behavior in relation to role it plays in its society (its "purpose" as seen by members of its society)

115

Bali, 1930. Form: *a monstrous, lion-faced, human-bodied figure.*
Meaning: *Holds a fierce spirit guarding the community's temple.*
Use: *Decorates temple entrance.*
Function: *(1) communicates the sacred nature of the temple it guards; (2) its production is the means through which the community supports talented artists enabling the congregation to visualize religious beliefs.*
Credit: Milwaukee Public Museum.

pants in a ritual or festival dance, and *mean* that the wearers remain loyal to traditional culture. We could look, too, at tin cans in highland Bolivia, where discarded cans are salvaged by peasants who put a strip of rag and some kerosene in the can to make a lamp. The cans retain their form, their use now is to give light, their function is to permit people to continue some of their activities and socializing after dark, and their meaning is a sign of poverty, for only the very

Form, Meaning, Use, Function *in an American city university campus:*
Form*: Large church and two large classroom buildings in late-medieval European style, fronting a main avenue of the city.*
Meaning*: The powerful authority of a long cultural tradition dominates the campus and city.*
Use*: Church is used to hold religious services, classroom buildings to house classes and offices.*
Function*: University selects and trains generations of Catholic Americans for managerial and professional employment, consolidating political and economic power for middle-class Catholic Americans and perpetuating the Roman Catholic American cultural tradition.*
Note how the architecture, deliberately imitating the style of the era when Roman Catholic leadership dominated European politics, symbolically portrays the persistence and power of this cultural tradition. The university further communicates its graduates' influential position in the political economy of the region by positioning its principal buildings fronting a main avenue of the city, where they will loom above thousands of passing vehicles daily. The message is emphasized by positioning the Law School, the building on the left, on the most visible corner of the campus.
CREDIT: Marquette University

poor, who have no electricity and can't afford even candles, use these lamps. Linton's distinction between form, use, function, and meaning should be kept in mind when cross-cultural comparisons bring up what may appear to be bizarre uses of objects.

Anthropological Linguistics

Anthropologists who study languages may specialize in one or another aspect of human languages: the structure of languages, semantics, historical linguistics, and sociolinguistics. These several facets of anthropological linguistics somewhat parallel Linton's four aspects of a cultural object. Structural or descriptive linguistics describes and analyzes the form of a language, or languages. Semantics is the study of meaning, how it is created and perceived. Historical linguistics charts shifts in languages and identifies general processes in language change. Sociolinguistics observes the social functions of language, the messages unconsciously accruing to behavior in its social settings.

This chapter briefly surveys the several facets of anthropological linguistics, particularly as they may help students better understand daily experience in communicating. Historical linguistics is least touched upon here because shifts in language seem to be somewhat like biological evolution, generally occurring outside most people's conscious observation or control. These shifts are interesting, because they offer clues to the historic contacts of a land (in place-names) or society, and they raise the controversial question of how much any individual can control social behavior—the eternal question of how much free will a human can claim.

The Structure of Language

Human languages work by means of two basic principles:

1. Words name objects and actions.
2. Arrangement of words into sentences carries part of the meaning.

Linguists including Franz Boas and, a generation later in the first half of the twentieth century, Roman Jakobson drew a general model of how human languages are constructed: First, there are the *sounds* used in speech. These can be described according to how they are produced by the vocal chords, breath, teeth, roof of mouth, tongue, lips. The technical word for a sound in speech is *phone* (of course you know that word—it is Greek for "voice"). Over 200 sounds, or phones, have been recorded in use in one or another human language. Linguists record phones in the International Phonetic Alphabet, where each phone is defined by how it is physically produced. Jakobson said this basic foundation of speech is the *phonetic level*. Second, there are the sounds regularly used in meaningful speech in a particular language. Each of these is a *phoneme*. Out of the more than 200 possible sounds for a human to use in speech, each language has selected a few dozen. American English uses around 45 phonemes ("around," because different regional or class dialects may use

> phoneme: minimal sets of sounds used in a language to distinguish meanings

a few more or a few less). Some languages use as few as 30, some as many as 60. The phonemes of any one language are only about one-third out of the possible more than 200 phones. Apparently, around 40 or so sounds (phonemes) are sufficient to convey a rich variety of meanings, and many more in one language would be inefficient. A phoneme is actually a cluster of closely similar sounds, because in fluent speech a person shifts sounds slightly in relation to what is spoken just before or after. Slight shifts that do not affect meaning in one language may do so in another. That is to say, similar sounds heard as "the same" in one language may be distinguished as "two different sounds" by speakers of another language. Third, phonemes are clustered or combined into *morphemes,* the technical term for what we usually call "words." Morphemes carry meaning. A morpheme may be a single phoneme (English "I"), or more commonly a string of phonemes (English "me" [2 phonemes], "cat" [3 phonemes]). Morphemes may be combined in a word, for example "cats" has the *root* morpheme "cat" plus the *suffix* morpheme "s" meaning "plural." Another example: "schoolhouse" has two root morphemes, "school" and "house," and for plural, "schoolhouses" adds on the suffix "s." Fourth, morphemes are strung together into sentences according to rules of *syntax.* The grammatical rules you learned years ago are English syntax. Syntax gives human languages their amazing versatility. To take an obvious example, the sentence "Dog bites man" describes a commonplace happening. Reverse the order of the morphemes to "Man bites dog" and we have quite a different action, one likely to be featured in the newspapers. The same three morphemes are used, but the change in their order radically changes the story they tell.

> *phone:* sound (any spoken sound).
> *phoneme:* sound used in a *particular language*
> *morpheme:* word (meaningful combination of phonemes).
> *syntax:* rules of order (grammar) for morphemes.

Jakobson used the *method of comparison and contrast* to analyze languages. He would compare examples of speech or written text to find similar sounds, combinations of sounds, and order of combinations. He would then ask a native speaker of the language to tell him whether two similar sounds he had heard spoken are "the same" or "different," thus recognizing the phonemes of the language. (To a foreigner, a phoneme may sound slightly different spoken by different native speakers, or by the same speaker at different times. People who know the language accept certain closely similar phones as "the same" phoneme.) By comparison and then contrast, Jakobson would discover that in English, "bat" and "pat" carry different meanings, indicating phonemic status for "b" and for "p." The only physical difference between the two utterances lies in activating the vocal chords in forming "b" and not activating them for "p" (put your fingers on your throat and say "bat," then "pat"; you can feel the vocal chords activated for the "b" and not for the "p"). In many other languages, it doesn't make any difference whether the vocal chords are activated or not when the lips are pressed together for the b/p phoneme. Note that a language may have several dialects, with one or more phonetic differences between them; New York English, for example, includes the phone technically called "glottal stop," written as an apostrophe ('), spoken by New Yorkers between the "t" and "l" in the morpheme "bottle" (that is, New Yorkers say "bot'l" catching their breath for a moment in the glottal stop). Standard American English does not include this phone, the glottal stop, after the "t" in "bottle." (Standard American English, the officially preferred phonemes, morphemes, and syntax—the dialect—of newscasters on the national networks, among others in the educated professional class, avoids identifying the region or social class the speaker came from.)

Languages differ in the way they usually construct morphemes. Chinese is called an "isolating" language because its morphemes are generally short, just a consonant or two and a vowel, while German is "agglutinating" ("glues together"), combining several morphemes into one long word (example: *Weltanschauung,* "world" + "on" + "viewing" = "worldview"). Chinese differentiates morphemes in part by using different tones and pitches for two otherwise identical, consonant-vowel-consonant morphemes. German, and English, do not differentiate morphemes by tone and pitch, but we do employ tone and pitch in syntax: The difference between a declarative statement and a question comes from the rising pitch at the end of the question. (Try saying "The dog bit a man" flatly, and it is declarative. Let your voice rise on the last morpheme and it's a question, "The dog bit a man?" [Meaning something like, we thought that dog was only dangerous to cats.] And if you raise the pitch for the three last morphemes, it's an exclamation of surprise, "The dog bit a man?!" [We thought that dog would never bite anyone!])

Linguists argue over whether all human languages have the same basic syntax, or "deep structure," claimed by the contemporary American linguist Noam Chomsky to be "actor/subject" followed by "verb/action." Chomsky is accused of mistaking basic English syntax for basic human syntax. It does seem that the concepts of "actor," "action," "object of action," and "state of being" (no action, just being) are universal. What is basic, clearly shown by empirical (direct observation) research, is that human children learn to speak human language, whichever it may be, by a series of steps: first the toddler constructs simple one- or two-word sentences, verb ("Go!") or noun-verb ("Dada! drink!"). Then, a year or so later, the child figures out some more complicated syntax, for example in English that "-ed" signifies "past action," giving the child sentences such as "Daddy bopped the ball," but also "I drinked the milk." Another year, and the child is mastering the "irregular verbs" (actually regular, there are different rules for certain verbs) and can say "I drank," "Mommy drove," "Grandma went home."

Children learn a great deal more than phonemes, morphemes, and syntax as they acquire language. Body language—the way one holds oneself or moves—and gestures, tone and pitch of voice and appropriate noises, these are all culturally determined. Skilled actors are very much aware of how much they must control in order to effectively portray a person of a particular class and background. Supposedly WASPs ("White Anglo-Saxon Protestants") are often "uptight," hold themselves fairly straight. They use relatively few gestures and keep their arms close to the body, while African Americans are stereotyped as "hanging loose" with more relaxed posture and frequent, more sweeping gestures. Men, being on the average taller than women, tend to look straight out and women, averaging shorter, tend to look slightly upward in conversation, holding the head a little cocked, producing gender stereotypes that bother some short men—if they look up with head slightly cocked, it's "effeminate," and they may compensate by staring aggressively at other men. (Watch actor Dustin Hoffman in the film *Tootsie*. He first establishes his role as a man with scenes where his body language is strictly conventional manly behavior, then with brilliant subtlety uses *almost* perfect feminine body language and tone when he takes on a woman's role. Take this film seriously: it exhibits the *social roles* "man" and "woman.") American boys learn to prefer declarative sentences sounding authoritative, while girls observing women's behavior use the questioning pitch more often, conveying a non-challenging feminine attitude. American women learn to break into others' speaking, completing the sentence and constructing the next as if helping the other to build a story. (Is it extended from helping a child to learn to build an utterance?) American men learn to wait until the other guy has finished his say. Such learned cultural role behavior is seldom conscious but significantly affects communication.

The Sapir-Whorf Hypothesis: Language Affects Perception

Early in the twentieth century, Edward Sapir, one of Franz Boas's students and a poet, drew attention to how language affects perception. A blatant example occurs when you are asked to write down what someone is saying, let us say taking notes from a teacher who speaks with a strong foreign or regional accent. Do you write down what you actually heard—the phonemes that differ from Standard American English? Do you write down the "uh . . ." between words? the sniff or cough? You *heard* sounds different from Standard American English but your *perception* focused on recognizing morphemes, so that your written notes show only words in conventional spelling, not the dialect phonemes or the meaningless noises you actually heard. As little children, we learn to distinguish between morphemes and noises that do not carry meaning, and to figure out the standard phoneme overlying actual individual variations.

Sapir's student Benjamin Whorf spent most of his life employed in the insurance business. Analyzing how language conventions affect perception proved critical in that business. Whorf's most famous case was an airport employee who tossed a cigarette butt into an "empty" gasoline barrel. It exploded and caused a disastrous fire in the hangar. Was the employee negligent because he should have remembered that invisible gas fumes remain in a barrel after gasoline has been poured out? He argued that he had tried to be careful, that he had looked about for an empty metal container instead of dropping his cigarette on the oily floor. The word "empty" that came to his mind when he saw the barrel overrode his intellectual knowledge that fumes remain in gasoline containers. Thousands of dollars in insurance payment depended on whether the employee could be held to have been "negligent."

Whorf spent vacations in the American Southwest studying the Hopi and Navajo Indian languages. (These are quite different. Hopi is related to languages of Mexico, including that of the Aztecs, and Navajo to native languages of Western Canada.) He found that neither of these languages uses the actor-action-object sentence as frequently as does English. A sentence with only a verb is permissible in Navajo. This means that Navajos more accurately describe what they see when they say (in Navajo) "Raining," contrasted to English speakers whose rules of syntax force them to say, "It is raining." (What actually is "it?") Whorf's point was that English speakers are likely to *think* in terms of agents (actors) causing actions, to look for cause, even when it is not appropriate. Navajo speakers, he thought, should be less likely to assume that everything they see is caused by an agent.

The Sapir-Whorf hypothesis that language structure affects perception and thinking is very difficult to prove, although it sounds reasonable. A considerable advance has been made by the contemporary American linguist George Lakoff, approaching the question by way of studying metaphors. In Whorf's time, in the 1930s, philosophers were busy trying to make language more precise in hopes of better clarifying the issues they discussed. Using metaphors, it was generally believed, messed up thinking by mixing dissimilar things. Philosophers' ideal, at the time, was symbolic logic whereby algebra-like symbols are substituted for words. Engineers'

> metaphor: speaking *as if* something shares a characteristic of a different thing.
> Example: "Speech is golden." Speech has no color but it is valuable *like* gold.

successes with precisely defined and designed machinery and building projects suggested the possibility that social behavior could be better ordered if definitions of words and phrases were sharper, like engineering formulae. This was the time when Nazi engineers carefully designed efficient gas chambers for killing millions of people. Gas chambers are monsters! The metaphor effectively expresses the *significant* meaning of the Nazi operation, whereas a precise definition of the constructions misses the horror. Lakoff, beginning his work in the 1960s, decided to reconsider the role of metaphor in thinking.

Metaphors We Live By, published in 1980, is a small paperback with big print and exploding ideas. In it, Lakoff and his collaborator Mark Johnson examine our most basic notions about communicating and thinking. Their conclusion is that all thinking is ultimately grounded in real experience. We form concepts out of our actual experience, then extend the concept metaphorically by identifying similar aspects of other experiences: for example, little children get up, feel bouncy, when they are healthy and well rested; they lie down, drag, when they feel ill. So, we learn early that "happy" is "up," "misery" is "down." It seems natural to say, then, that "things are looking up" when you mean to communicate the likelihood of happiness (what things? real things? can those things, if any, *look*? have they eyes?). Likewise, you say, "I'm really down today" when you mean to communicate sadness, never mind that in actual fact you've been on your feet maybe on the top floor of a high-rise building all day. And computers are "up" when they're working, making their users happy, and "down" when they won't work and everyone is frustrated and unhappy. Physically, "up" or "down" has nothing to do with computer operation. Projecting from early experiences is the way we build understanding.

Expansion of concepts from our early experiences structures language. "Up" from feeling well develops into "up" equating with "good" and "desirable," so that we speak of "high" status, "high" quality, "high" standards. We put "high ranking" people on platforms higher than the common throng, we portray God "on high" on the upper portion of a painting with humans below him. Subordinates bow down, lower themselves, before their "superiors" (Latin *super:* above, *sub:* below). Early experience induces us to readily accept reifications such as thinking of "an idea" as "a thing," leading to the metaphor that communication is "sending ideas" from one person to another, as if in boxes via a mail carrier.

> *reification:* speaking of an abstract idea or intangible as if it were a physical thing

It isn't necessary for each one of us to have all the same early experiences to understand basic metaphors. Because one simple metaphor such as "idea/is like/a thing" is extended in many ways, we can figure out related meanings from more-or-less similar experiences. You can say, "I'll send this idea by electronic mail" and someone who had never seen a computer working could easily understand because "send" and "mail" are metaphors referring to very common experiences.

Lakoff's claim that metaphors are basic to human thinking is supported by studies of how scientists work. It used to be said that scientists must think logically ("given A, then B is likely"), but anthropological studies of actual scientists in laboratories revealed that many breakthrough ideas come through a new metaphor occurring to someone. In the early nineteenth century, researchers conceptualized many invisible phenomena—light, heat, electricity, magnetism, and the movement of atomic particles—as if they were waves, metaphorically extending their knowledge from seeing the behavior of water. Once electricity was thought of as a current (that is, electricity "flows" through a conductor *like* a current flows through water), scientists devised a number of fruitful experiments. A physicist interested in weather invented an apparatus for creating miniature clouds in a glass container, and then the basic metaphor "wave" conceptually connecting electricity and atoms with water gave scientists studying atoms the idea to use the cloud chamber apparatus for experiments in molecular physics.

More support for Lakoff's claim comes from American linguist Mary LeCron Foster's analyses of common features in languages worldwide. Certain general ideas seem to be regularly conveyed by speech movements that mimic the idea: for example, the sound "l" involving a relatively relaxed movement of the tongue seems to correlate with words meaning *loose, limp, fall, let,* and so on; the wider stretching of the lips to produce "y" sounds correlates with meanings having to do with the concept of "extending," such as *yet, yield, yard, yawn, yell, yearn.* Foster hypothesizes that primitive human language development in the Lower Paleolithic used these mouth movements metaphorically to convey somewhat abstract ideas. The repetition and symmetry of many Acheulian artifacts of the Lower Paleolithic evidences intellectual recognition of pattern and may have been associated with development of syntax (that is, order and pattern) in languages. In the Upper Paleolithic, Foster hypothesizes, after thousands of years of slow extension of the capacity to conceptualize and communicate abstract ideas, people realized that patterns can be inverted, reversed, repeated after intervals, disassembled and reassembled. That sophisticated grasp of pattern accelerated the development of more complex syntax, the creation of new words, and the invention of other media of communication such as painting, Foster suggests.

Sapir and Whorf were onto something when they postulated that basic features of languages influence the thinking of speakers of the language. Lakoff and other more recent linguists have expanded our understanding of how language and thinking are inter-related. The Sapir-Whorf hypothesis suggests, for example, that speakers of Indo-European languages such as English will be highly conscious of people's gender because Indo-European languages' syntax requires speakers to select pronouns according to the gender of the noun referred to ("he" versus "she"). Algonkian Indian languages such as Blackfoot do not require attention to sex gender: their pronouns differ according to whether the reference is alive or inanimate ("live being" versus "it"). Lakoff's work adds that Indo-European language speakers are likely to stereotype a great many phenomena as "masculine" or "feminine" according to whether we would stereotypically use a masculine or feminine pronoun; for example, "dogs are rough, cats are sweet" or "police work is heavy, typists' work is light." Blackfoot speakers are likely to stereotype a phenomenon such as thunder, which takes an animate pronoun, as having qualities of a live being, something unlikely to be conceptualized by an Indo-European speaker. All this being so, nevertheless we must remember that humans can consciously compensate for the basic structuring of their particular language. Being aware that linguistic structure does have some influence on thinking, is itself helpful in developing our ability for critical thinking.

Language and Speaking

Early in the twentieth century, the French linguist Ferdinand de Saussure noted the important difference between a language, in the sense of one taught in school from textbooks, and speaking. Saussure called formal language *langue,* and speaking *parole,* these being the French terms. We think of language as if what we've seen in schoolbooks is the real language, with rules of syntax and spelling and series of paradigms of irregular verbs. What we effortlessly speak, picked up from babyhood, doesn't exactly match the formal English we learned in school. Speaking, *parole*, should not be thought of as messy imperfect *langue* but parallel to it. Saying "I gotta go" instead of "I must leave now" is not the mark of a stupid uneducated person, it's normal *parole*. Linguists must study both formal *langue* and actual *parole*, respecting both.

Pursuing research related to *parole*, many anthropologists and linguists challenged stereotypes of "good" and "poor" speech. They realized that pidgin languages, created out of two quite different languages where speakers of each must interact frequently in business but neither has incentive to really learn the others' language, are efficient means of fulfilling business communication needs. They realized that languages and dialects have a political function in signaling class and ethnic group affiliation; from the point of view of the dominant social group, speaking with a lower-class accent or dialect appears disadvantageous, marking the speaker as subordinate, but to the lower-class speakers it may demonstrate pride in their family and heritage. Some years ago, the English sociolinguist Basil Bernstein contrasted what he termed the "elaborated" speech of upper-class English people, who teach their children to use complex sentences and to develop a paragraph logically, with what seemed to him the "restricted" speech of working-class people. "Elaborated" speech fit a professional class performing in law courts and executive offices and living in multi-roomed homes where children were taught to separate themselves from the servants surrounding them. Listening to working-class English people, it seemed to Bernstein that they more frequently used incomplete sentences and a smaller vocabulary with their children. Bernstein believed this handicapped working-class children in school. Subsequent studies of working-class teenagers in England brought out how the "lads" deliberately rejected using the "proper" English their teachers attempted to instill. The "lads" realized that the likelihood of their getting high-class jobs was poor, even if they graduated with good grades from their working-class secondary school, and rather than alienate the friends they could count on, they affirmed their loyalty by sharing working-class dress, recreation, and speech. Not long after Bernstein's initial studies, this aggressive working-class punk cultural pattern was noticed by disaffected young people of other classes and achieved wide popularity as punk rock. The direct, simple, four-letter-word style, teamed with a powerful hard-hitting rock beat, expressed the emotions of young men and women of all classes crowded in cities.

While millions of young people grooved to Sting, the Sex Pistols, Eric Clapton, and Mick Jagger, several scholars including the English anthropologist Jack Goody were thinking about the role of writing and literacy in societies. This attention, too, stemmed from Saussure's fruitful distinction between formal language and speaking. Writing tends to "fossilize" language (in the sense of *langue*): A standard form is presented and preserved. The standard is accessible to all literate people but not to the illiterate, and formal education separates the literate, making them a social class, from the illiterate. From the earliest historic periods, in all societies developing writing, literacy has been a marker of higher social class. Sometimes laws forbade teaching slaves or peasants to read. Writing makes it easier to classify long lists of things, including behavior classified under legal codes, and makes it easier to declare that written rules define the norm, labeling variant behavior "deviant." It is no coincidence that writing developed with the inception of complex state societies ruling hundreds of thousands, or millions, of people. The American movement, beginning in the mid-nineteenth century, to provide schooling at taxpayers' expense for all children—and backing up the opportunity with laws enforcing school attendance—was indeed revolutionary. It is true that much of the enthusiasm for mandatory public schooling came from industries' need for literate workers, but the expansion of literacy did facilitate democratic procedures.

Universal public education raised the issue of class differences in language, as Bernstein realized. In the United States and Canada, controversies flare over whether children must use Standard American English. Standard English facilitates social mobility, since it is heard and taught all over the continent and someone speaking it can fit in with educated people in any business or profession. But Standard English seems to some people to be like packaged sliced white bread, uniform and bland, in contrast to regional or class dialects that trigger memories of generations of one's own people, of the land one grew up in, its sounds and way of being. Regional and class dialects carry a group's heritage, incorporating words and some syntax from foreign languages and phrases drawn from the group's surroundings and activities. African American dialects, for example, differ from Standard American English in part because they are likely to use an African language syntax form as a variant on Standard English (e.g., "be. . ." instead of "is . . ." or "was . . ." when long duration of the action is meant). Should people be urged to drop a variant reflecting their ancestry, in order to sound like an ad for sliced white bread? Should children from Spanish-speaking American or American Indian families be forced to speak only a language brought here by invaders who fought their ancestors? On the other hand, employers, landlords, and police may associate dialects other than Standard American with ignorance and immorality. Should children be permitted to put themselves at risk of suffering prejudice? It doesn't have to be either/or; most people can "code-switch," if they wish, once they've heard the differences. The controversy continues because it is the tip of the volcano of societal conflicts over privilege versus rights.

Studies of class and gender differences in dialect, and of the uses and effects of literacy, have become part of a broad sociolinguistic interest in the languages of "muted groups." A number of linguists are assisting subordinated ethnic groups to maintain their languages. Nationalists in Wales demanded a television channel broadcasting in Welsh. At first, the British Broadcasting Corporation dismissed the requests, claiming few people speak Welsh and even they understand English. When one leader in desperation went on a hunger strike, the BBC gave in. Along with their own language on television and radio, the nationalists have persuaded schools in Wales to use the language, and one can hear parents speaking Welsh with their children to encourage it, then lapsing into the English they grew up with when the kids are out of earshot. Speaking Welsh powerfully reminds people that England had conquered their country, had exploited their people (labor conditions in Welsh coal mines were notorious), and that greater Welsh sovereignty might be to their benefit. American Indians similarly are tying parental insistence on maintenance of the native language through its use in local schools, newspapers, and radio to increased demands for sovereignty as recognized in the treaties made between the United States and Canadian governments and the Indian nations they encountered in their expansion. Having the Indian actors speak Lakota in the movie *Dances with Wolves* was hailed as a breakthrough in forcing the American public to respect the reality of Indian nations. Contrast those scenes with older films' Indians grunting "Ugh" or speaking broken English. Languages are instruments for communicating not only overt messages through morphemes and syntax but also political statuses through popular association of particular language forms with class and ethnic groups.

RECOMMENDED READINGS

In the Case Studies in Cultural Anthropology Series (Fort Worth: Harcourt
    Brace)

Esman, Marjorie R. *Henderson, Louisiana: Cultural Adaptation in a Cajun Community.*
    1985.

Hostetler, John A. and Gertrude Enders Huntington. *The Hutterites in North America.*
    1996. (Hutterites are a Protestant religious sect that uses their forebears' German
    language to maintain their culture and separation from nonbelievers.)

Parman, Susan. *Scottish Crofters: A Historical Ethnography of a Celtic Village.* 1990.

Wong, Bernard. *Chinatown: Economic Adaptation and Ethnic Identity of the Chinese.*
    1982.

REFERENCES

Foster, Mary LeCron. Symbolic Origins and Transitions in the Palaeolithic. In *The Emergence of Modern Humans: An Archaeological Perspective,* ed. Paul Mellars. Edinburgh: Edinburgh University Press, 1990, pp. 517–539.

Goody, Jack. *The Domestication of the Savage Mind.* Cambridge: Cambridge University Press, 1977.

Lakoff, George. *Women, Fire, and Dangerous Things.* Chicago: University of Chicago Press, 1987.

Lakoff, George and Mark Johnson. *Metaphors We Live By.* Chicago: University of Chicago Press, 1980.

Linton, Ralph. *The Study of Man.* New York: Appleton-Century-Crofts, 1936.

9

Analyzing Societies (I): Cultural Ecology

```
                              D
                 L                      V
          R          V A L U E S              I
     expression        and        recreation
                    SOCIALIZING
     A R T S   (visual, musical, dramatic, literary)   G A M E S
                         N  O  F
                 T            S
          G U  L                 O           E
     R                             C
                                     E T  Y
     W    law    politics    religion    kinship    W
          MANUFACTURE      and      DISTRIBUTION

          P R O D U C T I O N    O F   R A W    M A T E R I A L S

               E N V I R O N M E N T
```

A Framework For Analysis

How do anthropologists understand living societies? In contrast to the tantalizingly fragmentary archaeological record, living societies are overwhelmingly rich in data. Participant observation is like parachuting into Disneyland, all kinds of people bustling here and there. Some of them, you're sure, are masking their real selves, and you suspect that some of the structures around you may not really be very true to the past they supposedly represent. Anthropologists try to follow the basic scientific method of recording careful observations, organizing them according to what seems likely to be significant principles of classification, and checking the validity of these hypothesized principles by seeing how well they accommodate new data. This mode, of scientific analysis, is one of *our* modern Western worldviews. It won't closely match perspectives of people in the society, although there will be overlap. Both descriptions, the scientific and the native, are worth presenting: The scientific uses terms and looks for principles of organization that may be universally valid, the native highlights concepts that the particular society tends to believe are important.

> *participant observation:* living in a community in order to learn and understand their culture

The chart beginning this chapter is a visual map for ordering observational data on living societies. The base for the society is mapped as the base of the chart: the environment. We make it big and bold to indicate how important it is. Out of the environment, people produce raw materials—food, fuel, materials for housing, clothing, cooking, tools. The arrow connecting the environment with production of raw materials goes both ways because production always affects the environment. Out of produced raw materials, people manufacture all their artifacts. "Manufacture" means processing food as well as making objects. "Distribution" is on the same line as "manufacture" because these are two aspects of getting items to people who want them. The eighteenth-century Scottish economist Adam Smith called production of raw materials the "primary sector" of the economy, manufacture the "secondary sector," and distribution and service occupations the "tertiary sector," a reasonable mapping but one that pulls apart the actually tightly linked manufacturing and distribution activities ("supply and demand").

Manufacture and distribution, as well as primary production from raw resources, are connected with what Karl Marx called the "social relations of production," relationships between workers and managers, suppliers and consumers, all historical actualities affected by location, wars, climate, health factors. Above the physical components of human societies we have placed laws, political structures, organized religious groups, and prescribed family relationships. These all regulate how people in the society are to act toward others, naming social roles and procedures to assign persons to them. These several systems of regulating society are held to be necessary. On a higher plane, socializing, expressing emotions and poetic images, the pleasures of experiencing beauty and playing games, are what make living worthwhile to humans. In these activities we can glimpse the values that guide people, and their worldview framing all behavior.

This and the following chapters will discuss these several levels, or focuses, for analyzing societies.

Level One: Cultural Ecology

E N V I R O N M E N T

The environment is the foundation of all organic life. Out of it come the biochemical molecules with which we build and move our bodies. We couldn't live for even a few minutes in the emptiness of outer space—unless, of course, we were to use our technology to construct an environment in a capsule and stay inside that simulation of an earth environment. We and our environments are interactive.

Ecology is the term for the concept that living organisms and their environment interact. Any organism, even a tiny bacterium, affects its environment simply by breathing, consuming nutrients, eliminating body wastes, and becoming a decaying corpse. Big organisms such as humans affect their environments even if they live entirely by collecting wild foods and sleeping in natural shelters: humans' food needs affect the numbers and probably the growth and reproductive success of the plants and animals collected, and human body wastes change the chemistry of the soil on which they fall.

> Ecology is the study of the interaction of living organisms and their habitat. The word was first spelled "œcology," from Greek *oikos,* "house," + *-logia,* "speaking with a certain knowledge." We think of the environment as an organism's "house." Ecology describes the "house" —the environment—and how organisms live in it.

With Neolithic farming, human groups began consciously to change their environments. As the French anthropologist Claude Lévi-Strauss put it, societies that lived by collecting natural resources were like the neighborhood handyman who picks up stuff laying around that might be useful, and can knock together a shed or shelf out of what's piled up in his backyard. In French, the fellow's called a *bricoleur,* and what he cobbles together is *bricolage.* In contrast, said Lévi-Strauss, people who consider themselves modern decide what they would like and design it, inventing materials such as plastics if no natural materials will enable them to complete the design. Lévi-Strauss calls this approach to life "engineers' thinking." Bricoleurs can create some very beautiful and efficient artifacts—think of the delicately flaked, sharp, leaf-shaped javelin points made by Upper Paleolithic people and their contemporaries, Paleo-Indians in the Americas—but there are limits set by the characteristics of the raw materials. "Engineers' " minds overturn natural limits. The Holocene has been the

This man in India using an elephant, something he's seen around, to do what an engineer constructed a bulldozer to do, is an example of bricoleur *thinking.*

Photo credit: Milwaukee Public Museum.

heyday of the engineers, beginning with radically changing organism populations in selected localities through agriculture, then building those gigantic human anthills we call cities, and finally erecting those enclosed mall complexes where people ice skate in summer around tropical foliage as the long-dead Elvis's voice booms through the filtered air.

It's all ecology, whether you study owls in remote forests or sparrows thriving on the crumbs from McDonald's in mall parking lots. When you focus on the interaction between humans and their environments, with particular attention to people's beliefs about their world and the way their customs affect their environment, you are studying *cultural ecology*. Anthropologists have been fascinated by the variety of interpretations of the nature of the world. If the world is things out there and we go out into it to get a living, why should there be any differences in conceptions of the world? Nineteenth-century anthropologists assumed nonwestern peoples were either of lesser brain development or ignorant because they were cut off from the discoveries of modern science. Hundreds of anthropological studies show that a scientific way of thinking—careful observations from which generalizations are drawn and tested—is characteristic of some people in every society, and that much scientific knowledge is incorporated in every cultural tradition. Simply to survive, every society has to do some study of its ecology. Differences in interpretation come partly from differences in the environments in which people live, and partly from profound philosophical ideas that suggest how the world should appear.

Historians formerly believed that science was invented in Classical Greece and developed in the western cultural tradition. A prominent biochemist, Joseph Needham, became curious why science "had not developed" in China, and began researching Chinese history. Needham found that in fact, China has a long and impressive tradition of scientific research. It had been unknown in the West because the few western historians able to read Chinese hadn't been interested in documents on science. At the same time, in the 1960s, that Joseph Needham was discovering the history of Chinese science, astronomers were recognizing the scientific knowledge behind Neolithic and American Indian sky observatories; linguists were recording the science embedded in "folk" classifications of plants, animals, and geology; and medical anthropologists were demonstrating the scientific basis of much "folk" medicine. Scientific observation and experimentation are practiced in all cultures.

French anthropologist Pierre Bourdieu gives us the term *habitus* to refer to a "way of being," covering both the ecology of a society (its environment and interaction with that environment) and its habitual interpretation of the nature of the world and its people (worldview). Bourdieu emphasizes the dynamic interactive relationship between a society and its environment, how the environment limits what people might do and at the same time stimulates us humans to get around the limitations, to invent technology and social practices that open options. Bourdieu's concept of habitus goes beyond active interaction to cover also how people in a society perceive their accustomed environment, the features they pay attention to, features they use in metaphors (e.g., "His heart is as hard as a rock"), and how they teach their members to regard their environment—for example, is the deep forest threatening, as in European fairy tales, or an embracing parent, as the Mbuti in the Congo believe.

worldview: people's belief about the universe and humanity (*not* people's notions about foreigners!)

Children are socialized, in their communities, to accept certain conditions as "natural." In traditional middle-class American homes, children have been

Eight photos illustrating "habitus"

Nias, Indonesia, 1930. Tropical coastal habitat. Dress and houses adapted to local conditions; the government-recognized village headman wears a foreign hat to mark his office, but keeps clothing suited to the climate.

Photo credit: Milwaukee Public Museum.

Port Moresby, New Guinea, 1928. Another tropical coastal habitat. Fishermen's houses here are raised above high-water level. (Note dugout canoe at left between homes.) Women and girls wear cool, shredded-fiber skirts like those of women in the nearby Trobriand islands.

Photo credit: Milwaukee Public Museum.

Cameroons, Africa, 1959. Bafut house. Another tropical habitat, this one an agricultural state where leading families even in villages build more imposing houses to mark their social power.

Photo credit: Milwaukee Public Museum.

The Acropolis, Athens, Greece. Classical Greeks took basic building forms and expressed them on large scale in local stone, to symbolize the power and permanence of the Athenian state. Even the common sight of women bearing loads on their heads is translated into huge female figures bearing the gods' temple.

Photo credit: Milwaukee Public Museum.

Near Pisa, Italy, 1928. The barefoot women bearing loads on their heads, the oxcart and horse-cart, the plastered houses with tile roofs and stone-faced temple (church), exhibit a cultural tradition several thousand years old adapted to the Mediterranean habitat.

Photo credit: Milwaukee Public Museum.

Indigenous Ojibwe Indian homestead near Lake Superior, with wigwam made of mats roofed with birchbark sheets.

Photo credit: Milwaukee Public Museum.

Ojibwe homestead, 1925. The family now lives in a European-style log cabin on its homestead.

Photo credit: Milwaukee Public Museum.

1936, Ojibwe family constructing a traditional wigwam in a city park for an ethnic-heritage festival.

Photo credit: Milwaukee Public Museum.

socialized to believe that men are born to be strong and aggressive and women born to easily cry, be silly and vain. Not only drama (including television shows like *I Love Lucy* and *Leave It to Beaver*) but also social practices reinforce the stereotypes in the worldview. Traditional middle-class American families pushed their boys to be active exploring the neighborhood and in competitive sports, while they kept girls close to the house and out of sports. Girls were smiled upon if they giggled a lot, boys were not. In restaurants, men ordered for women at the table as well as for themselves, and paid the bill, as if women couldn't handle speaking out or simple arithmetic. Since most people, wanting to be liked, more or less conform to what is prescribed for their role in society, the usual way of interpreting the natural world and human fate seems to be supported by people's experience. It's circular: Children are taught that boys "naturally" don't cry and girls do, so boys repress tears and girls readily weep. So see! you hardly ever see a boy cry and you do see girls cry. To challenge your society's worldview and habitus would seem the act of a crazy person who can't recognize the way the world is, the normal "way of being." The value of cross-cultural comparisons is the revelation of what behavior is the result of socialization in particular societies, and what behavior seems species-specific to *Homo sapiens sapiens*. Among Lakota Sioux, both men and women have been socialized that adults "naturally" break into tears during a speech expressing strong emotion. European visitors were surprised, and disturbed, when dignified men wept openly as they orated—and Lakota thought European men were "naturally" stony, "naturally" unlike fully human people such as the Lakota.

Worldview and habitus may not be challenged often, but they can be challenged, and they can change bit by bit. No society is static, unchanging. Any society that tried to prevent all change, never allow any modification, would be unable to survive more than a few generations at best, for the natural environment changes, and so do the society's demographics (population characteristics such as birth and death rates, number of people of various ages, of men and of women), and so do neighboring societies. The nineteenth-century opinion that only western societies are dynamic and changing, and nonwestern societies are rigidly "traditional," was simply propaganda for legitimatizing conquest—the "benighted heathen" supposedly blindly followed their traditional practices and needed to be freed by the colonial powers, sort of like a slew of Sleeping Beauties waiting for their Princes. The historian of science Arthur Lovejoy found that at the beginning of western history, by 700 B.C. in Classical Greece, already there was the stereotype that remote tribes had primitive cultures, which were either innocently good or horridly cruel, and "civilized" Greeks could journey to these places to observe pure Natural Man. Over on the other side of Eurasia, Chinese had similar stereotypes. The stereotype of one's own society being dynamic, creative, full of intelligent people, while foreigners are dull slaves to custom, functions very well to keep people working within their society—maybe not contented, but sure that they'd be worse off among the barbarians.

Cultural ecology tries to break out of the value judgments conventionally made about cultural practices. It begins with the premise that any society that survives over generations has adapted reasonably well to the conditions and resources of its environment (see the lower part of the chart, Fig. 9.1) and that its worldview, values, and customs (see the upper part of the chart, Fig. 9.1) reflect its environmental situation and support the ecological interaction. The nonhuman ecology of the region must be observed and analyzed: the landforms and soils, climate, water supply, animals and plants. The human population must be observed: numbers of people, their density per unit of land, their mode of subsistence, housing, transportation. The interaction between humans and the land—the human ecology—must be plotted out. Is the population low in relation to resources? high? well adjusted? Is it stable in numbers, or rapidly changing? Are its techniques of resource extraction sustainable over a long period or wasteful, damaging to the land's capacity to regenerate? What is known from archaeology or historical documents about the region's earlier human ecology? When the ecology is described, the anthropologist can get to the fun part, teasing out the way the culture is molded by its natural situation and in turn molds that situation (the interplay Bourdieu terms *habitus*). Anthropologists noted a century ago that we can map out *culture areas,* geographic regions each with its distinctive cultural pattern reflecting adaptation to the region's natural attributes *plus* the influence of neighboring societies.

Sometimes cultural ecology shows a straightforward relationship between a society's culture and its ecology. On the Northwestern Plains of the United States and adjacent Canada (Wyoming, Montana, Alberta, Saskatchewan), grasses are the principal plant cover and bovines (bison and cattle) the principal food animal. Before the Eurasian grass, wheat, was imported, grain agriculture was impossible; the region is too dry for the native American grain, maize (corn). The best way for people to gain a living from this land was by hunting bison, the native bovine. To balance the diet, camas (a native tuber) was cultivated in its natural habitat, other native roots such as the prairie turnip were collected, and surplus meat and hides could be traded at the farming towns along the Missouri River and its tributaries in North Dakota for maize, as well as for pipe stone, for a glassy rock that makes excellent, sharp arrowheads and knife blades, and for ornaments. The cultural ecology of the Northwestern Plains nations—Blackfoot, Gros Ventres, Sarsi, Cree—focused on the bison herds until European invasions drastically altered it. Communities were small and nomadic, moving camp in a pattern resembling the movements of the bison, wintering in sheltered valleys or parkland and traveling farther in the warm months. Each year, bison congregated by the thousands in summer, socializing and finding mates, and the people congregated at the same time, socializing, trading, holding religious ceremonies, mediating conflicts, gambling, courting. As the snows approached, the lively rendezvous camps, like the bison herds, divided again into small village groups that returned to the wooded spots where they could be protected from the worst storms and find firewood. Bison and humans were in symbiosis, the humans surviving on bison meat and the bison population thriving because the humans burned over the land each year to foster growth of the nutritious grasses the bison grazed. This symbiosis, and the similarity between bison herds and human communities in size, habitat, and annual cycle, were recognized by the humans, whose worldview held that the bison (and other animals of the Plains) are other nations, each with its particular customs and language. Bison were believed to feel kinship with human communities, occasionally in the past to have visited them transformed in appearance to humans, and to willingly enter the humans' corrals to enable their human friends to survive.

European invasions broke this habitus, this way of being. Competition for land in eastern North America between what would total millions of immigrants from Europe and the native American nations drove Indian nations westward. More and more Indians tried to make a living hunting bison, west of the colonies of Euro-Americans. In the nineteenth century, that colonization reached the Plains, plowing up bison habitat and bringing in a competing bovine from Europe, cattle. The bison herds were exterminated and the Indian nations forced to surrender their lands in exchange for famine relief.

Now there is another habitus on the Plains. The majority of the people now living on the Plains have been socialized in a cultural tradition that declares animals to be very different from humans, to lack souls and be of low intelligence. Animals and plants are to be controlled wholly by humans. Radically altering the landscape, replacing natural forms with clearly artificial rectangular shapes (fenced fields, houses and yards, street grids, shopping malls), is highly valued. Cultural ecology points out that a key factor in the difference between the two habituses, the two ways of being, is wheat: With no native American cultigen (crop) able to sustain full-scale agriculture on the Northwestern Plains, its original human inhabitants had to adapt to the principal available resource, bison herds, developing symbiosis with them for maximum utilization of the region. Bison apparently can't be tamed, so they couldn't be domesticated and their independence had to be respected by their human neighbors. Then came a new ingredient in the ecology. Wheat, once it was imported, grew well on the Northern Plains. To grow it, the native grasses were destroyed so wheat could be substituted. Domesticated cattle were substituted for the independent bison. Such wholesale substitution of Europeans' preferred resources, carried out through destruction of the native resources, fit and reinforced a worldview that claimed humans are meant to command the world. Cultural ecology explains the differences between Blackfoot and Euro-American worldviews as stemming from their different resource bases, from which people develop a habitual mode of subsistence, social relations, and values.

Cultural ecology as a research strategy is not supposed to make value judgments. A nomadic life of bison hunting and root and berry gathering, with its worldview of respect toward the other animal nations sharing the habitat, is not *in itself* better, or worse, than the European-derived radical substitution of rectangular fields and yards and houses and street grids for a less obviously modified native grassland with scattered clusters of conical tipis. Recent studies urge us to add another dimension to cultural ecological studies: Is the habitus sustainable? We learned the hard way, during the 1930s' Dust Bowl drought, that plowing let precious topsoil blow away, or run into streams after rains. Thousands of families were beaten by the inadequacy of their technology to maintain the resources they depended upon. The ecological disasters we have watched in the twentieth century—the Dust Bowl, the creep of Sahara sand dunes over destabilized African farmlands, the rapid rise in river-borne diseases in Egypt once the Nile floods were contained in back of the Aswan Dam, the destruction of temperate-zone forests and lake life by acid rain, the massive erosion of tropical lands after clear-cutting their forests—all these and so many more examples of overwhelming impact teach the basic lesson of cultural ecology, that human societies *adapt to their environment* and *adapt their environments to them*. For long-term security, we must weigh the effects of our customs on the world we live in, and seek to construct a "way of being" based on real symbiosis. From that perspective, restoring native Plains grasses and bison herds in place of the wheat farms makes sense; geographers from Rutgers University proposed doing that, turning the western Plains back into a "Buffalo Commons." Ranchers would cull the herds and sell the lean, healthful bison meat to cover the mini-

---

"The reason there are no more elk in the mountains is that prairie chickens don't dance on the prairie anymore."

Anthropologist Alan Marshall had mentioned to his Nez Perce Indian teacher, Cyrus Red Elk, that Idaho game wardens were concerned about how few elk remained in the mountains. Marshall remarked that the increase in logging no doubt was responsible for the reduction in elk in the mountain forests. Mr. Red Elk replied, "No. The reason that there is no more game in the mountains is that prairie chickens don't dance on the prairie anymore."

This must refer to a Nez Perce myth, Marshall thought. Nez Perce had pointed out to him that prairie chickens (sharp-tailed grouse) and humans are the only species that prepare special places and gather there to drum, sing, and dance. Nez Perce believe that when they drum and dance ceremonially at these time-honored dancing grounds, spirit beings dance with them, renewing the bonds that bring blessings and prosperity to the people. Presumably, when prairie chickens dance, their spirit friends are with them, too. Did Mr. Red Elk believe that the elk population depends on the prairie chickens' spirit friends?

Marshall discovered that prairie chickens no longer danced on the prairie in Idaho because large-scale Euro-American farming destroyed the native grasslands in the broad valleys. These grasslands had been the principal wintering grounds of the elk. The critical factor in elk survival was not the mountain forests where they summered and were hunted by sportsmen, but the prairie valleys and the deep, warm sheltering canyons cutting through them. Mr. Red Elk knew why there is no more game in the mountains; he explained it succinctly. There was nothing mystical in the explanation: Red Elk thought Marshall would realize that the disappearance of prairie chickens was the clue to radical changes in the ecology affecting other species, such as elk, that utilized prairie chicken habitat.

mal costs of sustaining the Buffalo Commons. Long-term sustainable subsistence practices aren't pie-in-the-sky, they will be inevitable.

The best way to understand human ecology is to read several ethnographic studies. Ecology has been given a prominent place in most ethnographic work since the mid-twentieth century. One landmark book in cultural ecology was *The Nuer*, by British anthropologist E. E. Evans-Pritchard, published in 1940. Nuer live in the Sudan region of East Africa. Much of that country is range land suitable for cattle but, except for limited areas, not for agriculture. Consequently, Nuer economy has been based primarily on raising cattle, and the people much admire fine cattle, give cattle as wedding gifts and to seal contracts, sing songs about how lovely a herd is as the lowing cows enter their pen in the evening, etc. The leader of a Nuer village is called its "bull" (even when the leader is a woman). Nuer habitus is organized around the needs of cattle, for if their cattle sicken, the people may starve. Neighboring the Nuer are the Dinka, whose land is better for farming. Evans-Pritchard described the Dinka as perpetual victims of Nuer raids to capture cattle. Later anthropologists, including Francis Mading Deng (who is himself Dinka), picture the Dinka more favorably, recording many instances of Nuer settling peaceably among Dinka. A cultural ecological analysis, of which Evans-Pritchard's work was the pioneer, clarifies the situation. Environmental conditions in the southern Sudan can be harsh and fluctuating, with extensive prolonged flooding from the upper Nile in some years and drought in others. These fluctuations threaten farmers, who are fixed in one place. Cattle, because they are mobile, are a kind of insurance against crop failure. The labels "Nuer" and "Dinka" refer to complementary economic adaptations, primarily cattle herding or primarily farming, that allow the human population to fully utilize the region over the long term.

The power of ecological analysis to illuminate the foundation of a society has made this approach popular among anthropologists since *The Nuer* was published. Colin Turnbull described how well adapted the Mbuti of the Congo, in Africa, are to their environment, their unusually small size (they are the African "pygmies") letting them run nimbly through the tropical forest that continually caught the big Britisher Turnbull in its tangle of branches. The Mbuti think of the forest as their parent, providing food, shelter, and safety. They respect it as children do their parent, even sing to it. Mbuti trade meat from their hunting and other forest products to neighboring Bantu-speaking agricultural villagers for metal knives and palm wine, and are happy to visit if a villager is hosting a feast, but they consider farming hard, hot work and they enjoy greater freedom in their shady forest. A comparable study has been provided by Richard Lee, an American anthropologist, of the Dobe Ju/'hoansi (formerly called !Kung), a Basarwa group (popularly called Bushmen). The Ju/'hoansi live in the Kalahari Desert of South Africa and adjacent Namibia and Botswana. Like the Mbuti, they hunt and gather wild foods. Like most Mbuti, most Ju/'hoansi desire little in the way of material possessions, prizing their independence from outside government. Intensively recording Ju/'hoansi daily activities, Lee found that they enjoyed more leisure than most working people in larger societies. Turnbull's and Lee's ecological analyses demonstrated that the standard western notion that hunting-gathering people live lives that are "nasty, brutish, and short," as the seventeenth-century English philosopher Hobbes put it, is quite wrong. Turnbull and Lee showed, also, that the values of freedom and respect may be more important to some people than material possessions: Many Mbuti and Ju/'hoansi who did want clothes, radios, beer, and cigarettes left their nomadic bands to work on farms or in towns; the bands Turnbull and Lee observed were the people for whom liberty was worth more. A depressing postscript to Lee's work is that the South African government insisted on "civilizing" Basarwa, forcing many bands to remain permanently in reservation villages where they were supposed to raise goats and farm. Since the Kalahari is a desert, farming requires irrigation and the government skimped on developing this, leaving the Basarwa to depend on welfare payments. The Mbuti are threatened by the widescale destruction of the African forests. Demands of large national populations for resources may leave no space for small societies to sustain different ways of being.

Cultural ecology takes into account social factors in a group's environment. Imposition of South African rule on the Basarwa changed their habitus, willy-nilly. The woman whose practiced eye can find nutritious roots in the dry land-scape and the sure-shot bowman no longer garner admiration. In their place, the smart guys who can speak English and read and promise votes to politicians influence the community. The Kalahari itself hasn't changed much, especially the sections now incorporated into a nature preserve; it's the political condition that has changed. In his 1940s' pioneer work, Evans-Pritchard had initially ignored the political aspect of Nuer ecology, writing as if there were no British colonial power recently extended over Nuer country (though it was only because of that conquest that he was given funds to study the Nuer). Subsequently, Evans-Pritchard insisted on acknowledging historical circumstances. A look at historical circumstances for Basarwa by anthropologist Carmel Schrire revealed that in the seventeenth century, when European and African Bantu colonization hit South Africa, Basarwa generally lived in villages raising cattle. Squeezed between two invaders, one from overseas, one from the north, each with much greater population and better weaponry, the Basarwa moved out of the desirable cattle-pasture lands into the Kalahari. Their hunting-gathering way of life was not the continuation of a Paleolithic culture, but a historic adaptation. This revelation underscores the dynamic nature of the ecological relationship. No historic society is simply a remnant of Paleolithic culture; all the living societies we have observed are adapted to modern conditions.

RECOMMENDED READINGS

In the Case Studies in Cultural Anthropology Series

Lee, Richard B. *The Dobe Ju/'hoansi* (earlier editions use the title The Dobe Kung), 1994.
Turnbull, Colin. *The Mbuti Pygmies: Adaptation and Change*, 1983.

Other case studies highlighting cultural ecology include:

Goldschmidt, Walter. *The Sebei: A Study in Cultural Adaptation.* The Sebei of East Africa are comparable to the Nuer and Dinka in carrying on both farming and cattle pastoralism. 1987.

Hallowell, A. Irving. *The Ojibwa of Berens River, Manitoba.* The ecology of Northern Canada makes fishing, hunting, and commercial trapping a viable twentieth-century economy for the Ojibwa; Hallowell in the 1930s and the editor of his notes, contemporary ethnohistorian Jennifer Brown, clarify the interrelationship between history, ecology, and Ojibwa worldview. 1992.

Kintz, Ellen M. *Life Under the Tropical Canopy: Tradition and Change Among the Yucatec Maya.* Kintz skillfully shows the interaction between the Yucatec tropical environment and the Maya who have populated it for many centuries. Since the Maya habitus was first their independent kingdoms, then the imposition of Spanish colonization, and now greater integration into the international economy, Kintz can bring out the interplay of values and environmental potential. 1990.

Parman, Susan *Scottish Crofters: A Historical Ethnography of a Celtic Village.* Gaelic-speaking Highlanders in Scotland were supposed to be another unchanged primitive way of life, but historical research indicates that much of the crofting culture is the effect of nineteenth-century agribusiness development by wealthy landowners. With the sea on one side and the laird's sheep range on the other, the residents work to keep their niche. 1990.

Tonkinson, Robert. *The Mardu Aborigines: Living the Dream in Australia's Desert.* It is instructive to compare the Australian Aborigines with Basarwa (Ju/'hoansi). Both have been pushed out of their most productive land over the past couple of centuries. The Aborigines are famous for their devotion to their own religious traditions, teaching that their rituals and actions are necessary to the perpetuation of the world as they know it—part of the "business" of men and women, they say. This understanding gives an interesting ecological sophistication to their culture. 1991.

REFERENCES

Bourdieu, P. *Outline of a Theory of Practice.* Cambridge: Cambridge University Press, 1977.

Lévi-Strauss, C. *The Savage Mind,* Chicago: University of Chicago Press, 1966.

Lovejoy, Arthur O. and George Boas, *Primitivism and Related Ideas in Antiquity,* 1963. (First edition 1935.) Baltimore: The Johns Hopkins University Press, 1997 reprint.

Marshall, Alan G. " 'Prairie Chickens Dancing'. . .": Ecology's Myth. In *Idaho Folklife: Homesteads to Headstones,* ed. Louie W. Attebery, University of Utah Press. Pp. 101–107. 1985.

Needham, Joseph et al. *Science and Civilization in China,* Multi-volume series. Cambridge: Cambridge University Press, 1954 et seq.

C·H·A·P·T·E·R   **10**

Analyzing Societies (II): Economics

In this chapter, we focus on the next level up in our chart:

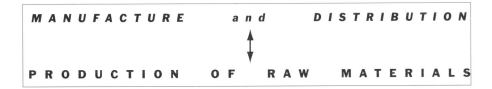

MANUFACTURE	and	DISTRIBUTION
PRODUCTION	OF RAW	MATERIALS

Getting a living is economics. "Production of raw materials," "manufacture and distribution" are *economic* activities. A community's economy involves the resources available to its members, their technology, and social organizations for utilizing the resources.

Economics is embedded in ecology, which is why the sentences above sound much like the preceding chapter. Focusing on economics, the production of raw materials including food and manufacture and distribution of the material culture of a society, this chapter lifts the human activities out of the ecological matrix for a finer-tuned examination of the social relations of getting a living.

Comparing Anthropological Economics to Formal Economics

College courses in economics tend to limit their field to *formal economics,* models of modern western economic systems recognized in government planning.

The discipline of formal economics was created in the late eighteenth and the nineteenth centuries by European philosophers and politicians setting out a rational explanation for the social changes we call the Industrial Revolution. Early modern (seventeenth-century) European states replaced the medieval feudal structure of personal loyalties and little choice of occupation with the impersonal structure of centralized political power enforced through codes of law. Citizens were no longer expected to seek aristocratic patrons and serve, if requested, in their private armies battling for the throne (vividly dramatized in Shakespeare's historical plays). Earning a living moved into a national framework, with people free (as medieval serfs had not been) to change jobs and move to where there was a market demand for their goods or skills. Personal mobility prompted people to think of the national state as their arena, and their protector against tyrannical local lords. In the first phase of modern state-building, English philosopher Thomas Hobbes argued that humans "naturally" fight like dogs for a bit of meat, and that such a "war of all against all" is controlled by enlightened people realizing that to escape "nasty, brutish and short" lives they must contract (formally agree) to establish offices of authority entitled to enforce laws for the common good. A century after Hobbes, Adam Smith thought he discerned "the invisible hand" of the market manipulating social relations. The form of the modern European state with its central authority enforcing written laws over all persons in its territories was no longer controversial. It now seemed "natural" that people should choose their occupation and residence and base their choices on opportunities to obtain maximum price or profit from whatever deal they could get from their money, property, or labor. *Given the habitus of eighteenth-and nineteenth-century Western Europe,* this was rational and appeared "natural." Formal economics analyzed the relations between state authority and free markets and the behavior of individuals in a society that assumed every person had as "property" either land, goods, and money or energy and skills, with any one of these freely exchangeable for any other.

> Anthropological economics examines social relationships, rather than supposing individuals coldly make "rational" choices.

Substantive economics takes a different position. It studies actual resources, skills, and relations of production. These vary greatly around the world and through history. In the middle twentieth century, economist Karl Polanyi, with anthropologists Conrad Arensberg and George Dalton, argued that the relatively unregulated, competitive market so dominant in modern European and U.S. political economies is a particular historical formation. Many of the assumptions of formal economics don't hold for most other societies: People don't universally or "naturally" want to maximize their material possessions, or believe that desired objects are in scarce supply and must be aggressively competed for. Blackfoot Indians on the Northwestern Plains, for example, despise people who selfishly accumulate possessions. Leaders among the Blackfoot are expected to live modestly and use their time and energy to assist the less fortunate. Men and women work to obtain large amounts of food, horses, and goods

THE INFORMAL ECONOMY Weekend market in a Midwestern town. Note the vendor's home-made cider press.

Photo Credit: Aldis Strazdins

in order to frequently invite others to feast and receive gifts. Traditionally, when a much-admired leader died, people constructed paths of stones leading from several directions to the grave, symbolizing followers coming from all directions to benefit from the leader's generosity. Indians today contrast their value system with that of whites—when Indians wish to honor someone, they give gifts *away* in their name, while whites, they say, give gifts *to* the honored person. The contrast is a bit unfair, of course, since many whites honor others by giving to charity in their name, but the basic point is that Blackfoot life can't be understood through formal economic analysis based on European values and political institutions.

Formal economics tends to overlook some important aspects even of modern Western societies. The extensive, important "informal economy" of families and friends exchanging services and lending money; of garage sales, flea markets, home-based small businesses; plus the businesses of burglary, fencing stolen goods, illegal gambling, and other crimes including shoplifting and embezzling from employers, cannot be quantified like legal, taxed enterprises and may be neglected in formal economics courses. These, like the economics of nonwestern or earlier western societies, can be studied through the substantive approach of anthropology. Anthropologist Rhoda Halperin, for example, observed vendors at weekend markets and documented their reliance on the "extra" cash they earn to support themselves. Gracia Clark studied garage sales in the United States, Sybil Wolfram the similar "jumble sales" in Britain. Wolfram learned that cooperating to put on, and attending, a jumble sale maintained a sense of community among residents in a village or neighborhood, and that although the fee to enter the sale was nominal and everything priced ridiculously low, considerable sums could be made because there was no investment or overhead. Garage and jumble sales, like weekend markets, don't get reported to the IRS and often are thought even by participants to be minor activities, but the sums of money earned can make a real difference in whether a family manages to get along. Lillian Trager and a sociologist colleague, Jim Stills, wondered how people in a small industrial city coped after the largest employer, an automobile plant, closed. They found a shift toward greater involvement in the informal economy compensated to a surprising degree for the loss of unionized jobs in the big factory.

> Using the method of participant observation, anthropologists research informal economic behavior that isn't officially reported.

Karl Marx, and those who follow his approach, have emphasized the societal relationships channeling production and distribution. Marx studied history closely and saw that political statuses, for example aristocrat or slave, and laws restricting production or consumption to certain social classes strongly affected the workings of "the market": Adam Smith's "invisible hand" might be quite visibly attached to a titled lord or judge. Marx's collaborator, Friedrich Engels, operated a factory where he dealt with the demands of his employees as well as those due to his competitors. Living in nineteenth-century England, Marx and Engels witnessed mobs again and again storming the gates of Parliament, yelling for reforms in the laws that gave the vote only to men who owned property, that taxed the poor, that tolerated dangerous and degrading conditions for workers. Class conflict became a key point in Marx's analyses. Anthropologists share with Marxist economists, political scientists, and historians a focus on societal structure and social relations, but class conflicts may seem less significant to anthropologists. There are some anthropologists who label themselves "Marxist" and do highlight class conflicts; there are many anthropologists who, plunged into a peasant rebellion or observing an agency where middle-class professionals experience difficulty dealing with lower-class clients, find class conflict is part of their analysis. "Marxist" interpretations may appear in the work of anthropologists who dislike "schools of thought" labels, preferring an open approach to their data. Our holistic perspective tends to encompass a variety of explanatory factors.

Reciprocity

Studying economics as a participant observer in a community, the anthropologist soon realizes that we can't separate out "economic" from other behavior of humans in their societies. Cooperation is essential for long-term survival (who will provide food and shelter when you're ill?). Economics is not a simple question of individual choices in a market, it's a web of obligations and opportunities.

The thread that forms the web is, as the early twentieth-century French anthropologist Marcel Mauss pointed out, the principle of reciprocity. People mark their relationships by exchanging items. Husband and wife give each other food, help, gifts, and those most precious creations, children. Parents give their children the necessities of life and when the parents are elderly, the children should reciprocate by providing support to the parents. Friends exchange gifts, taking care that the cost and type of gift suits the relationship—you can give your roommate a sweater, but if you gave an expensive leather jacket, people would suspect there was more than just friendship between you. We know all too well how we consider our lists of holiday gifts and cards, matching the depth of the relationship by an appropriate outlay of money or effort. If someone to whom we gave a gift fails to reciprocate, at least with a thank-you note, we figure that's a signal the relationship is at an end. Gifts, Mauss emphasized, are not simply outpourings of the heart, but symbols of the cooperation essential to human survival.

reciprocity, from the Latin *re-,* "go back" (as in "return") and *pro-,* "go forward" (as in "progress"): "go back and forth" as exchange of gifts or services.

Two anthropological studies excited interest in the meaning of gifts and reciprocity. In the 1880s, Franz Boas began learning about the culture of the Kwakiutl and other indigenous Indian nations on the Pacific coast of Canada. Collaborating with a trader's son who had married into the Kwakiutl community, Boas transcribed thousands of pages of descriptions of Kwakiutl behavior, particularly the memories of aristocratic men. Much of the descriptions concerned the feasts these men had hosted or attended. "Potlatch" is a native term for the public feasts. What intrigued Boas was the aggressive gift-giving reported for the potlatches: Guests were given a superabundance of food, thousands of dollars' worth of presents were pressed upon them, people boasted of their excessive generosity. What was the point of this display of conspicuous consumption?

potlach: Northwest Coast Indian term for feast with gift-giving

Let's answer that by reminding you that some Americans today indulge in potlatch-like conspicuous consumption feasts. Not long ago, a rich Chicago father gave a party for his son's thirteenth birthday. The boy liked Ferrari racing cars. At thirteen, he couldn't drive one, but his doting papa rented a Ferrari dealer's showroom for an evening, had caterers bring in the birthday dinner, and let his boy's friends eat their hot dogs and pizza surrounded by the luxury cars. This outlay of cash signaled to the children's families the great wealth and social standing of the host family. So it was with the Kwakiutl. The impressive outlay of expense, ostensibly to please the guests at a potlatch feast, actually signals the high status and accompanying power of the host. Ambitious guests will try to top the outlay at the next feast they give, signaling their status to be higher than that of the previous host. Potlatches, big hotel weddings to which a couple thousand "friends" are invited, debutante balls, and the like, are means to publicly display the financial power of the giver.

The other landmark anthropological study of gift-giving was published in 1922 by the Polish-born British anthropologist Bronislaw Malinowski, reporting on his two years' study of the Trobriand Islands off the southeastern coast of Papua New Guinea, in the South Pacific. Malinowski was deeply impressed by the long, dangerous sea voyages Trobriand men undertook in their outrigger canoes to exchange shell ornaments with friends on distant islands. Necklaces with a large, polished red central shell are always passed on from island to island in a clockwise direction, and armbands made from a broad white shell are always passed on counterclockwise; exchange of these ornaments is called *kula*. The best of these necklaces and armbands are heirlooms known to have been treasured by particular famous chiefs in the past. Ambitious men want to be ranked among the owners of the acclaimed treasures, to be talked about when people discuss who is important. Demonstrating the courage and skill to sail so far, the knowledge of the treasures' history and the confidence and persuasive manner to induce an owner to part with the desired valuable, brings fame to a man. The exchange of *kula* treasures marks men to be reckoned with. Like golden crowns, *kula* necklaces and armbands have no utilitarian value but immense symbolic use. Malinowski recorded that Trobrianders say they "give," not "sell," *kula* valuables. Marcel Mauss noted Trobrianders' emphasis on *kula* as an exchange of gifts, not market barter (ordinary items such as pots, axes, pigs are carried on commercial trading trips, separate from *kula* voyages). Such an exchange of beautiful treasures between two highly respected men seemed to Mauss to perfectly illustrate the principle of reciprocity and its role in structuring societies: each man, and his followers from his own island, can be actually seen by onlookers to be linked to the other. Through the visible alliances of leading men, *kula* links hundreds of island villages into a nation.

kula: in the Massim islands off Papua New Guinea, voyages to exchange prized shell ornaments

Half a century after Malinowski's research, American anthropologist Annette Weiner went to the Trobriands and found Malinowski hadn't noticed another kind of reciprocity important to structuring Trobriand societies. Local women insisted that Dr. Weiner accompany them to funerals where they spent hours collecting together and then giving out hundreds of bundles of dried banana leaves and the traditional skirts made out of the shredded leaves. Women don't usually go on *kula* voyages, but they too seek fame through public gift-giving, in their case the distribution of skirts, or the material to make them, to women relatives and friends attending the funeral of a family member. The more bundles and skirts given out, the more friends and relatives a family counts. Male leaders are known by the *kula* treasures entrusted to them by important men on other islands, women leaders are known by the numbers of people who come to pay respect to their family at a death. Public gift-giving is the physical measure of social status and the power it brings.

That thread of reciprocity, so often symbolized by gifts, is valued in all human societies. Presidents and prime ministers paying official state visits to each other exchange beautiful objects made by their countries' artists. Little girls in grade school exchange plastic bracelets. Whatever the scale, there is the promise that a productive relationship has been instituted. Reciprocity may involve actions rather than objects: "You scratch my back, I'll scratch yours." In politics, "You vote for my constituents' pet project, I'll vote for yours" and "Vote for me, and I'll get the potholes on your street fixed." Give the bank your money in a savings account, and it will reciprocate by paying you interest. Give a company money, and it will reciprocate by paying you dividends. Reciprocity is an essential component in most economic transactions.

Value

Anthropological economics looks at the *social* use of material objects. Beyond the bare necessities to stay alive, material goods primarily serve social functions. Formal economics assumed that people "naturally" (invariably) want more and more and more, that their appetite for goods and services can never be satiated. Like the dictator's wife who had thousands of pairs of shoes in her closets, enough could never be enough. Furthermore, because population tends to increase, in time a greater number of people will be attempting to fill their needs from a limited planet. Therefore, formal economics postulates a principle of scarcity from which cost, or value, derives from the difficulty people meet in attempting to obtain desired goods and services. Difficulty can arise from the time and energy required to obtain the good, or from competition for it. The problem with the principle of scarcity is that no one "naturally" wants thousands of pairs of shoes. The dictator's wife, an ex-beauty queen, filled her closets with shoes and other fashionable clothes to draw admiration: what she wanted was *approbation*.

> Historian Arthur Lovejoy noted that the desire for *approbation*— to be thought well of by those one associates with—seems a universal human need.

The natural needs of humans are modest: plain food, water, fire, a simple shelter from rain. Humans evolved in warm climates and "naturally" might stay there, having no need for clothing. Societies like the Dobe Ju/'hoansi and the Mbuti show us that living off the land in a tropical climate takes only about half what the rest of us call a work week. Most days, both men and women enjoy leisure to nap, chat with neighbors, play with the children. When, at the end of the Pleistocene, larger human populations required the organization of more complex societies, workers needed to produce more than their own families' needs in order to give the surplus to full-time managers. Possessing power over people's productive time came to be signaled, or *symbolized,* by the display of objects requiring much time to be produced, for example by clothing fabricated through hundreds of hours of weaving and embroidery, by fancy cakes, by large houses involving numerous construction workers, by ornamented furniture, by entertainment from musicians and dancers who practiced for years to perfect their art. Conspicuous consumption of time- and labor-consuming articles signals the owner's social right to command that labor. Lack of such objects signals the poor person's subordinate status. Societies with managerial and laboring classes look quite different from societies such as the Mbuti and Ju/'hoansi, who reject class stratification and demand that everyone share the

YOUNG AMERICANS' "NECESSITIES"
The small apartment of a young American couple displays the many manufactured goods they have been socialized to believe necessary.
Photo credit: Aldis Strazdins

resources brought into their communities. Small societies such as theirs can operate through informal, flexible organization, giving people the feeling they are freely conforming to social expectations.

The question becomes, what motivates *both* manager and laborer, in class-stratified societies, to do their jobs? It's seldom a simple matter of work or starve—people who can't work are usually fed, and in many societies, people who can and want to work may be prevented by a political structure that limits their opportunities. Managers and laborers work at their socially appointed jobs in order to gain the good opinion, the approbation, of the people they associate with. For some, it will mean prestige or power, but for most it's just seeing respect from other people. If we remember that we humans are gregarious mammals, we realize that millions of years of natural selection for living in a social group have bred us to be sensitive to our fellows' attitudes toward us and to feel impelled to gain their approbation. Without the approbation of the others in our social group, we would be ignored or outcast and without a mate. The genes of antisocial hominids weren't likely to be passed on. Our ancestors were the ones who did care about others, did seek their approbation.

In the final analysis, value is set by one's social group. No material or object has value in itself. Only when a society recognizes a material or object as *signifying* high social status, prestige, or power does it become precious. This is well shown in the Trobriand Islands, where the actually rare well-cut and beautiful shell ornaments exchanged in the *kula* are not the only valuables; bundles of banana leaves are also valuable, though very plain to look at. Both *kula* shell ornaments and banana-fiber skirts are time-consuming to make, and are likely to have been gifts. A man wearing a rare shell ornament and a woman wearing a painstakingly constructed full-length banana-fiber skirt exhibit a sign of the respect, the approbation they have earned from their peers. Only respected men, judged responsible and intelligent, are accepted as *kula* trade partners; only respected women, judged responsible and intelligent, will own skirts made from quantities of laboriously shredded and woven banana fiber. These valuables are badges of good character, calling forth respect. In each case, the man and woman wearing the valuable item signals not only their personal worth, but also the fact that family and friends stand behind them.

> a U.S. woman sued the BMW automobile makers for $10 million because they did not limit import of their M5 model to 500 cars per year. By selling more than this arbitrary limit, she claimed, BMW cheapened the value of the M5, causing her and other buyers to lose money in resale value—and M5 as a sign of high status.

Anthropologist Mary Douglas observed the BaLele, a group of communities in the Congo in central Africa, make and use a valuable much like the Trobriands' banana-fiber skirts. BaLele raise raffia palm trees for the leaves, which they shred and weave on looms for skirts. Like the Trobriand skirts, raffia cloth is laborious to make, and an appliqued dance costume of ten lengths of raffia cloth represents much time and skill. Lengths of raffia cloth are valuable, and they are given as gifts on occasions marking a person's social value: by a husband to his wife upon the birth of their child, by a youth to his father when

Papua New Guinea, 1928. A handsome young man seeks the approbation of society through cosmetics, coiffure, ornaments, and offering a business deal for local products.
Photo credit: Milwaukee Public Museum.

the boy attains adulthood, to a bride's family upon her marriage, at the funerals of a man's parents-in-law, as tribute to chiefs, and as fines (communicating the offender's respect for the community). Young men beg older men to lend them raffia cloth to get enough for a proper bridal gift, and the older men can keep rambunctious or disrespectful young men in line by threatening to refuse the cloth, dooming the young man to bachelorhood or a no-account girl for a wife. Douglas saw raffia cloth sold for francs, the national currency, but francs alone were not considered suitable gifts on important social occasions. Nor could factory-made cloth substitute. The BaLele had selected the local skilled craft product to *represent* value, to be the standard unit in counting wealth.

American society has selected currency to be our unit of wealth. Market economies like ours use arbitrary standardized items to represent units of labor time (the basic real valuable): people are paid so much per hour, the rate supposedly reflecting the amount of their training and skill. We also have selected time-consuming skilled craft products to signal high status: Rolls Royce limousines, gold jewelry, fine china, designer-made clothing. The difference between luxury goods and standard items lies in the amount of labor time invested in the object. Limousines have hand-polished leather interiors that represent a great deal of labor time—in raising the animals from which the hides came, in slaughtering, skinning, tanning, shipping, inspecting, cutting the hides, in installing the leather. A stranger from Mars might very well think that a heavy vinyl covering, rapidly machine produced and assembly-line installed, looks prettier than leather; it may be as durable and it will require less upkeep. We have to learn, from others in our society, that vinyl is a sign of mediocrity. We learn to recognize symbols of low status as well as those signaling high status.

Understanding that approbation, and not simply a goal of amassing signs of high status or power, induces people to conform to their social group's cultural pattern explains the behavior of those who refuse to accumulate goods. Monks, Hindu holy men, 1960s' hippies, ostentatiously reject owning goods, seeking the approbation of others (perhaps including God) whom they believe agree that seeking material objects interferes with the pursuit of a greater good. For such ascetics, distinctive unfashionable clothing signals their peculiar group, and begging for daily food becomes their occupation, their socially patterned way of earning a living. Their costume has a value, as much as any corporation executive's business suit or jet-setter's high-fashion outfit. Value is not inherent in any object, and the signs that elicit approbation from members of one social group may signal others to reject the person. Some Americans respect people wearing expensive fur coats, other Americans spit upon anybody who they see has encouraged the slaughter of so many helpless animals. Members of a social group learn a rationale supposedly explaining why one item is desirable and another to be avoided. (Fur coats are warm, say some; fur coats are dead animals and death is tragic, say others.) Our society claims that scarcity is the reason goods such as gold or Rolls Royce limousines are valuable, but the production of gold, Rolls Royces, and other high-status symbols is controlled to maintain scarcity. It is important to cut through the rationales and understand that value is arbitrary, at bottom the value is measured by the approbation of one's peers.

> the social group's assignment of value teaches members to perceive beauty in the valued items and ugliness in items that are labeled low value.

Subsistence versus Market Economies

Logically, there could be a distinction between producing only necessities for one's own family consumption, and producing additional items to trade with others. The importance of reciprocity tieing together people blurs the logical distinction. Small societies that prize independence over material goods, such as the Mbuti and the Ju/'hoansi, value sharing highly, for without day-to-day cooperation and sharing of food, families would suffer every time a hunter had poor luck or a plant gatherer had to tend to a new baby. Agricultural villagers must also cooperate—to manage peak labor needs; to assist households struggling with illness, death of an active adult, or disability; and to deal with the demands of governing agents from the larger political unit. Exchange of food and material goods functions as the sign of good will and willingness to cooperate. Thus even those whose households produce all their own necessities keep in mind the social obligation to have ready food or items to share or give as gifts.

There is a useful distinction between social groups whose working households *primarily* produce nearly all their necessities, and those whose *primary* plan is to produce only particular items, depending on regular exchange to obtain other (or all) necessities. Households that expect to be basically self-sufficient are said to have a *subsistence* economy; those that depend upon regular exchange are said to be in a *market economy*. The distinction is not whether somebody makes an item or gathers extra food to exchange; the distinction is whether the person expects their household to produce its own needs, or expects someone in the household will be going to the market to obtain some of the necessities. Dependence upon the market requires a society to structure social relations to ensure that the necessities they don't themselves produce will be reliably available to workers.

> subsistence economy: households produce all their basic necessities
> *market* economy: workers produce quantities to exchange for necessities they don't produce

One point to keep in mind: Subsistence economies may be *imposed* upon communities by governing agents. Rural farmers or conquered groups may be denied access to a variety of occupations in order that the power and wealth of upper classes will be protected. Peasants may be forced by law to wear home-made cloth, eat home-baked bread from their own fields' grain. Within one nation, upper classes can live within a market economy, exchanging wealth or professional services for food, clothing, and skilled labor, while in the countryside, serfs or slaves are required to grow their own food and fiber and make their own household goods from local resources. Of course, the serfs or slaves must also produce more in order to provision their masters' households, or must labor in the masters' enterprises in addition to their own subsistence work. Hunter-gatherer groups may appear to have chosen subsistence economies, when historical expansion by military powers drove them into marginal regions and gave them the hard choice of serving masters or subsisting in a minimal economy where resources for market production are lacking.

Market Economies

Markets are a common means for people to exchange items they may not produce themselves. Markets thus depend upon production beyond the producers' consumption needs. A true market economy exists when every worker produces a surplus of some product instead of investing time and labor in directly filling subsistence needs (food, shelter). Workers then must exchange their surplus for others' surplus in order to survive: wheat for house-building materials, meat for knives, labor for clothing. Market economies can exist without money, but some medium of exchange is likely in a market economy; cacao (chocolate) beans functioned as money in the Aztec empire in Mexico, cowrie shells did in Africa, and dentalium shells in the Pacific Northwest of America, all these

*Sri Lanka, 1930. Professional potters with bowls mass-produced by hand for the local mar-
ket. There is no simple distinctin between "handcraft" and "mass production."*
Photo credit: Milwaukee Public Museum.

Roadside restaurant, Bali, 1930. The operation looks simple but the enterprise is a business operated in a densely populated state.
Photo credit: Milwaukee Public Museum.

objects being standard sized, numerous, countable, and durable like coins. Societies with market economies must be able to assure people reasonable stability and security when they engage in market transactions; feudal societies protect "market peace" on scheduled market days. Without the expectation that surplus production can be exchanged for other necessities, workers would be forced to get their food and other requirements directly rather than plan to produce surpluses.

In North America today, almost no one lives by what they raise and build, or weave and sew, themselves. When a hydroelectric dam project ruined the hunting territory of Cree and Inuit in the James Bay region of northern Quebec, Canada, negotiators agreed to a program designed to protect the native families' way of life in the remaining undeveloped area. To continue to live by hunting and fishing, families said they needed a guaranteed minimum cash income. James Bay Cree take nearly all their food and shelter directly from their environment, but they have been part of the international economic system, selling furs they trap, for over 300 years. To live traditionally in the bush, they require money to buy trapping equipment, rifles and ammunition, tools, industrially manufactured clothing, and motor transportation to bush localities. Most of the millions of other North Americans couldn't produce even food and shelter for themselves. Anthropologist Robin Ridington, who has lived for many months with northern Canadian Dené Indians, remarks that while most Americans carry technology inefficiently in bulky tool boxes, his Dené friends carry their technology in their heads: that is, they know how to make snares, fishing lines, containers, and other implements for obtaining necessities from local resources. One effect of a commitment to a market economy is the inefficiency of having to purchase all kinds of implements and services because one's own education has been limited to one's specialty.

> "Know-how" is an economic asset that's hard to quantify.

Over the past several thousand years, and in much of the world today, a majority of people have lived in mixed economies, some based on production for the market and some on subsistence production. A village in Bolivia, in the center of South America, is typical. The basic work unit is husband and wife, living in a one-room adobe home with their children. The couple farms a few acres, the husband guiding an ox-drawn plow as the wife walks behind, sowing seed. The wife, or sometimes a child, takes their little flock of sheep out to graze, spinning wool into thread as she guards the animals, and the husband or an older child takes the cattle to other pasture. A pig will be tethered in a muddy spot so it can dig its food and wallow. Chickens in the farmyard pick up scraps of grain. The family seldom eats meat: The sheep provide wool for clothing, the cattle provide milk to be made into cheese, the pig will be sold to gain some cash. There's a donkey that can carry big bundles of roof thatch or grain or potatoes, and is lent or rented to other villagers who don't own a pack animal. (One villager owns and can repair a truck, but hiring a truck is expensive—gas costs cash.) Husband and wife both weave their homespun wool into cloth, blankets, and storage bags. They attend the village market held one morning each week, buying a few vegetables such as onions, a bag of bakery rolls and coffee for breakfasts, a small bag of detergent powder for washing clothes (in the river), and perhaps as a special treat a couple of apples or oranges that they will divide with the children. A few times a year, the couple will buy factory-made clothing from a market vendor; men today wear standard shirts and pants and baseball caps, and the women like T-shirts, blouse-and-sweater sets, and readymade petticoats and skirts—homespun wool is scratchy. To pay for their purchases, the husband looks for manual labor jobs and the wife sells her homemade cheese in the market. Another family in the village constructs an adobe bake-oven and spends a day or two each week producing the rolls their neighbors want to buy. One man has learned carpentry skills, has a few tools, and makes benches and stools out of scrap lumber, trading them for produce. A few men own small boats and net sardine-sized fish in the lake, selling them door-to-door in the village or on market day. When a house is to be built, or planting and harvest demand more labor, relatives help each other. The villagers value being their own boss and knowing that others in the community will help them if needed, but they don't see their lives as idyllic. They'd like electric lights and radios (some of the younger people have battery-powered ones), they'd like

A Village in Bolivia

A. Village in the highlands of Bolivia, on the shore of Lake Titicaca. Houses are of adobe brick, with thatch or tin roofs. At the right are cement-block clinic building and social-agency house (both seldom staffed), and behind them the public elementary school classroom buildings. In the foreground, a man plows with an ox while women in the center wash clothes in the little stream, and sheep graze.

B. Farmsteads outside the village. In the center against the farmyard wall is a round adobe-plastered bake-oven in which the family bakes rolls to sell in the weekly market. A few chickens and a pig are in the yard, left, and some guinea pigs inside the adobe-brick hutch beside the cookhouse, right.

C. Homes in the village, from the rear: In the patio (backyard) of the small home in the center, a woman is washing dishes beside a small wooden rack made by the village carpenter. The family raises guinea pigs, to sell as meat in the weekly market, in the thatched adobe-brick cookhouse on the left.

D. *Inside the same one-room home, the kitchen corner. Potatoes, the staple food, are in the basin ready to be cooked for noon dinner. Cooking is done on the kerosene burner in center (with pot on top), or outside in the patio on a small adobe-plastered stove burning dried dung (wood is very scarce). The Diet Coke can has been salvaged from tourists' discard, to serve as a container. Homespun, home-woven wool blankets are rolled up on chest at right, and the woman's spindle for spinning wool is tilted against the wall, lower right corner. Two kittens play behind the pots, right center. Their thin mother survives on birds she can catch and potato soup, all her owner has to feed her.*

E. *Market day in the village plaza, looking south. Vendors sell from cloths spread on the cobblestones. During her participant observation study, the anthropologist lived in the whitewashed house, third from left, in the background.*

F. *Market day, view looking north toward gravel highway running through village on far side of plaza, and beyond village, Lake Titicaca and the Andes Mountains. Woman in lower left is selling apples (imported from nearby Chile) and bananas from the hot lowlands. Vendors in upper left sell new and used clothing. Men in center cluster around vendor selling bicycle parts. Couple in right center background are looking at bolts of cloth. Trucks parked in right background along highway transport some vendors and their wares, other vendors come by bicycle or walk.*

G. Pick-up soccer game with teenage girls and boys playing outside village.

H. "Traditional" Spanish-colonial-style agriculture along Lake Titicaca shore. A pair of oxen pull the wooden plow guided by a man, while the women of his family plant seed potatoes in the furrows he plows. Much of these flat plains around the Lake cannot be used for Spanish-style plow agriculture because they are too marshy.

I. Women preparing seed potatoes to plant in traditional field. Glass bottle by woman's skirt, lower left, held a little distilled liquor sprinkled over potatoes in a ritual praying for a good crop.

J. *Reviving the ancient Tiwanaku culture agricultural system, abandoned 800 years ago when a decades-long drought lowered the water table in the Lake Titicaca plains. An archaeological project discovered the ancient method and recruited members of the village to rebuild the Tiwanaku raised fields (center).*

K. *Rebuilt Tiwanaku fields left background, a community team working on another field in background, raised fields and ditches in right center still in their abandoned state. In the foreground, a village family eats its noon dinner picnic style, carrying prepared food and bottles of beverage wrapped in homespun, home-woven cloths slung over the shoulder. The pickax (bottom right) and shovels behind the standing man show that this family, too, has been working on rebuilding the ridged fields.*

L. *Women take a break from restoring the ancient field system. Children accompany their parents to the fields and play quietly.*

M. Planting Festival. The ancient Tiwanaku ridged fields and ditches have been reconstructed and village women leave the village with seed potatoes in their carrying cloths. A band of local musicians goes with the women to the fields. Man on right has a drum in his carrying cloth.

N. Out on the ancient ridged field, women pile the seed potatoes beside a carrying cloth with popcorn (right lower center) for the celebration. People have put a green stalk in their hatbands as a symbol of the green plants to be grown.

O. Planting. Men use pickaxes to make furrows on the ridged fields, women follow, placing seed potatoes in the furrows and covering them with soil. Upper left corner, the professional agronomist who has been supervising the restoration of the ancient field system watches the planting.

P. In the background, the neat rows of raised fields and ditches, restored and planted after a lapse of 800 years. The Tiwanaku system raises plants above the Lake Titicaca normal high water table, draining the groundwater into ditches that protect against frosts by slowly radiating warmth after the sun goes down, and that can be used as fish ponds. Annual dredging of the ditches, piling the dredged muck on top of the fields, renews soil fertility—a productive, sustainable agriculture that does not require any imported fuel or machinery. In the foreground, children and some of the women wait for the planting to be completed in the background.

Q. Planting completed, everyone dances in celebration. One of the project archaeologists, facing camera wearing tractor cap, and a project assistant also wearing tractor cap, left foreground, dance with the villagers. This illustrates participant observation, *living in the village, participating in villagers' work, celebrating with them, recording their way of life with camera and words.*

R. At the end of a happy day, with every prospect of a bumper crop of potatoes to come. Villagers return to their homes, but although the drummer has packed up, two flute players will provide the tune for a couple of young women still dancing. Note the head of a baby, wearing a white knitted cap, in the carrying cloth on the back of the woman in lower left. Young children kept close to the mother in this manner enjoy secure yet stimulating care.

Credit: Alice Beck Kehoe and Proyecto Wila Jawira

a more varied diet, they'd like to be able to plaster their houses so adobe dust doesn't constantly fall on dishes and clothes, and most important, they'd like to give their children education and opportunities to pursue city careers if they wish or buy farms if they prefer. Even with limited access to modern medical resources, more children grow up than the village can accommodate. This is not a new problem.

Where do rural villagers' children go? They go to the cities. They work on construction, in transport, as maids and cooks and gardeners, in factories, and in the little shops in the slums. Migration from farm villages to cities has been going on for 5,000 years. Cities seem to be sponges soaking up excess population. Historically, cities have suffered very high mortality rates because the many thousands of people living close together, usually without sanitary water supplies or waste disposal, have been reservoirs of disease. A few societies provided carefully for these needs of an urban population. Harappa, in third-millennium B.C. India, built fine sewer systems, as did Classical Rome, and Rome and the Aztecs of Mexico brought clean water to city dwellers via long aqueducts from the hills. Even where authorities were concerned with cleanliness, epidemics spread disastrously. As a result, city populations did not reproduce themselves, creating a constant need—a market—for labor. Rural villagers may appear to be isolated from the cities, to be self-sufficient with their farms and crafts, but they are one component of national economic systems that require the surplus population from farm communities to be absorbed into the labor force in cities. Markets, for goods and for labor, integrate cities and countrysides.

Rural people may see the misery of the lower class in cities and seek instead to colonize new land. Expanding populations spread agriculture throughout the world, adapting technology and cultigens to previously uncultivated areas. Europe's cities could never have absorbed the millions of peasants and townspeople who moved to America over the last four centuries. This stupendous migration not only relieved pressure on Europe's farms and cities, it also fostered the growth of a global economy in which international imports and exports are basic to fulfilling people's needs. In the little Bolivian village, T-shirts and bicycle parts from China, fruit from Chile, radio batteries from the United States are always available in the weekly market. When the village celebrates its annual festival, some of the people rent parade costumes from shops in the city, and nowadays we see Bugs Bunnies and Sioux Chiefs out of Disney movies dancing alongside the traditional legendary bears and water monsters. Nor is this global economy so new: 300 years ago, Canadian Indians bought pretty glass beads manufactured in the Czech Republic, paying for them with beaver pelts that would be shipped to Europe to be made into fashionable hats. Jobs for thousands of Europeans depended on this trade. Five millennia earlier, Mesopotamia, Egypt, and India were shipping goods to each others' markets and exploring routes to untapped resources and consumers. Long-distance distribution of highly valued raw materials and finished goods is visible in the

Upper Paleolithic, when high-quality flint for cutting blades and ornamental seashells were taken hundreds of miles from their sources, and beautifully carved spearthrowers were apparently traded to adjacent regions. The spread of ideas, of techniques, of useful plants and animals, and of people occurs through trade, and the spread expands and strengthens trade.

Summary

Anthropological economics covers societies that do not have markets or money as well as those that do. Anthropologists suggest that *reciprocity,* that is to say exchange, is important in every society because it not only distributes goods and services but also symbolizes ties of mutual concern. Millions of years of natural selection for gregarious living have produced sensitivity toward others and a strong emotional need for the *approbation* of our peers in our social groups. Possessions and behavior label members in a group, signaling who is in the group and usually also each individual's status—leader, commoner, fringe. Value is assigned by the group to objects and behavior. Value is not inherent in materials nor determined by inevitable scarcity; scarcity is often deliberately maintained to prevent commoners from gaining signs of high status. Social value is the key to economic behavior.

REFERENCES AND RECOMMENDED READINGS

Douglas, Mary and Baron Isherwood. *The World of Goods.* New York: W. W. Norton, 1979.

Lee, Richard B. *The Dobe Ju/'hoansi.* Fort Worth: Harcourt Brace, 1984.

Lovejoy, Arthur O. *Reflections on Human Nature.* Baltimore: Johns Hopkins University Press, 1961.

Turnbull, Colin. *The Mbuti Pygmies: Adaptation and Change.* Fort Worth: Harcourt Brace, 1983 (Turnbull's earlier study of the Mbuti, *The Forest People,* is also available in paperback.)

Weiner, Annette B. *The Trobrianders of Papua New Guinea.* Fort Worth: Harcourt Brace, 1988.

Analyzing Societies (III): Regulating Societies

In this chapter we focus on the middle level of our chart

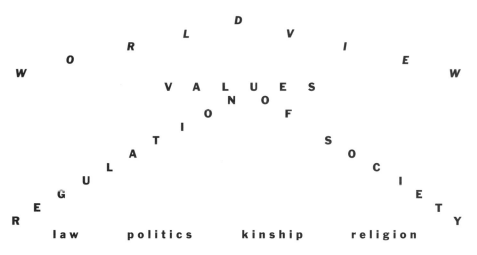

Human societies carry on patterned ways of organizing their members. Americans think of political structures, formal institutions, and job roles as means of organizing people. In addition we have the roles we think of as "natural," particularly those anthropologists term *kinship:* family relations. Cross-cultural comparisons reveal much variation in what societies believe to be natural relationships—in some, it seems natural to see a few children with women "fathers," or all the boys and girls in a large extended family as brothers and sisters. Analysis shows that kinship is a means of assigning roles to people, a form of regulation especially important because it gives a role to everyone, beginning at birth and continuing even after death. People may be given, or allowed to take, additional roles, and these may be what we conventionally call occupations, political positions, or social statuses. Giving names to roles helps to regulate people in societies.

Another way to think about regulating societies is to examine the distribution of power in a society. Who may act as he or she thinks best? Who must obey another? What are the laws or rules that people acknowledge? How are they enforced? A focus on power must, in an anthropological perspective, take in the society's worldview, the history it gives of the origin of its political structure and beliefs about the nature of humans and social relationships. Contemporary western people are likely to grow up believing that laws are established by governments and humans will not obey the laws unless coerced by police and the threat of punishment, whereas many other societies believe that humans naturally live cooperatively with others. The extreme of the western worldview is "spare the rod and spoil the child," a belief that humans are born full of sin and only beatings will keep them obedient to lawful authority; this belief horrifies many nonwesterners. Anthropologist Ruth Underhill questioned Tohono 'O'odham (commonly known as Papago Indians) until she learned their principle of child-rearing: "Draw the children into your own life. Give them from birth love, companionship, and responsibility." 'O'odham adults of course have power over their children but they don't *see* the parent-child relationship as involving power. Instead, their worldview posits power as an impersonal force pervading the world, outside ordinary human relationships, and humans as innately cooperative. We can recall Arthur Lovejoy's conclusion that people seek the approbation of their peers and will regulate their conduct in order to win approbation. Laws are codes of behavior that are supposed to win society's approbation, and power to enforce laws ultimately comes from consensus of the adults in the community—even in dictatorships, which always risk rebellion by the citizenry.

Regulation of society rests upon worldview. Describing political structures without describing the habitus—the entire way of being—that embeds it is short-sighted. From this perspective, religion is as much part of a society's political structure as are legislatures, laws, and police. Thomas Hobbes's concept that societies represent a kind of truce in the "war of all against all," a fragile agreement between citizens to pursue their interests jointly because the alternative is mayhem, came to him as he lived through the turmoil of seventeenth-century England, when the lawful king, a Catholic, was beheaded by Protestant Puritan rebels. Hobbes's England indeed was a society in a fragile truce, torn by conflict between those who believed kings ruled by divine grace and those who held power to come from consent of the governed. Each side was convinced the other sinfully ignored God's will. The final compromise (in 1688), a constitutional monarchy, reconciled what had appeared to be opposed religious beliefs and not incidentally encouraged greater religious toleration. Political events, religious concepts, and worldview influenced each other in what can be labeled a *dialectical* process of assertions posed against others' claims, and both subjected to efforts to discover a common ground. The eighteenth-century philosopher Georg Hegel argued that the course of history may be said to follow a dialectic, factions setting up oppositions and working these out as common needs are revealed, whereupon new factions appear and the process goes on.

Dialectic:
thesis (statement of idea)
antithesis (the opposite idea)
synthesis (the two ideas have some common features)

PART I:
SOCIAL ORGANIZATION AND POWER
Language and Power

Cross-cultural comparisons make us wonder why in some societies people put up with what seems to us to be oppressive situations. We can understand that slaves in the United States before the Civil War obeyed because the alternative was brutal flogging, but why did free married women at that time accept the handicap of being held legally incompetent to manage their own affairs? Pierre Bourdieu's concept of the habitus, in which, as he puts it, "history is turned into nature," helps explain oppressed groups' acceptance of their lot. Probably few slaves believed that Africans are biologically incapable of maintaining themselves as responsible citizens in a modern state, but many nineteenth-century women did believe that biology incapacitated them from filling the positions in government and professions taken by men. Scientists at the time measured skulls of men and women and proved that men had on average a larger brain capacity than women. Larger brain capacity equals greater intelligence—who could argue against scientific measurements? (The flaw in the scientific "proof" is leaving out the observation that overall brain size correlates with body size but not necessarily with intelligence. The larger average size of men compared to women meant men's skulls would average larger. But the enormous size of whales' skulls doesn't seem to equate with vastly greater intelligence compared to puny humans.) Politico-economic history had produced a United States where African immigrants were systematically treated like animals and women excluded from competing in business, and the habitus, the customary way of being, turned that history into assertions that the brains of Africans and women "naturally" stayed underdeveloped compared to European men's brains.

More ludicrous (to us) is the "knowledge" that a woman's uterus could get loose and float about inside her body, and thus, cause her to become hysterical. The word "hysterical" comes from the Greek word for uterus, *hustera*. Some medical authorities believed the uterus to be a parasitic animal that might choose to roam about inside its hostess. Medical treatment for hysteria included applying foul-smelling stuff to the woman's nose and sweet-smelling perfume to her vagina—this to induce the uterus to leave her upper body and return to its proper lower place. Men of course could not become hysterical because they lack a uterus. When Classical Greeks or nineteenth-century Americans said women must be excluded from professional or political roles because having a uterus made them liable to hysterics, this social decree was said to be dictated by "nature." There were no CAT-scan machines to show the uterus of a hysterical woman. Who could deny respected doctors' professed medical knowledge?

Who speaks authoritatively in a society? Here is the crux of political power. British anthropologists Edwin and Shirley Ardener reminded us that not only do respected authorities speak out, but also that disrespected groups are, in the Ardeners' words, muted. Muted groups—slaves, children, women—may talk a great deal and talk loudly but they are not listened to. Their talk is labeled "chatter," the same word that labels monkeys' vocalizations. Muted groups may speak in a dialect that marks them as different from the group in power, or use mannerisms that mark their lower status. Women in American society, for example, are likely to use question form more frequently than men. (A woman is more likely to say, "Will you do the dishes?" while a man more likely says, "Do the dishes.") Women are more likely to use "we" forms ("Let's see how this problem is worked," versus "This is how the problem is worked"). Subconsciously, American women tend to avoid sentence forms that indicate authority.

Legal scholars as well as anthropologists, sociologists, and linguists are examining the language of authority. The most powerful expression of authority is silence. ("Be quiet!") Emperors and presidents may sit silent on platforms while underlings read out decrees. Next we have the measured slow speech of judges and famous professors. Their audiences patiently listen. Low-status people often speak in a rushing babble of words, not because they are too stupid or immature to reflect, but because they're eager to get a word in before they're ignored. The same situation can be seen in written forms: Legal documents have the authority to *demand* close attention no matter how boring; writing that carries no authority such as comic books tries to please the reader with short snazzy lines. Analysis of discourse demonstrates how power, or its lack, is socially signaled. Modes of discourse used in spheres of authority such as the law and medicine are not, as we naively suppose, "natural" to men who go into these high-status professions or even "natural" to the work of these professions, but rather serve to mark authority.

Power

In the 1980s, anthropologists became increasingly concerned with the question of power in society. Exercising power, it had been assumed, was part of the role assigned to some social actors, that is, a policeman exercised power because that was his role in his society. Social actors were assumed to be selected for their ability to fill a particular role: Police were selected from big strong men, there couldn't be women police because women wouldn't be strong enough to overcome male criminals. Along came the 1964 Civil Rights Act, colonies were winning independence, a world power was unable to overcome the resistance of the small nation of Vietnam; and among these challenges, how power is obtained, how it is and how it should be wielded, became vital issues. Power could mean authority—*power over* others—or ability to effect action—*power to* act. The issue of power brought together anthropologists focusing on individuals negotiating the matters of social life, and anthropologists looking at symbols and rituals.

Victor Turner, a British anthropologist, gave a series of lectures published in 1969 as *The Ritual Process*. Here, at the heyday of the counterculture "hippie" movement, when it seemed a whole generation had gone to a meadow in Woodstock, peeled off their clothes, lighted a joint, and grooved to the heavy rhythms of rock, Turner described a cycle he could document over and over, cross-culturally: structure and antistructure. This is really a dialectic, with structure (or hierarchical organization) frustrating people who eventually rebel and try to live communally, sharing work and rewards equally. That second phase Turner termed *communitas,* or antistructure. What history shows, he wrote, is that pure communitas doesn't keep people happy, either. "From each according to his ability, to each according to this needs" sounds nice, until you have to decide whether Friend Joe's "inability" to remember to wash the dishes when it's his turn ought to be accepted. And what about housemate Steve's "need" for money to go hear his favorite bands, when it comes out of the pooled incomes of the house and there's never much cash? Hierarchy, structure, creeps into communitas living, Turner discovered, as leaders emerge and rules get made. Victor Turner's work in the 1960s and 1970s illustrates an approach that abstracts out of events the recurring processes and symbols characterizing social groups.

"Politics is power," say some anthropologists. Political institutions are seats of power, politicians are people eager to exercise power. Perhaps. Power is more than the business of politics. Power lies within any human relationship, whether that power is openly displayed or carefully avoided. That is possibly the most crucial aspect of the issue of power, to indicate when and why participants *avoid* openly exercising power over others. Victor Turner identified institutions in many societies, including our own, highly valuing mutual respect between the members, where no one is above the others ordering them about, no one is considered below, obliged to obey orders, but all are held to be equally deserving of respect, equally obliged to work and share. Avoiding the show of authority, Turner noticed, allows irresponsible members to sabotage the enterprise. Most groups in societies expect people to employ a repertoire of persuasion, negotiations, and assertive demands as occasions and company seem to warrant. Using these several means of moving others to satisfy one's wishes is labeled "politicking" when it occurs on Capitol Hill, or between statesmen at a summit meeting, or at a treaty council. Politics are obvious in public affairs, while potentially at least, power is a consideration in all human relationships. Every human has a repertoire of behavior learned as a member of a particular society.

Status and Roles

Societies have both statuses and roles. Status refers to "standing" (from the Latin word for "stand"), a fixed social position. People usually occupy a series of statuses, beginning with baby, then child, perhaps student, young independent adult, married person, parent, worker, elderly person, finally dead person. We can occupy more than one status at the same time, for example rich person, manager, professional, as well as married, adult, etc.

Role refers to behavior, how a person *acts*. The term comes from our familiarity with actors playing roles. Having the status of a child or a rich person doesn't itself guarantee certain behavior: Some rich people live very modestly, some children behave like little adults (and some adults behave like children). The role of "rich person" or "child" can be played by anybody, whatever their real status. The sociologist Erving Goffman emphasized how demanding our social roles are, how much like actors' roles in requiring us to create an appropriate appearance, voice, mannerisms, as well as accomplish appropriate tasks. Think of college students getting ready to go to class, taking care to shower, blow-dry their hair, apply deodorant, put on clothes of the style and brands worn by their peers, sling the fashionable backpack over one shoulder (*never* over both shoulders!). Goffman called it "the presentation of self in everyday life," but what he really meant was the acting of roles in everyday life. He implied that we don't have much "self," only roles. Think about it. Even the person who wants to be a nonconformist finds that is a social role, too, with its appropriate dress, mannerisms, and occupations—jeans, flannel shirt, work boots, handyman jobs.

Social Institutions

Between World Wars I and II, social anthropologists including Bronislaw Malinowski and his English colleague A. R. Radcliffe-Brown and the American sociologist Talcott Parsons presented a view of societies labeled "structural-functionalist." In this view, societies are built up of a number of "structures" that would include a kinship "system," political institutions, economic institutions, religious organizations, perhaps a class system. Each of these has roles or offices for people in the society. Each structure serves a function in keeping the society going. Kinship keeps new generations coming up, political institutions keep people orderly, economic institutions organize work, religious ones instill a moral order. Statuses and roles are part of the institutions.

After World War II, the radical political and economic changes in the world highlighted a big question little discussed by the structural-functionalists: How do societies change? The way structural-functionalists described societies, everything either kept going or broke down. They couldn't explain how people and groups muddled through. For a few years, anthropologists stayed with a 1930s term, *acculturation,* used to describe colonial peoples' changing from their native culture to that imposed by the colonial power governing them. American Indians, Africans, and Oceanic nations were said to have a functioning indigenous culture and then to abandon it institution by institution as they decided to follow the cultural pattern of their governors. There were thus degrees of acculturation from minimal to complete ("assimilation"). The concept of acculturation was flawed by the assumption that it worked *from* the indigenous cultural pattern *to* the colonial power's culture, which was equated with changing from "simple" to "complex." That was, unhappily, another way of saying from "primitive" to "civilized." Acculturation implied the racist nineteenth-century western idea that Western Europe and the United States were the most evolved societies and all others were "backward." American anthropologist Irving Hallowell showed how much had been absorbed in the opposite direction, *from* American Indians *into* U.S. culture—the people labeled "civilized" acculturating *to* the nonwestern societies. The term "acculturation" was also unsatisfactory because it didn't address how or why the culture changes happened.

Anthony F.C. Wallace, another American anthropologist, faced the inadequacy of the notion of acculturation as a simple replacement of one culture's institutions by those of another. First, in 1956, Wallace published a model he developed from his study of Iroquois Indian history. Contrary to simple acculturation notions, many Iroquois had changed from their preconquest religion to one introduced in 1799 in order to *preserve* Iroquois culture against the demands of the conquering government. The modified Iroquois religion, called the Gaiwiio ("Good Message," or "gospel") and the cultural pattern it promoted was preached by an Iroquois aristocrat known by his title, Handsome Lake. Wallace found evidence of demoralization after the Revolutionary War, in which a number of Iroquois allied with the British and subsequently lost much of their homelands. Drunkenness and violence consorted with unemployment in postwar Iroquois communities. Handsome Lake claimed he had been escorted to Heaven and instructed to carry back the Good Message advising how best to live in the postwar situation. Iroquois men, accustomed to travel to hunt and to trade, should take up occupations such as farming still available to them, though formerly performed by Iroquois women. Above all, Handsome Lake urged sobriety and peacefulness both within the communities and between Iroquois and others. The Good Message was eagerly listened to and, in Wallace's word, "revitalized" Iroquois societies. From this history, Wallace drew his "revitalization model" of, first, a stage or period of stress suffered by a few individuals because traditional behavior no longer was successful for them, next a stage in which the majority of people in the society suffered frustration from the inadequacy of traditional cultural patterns to meet the present situation, then the revitalization "movement" when a gifted individual (the "prophet") articulates a new culture pattern. Disciples help the prophet disseminate the message, modifying it to better fit the needs of a large number of people. If the new cultural pattern is well adapted to the people's situation, presenting them with guidelines to a reasonably satisfying life, it can become the dominant cultural pattern for the society.

Wallace's revitalization model, drawn from in-depth historical research and careful cross-cultural comparisons, charted how some societies, at least, have changed their cultural patterns, and it broke away from the assumption that successful change would invariably be simply from the non-western to the contemporary western culture. Wallace realized that in the course of his analysis he had slipped from a conventional to a more radical concept: Societies are not a device for "replicating" culture, cloning themselves, but somehow they manage to "organize diversity," he noted. Structural-functionalism saw variations within a society as "deviance" from "the norm." Wallace saw variety as the way life really is, and the challenge to anthropologists was to figure out how that gets organized enough to carry out some of the group operations contributing to individuals' and families' survival.

> Societies or cultures are not "things" that can be mechanically reproduced. We *reify* observations of behavior—think of behavior as "things" (Latin *res*, "thing")—as we try to understand our situation by organizing perceptions into categories.

During the 1960s, a number of anthropologists focused on the dynamics of social behavior. They traced "networks," discovering that whatever the official line may be, it's generally who you know that gets you a job, a date, into the club. They followed out "transactions," seeing social interaction as so many business deals. "Brokers" were identified, people who brought together other

> One example of ideal versus real came out of archaeologist William Rathje's project to understand the formation of prehistoric sites by analyzing how contemporary Americans create household garbage. Rathje's group interviewed householders at their front doors about their consumption habits, then sorted out their consumption discards from their regular garbage collection. People usually told interviewers that their households consumed few or no alcoholic beverages—our ideal behavior—in spite of the six-pack containers, gin and vodka bottles accumulating in their trash cans—their real behavior.

people's networks. "Culture brokers" were people such as interpreters and government-recognized village headmen who brought together representatives of different societies. "Case histories" were compiled, copying the way legal scholars discover social behavior through records of questions at law. An earlier concept, the important difference between the ideal behavior people claim to be their goal and their real behavior, was re-emphasized. Overall, the 1960s in anthropology, reflecting that period in the world in general, was a rebellion against the smothering notion of a static society in which people played assigned roles.

One of the most popular metaphors for social behavior in the 1960s was that life is a game that people play by means of strategies. Social behavior could

Angola, Africa, 1930. Men play a game similar to chess, thinking out strategies to overcome the opponent.
Photo credit: Milwaukee Public Museum.

be described as sets of strategies to gain one's needs and pleasures. The metaphor that life is a game goes back centuries, to the invention of games like pacheesi (originally from India) where little peg "men" move along a board according to throws of dice. Pacheesi mirrors the image of humans as pawns struggling through life plagued by the uncertainties of luck. "Game theory" was developed in mathematics, holding out to anthropologists the possibility that social behavior could not only be more precisely described through mathematical symbols, but also might be predictable through mathematical logic. Some fuzzy truisms came out of this, for example, that people tend to maximize satisfactions. Expecting that mathematical models could soon be devised to adequately explain all social behavior was taking a much too limited view of human life.

A lasting result of the radical shift in focus during the 1960s from prewar structural-functionalism has been recognition of the choices open to individuals. The abstract concept "social institutions" is only a way of mentally categorizing sets of patterns of behavior; people are not locked like prisoners within invisible walls in "social institutions." Game theory continues to have some application, especially where individuals or groups are clearly maneuvering against each other for a definite goal. Case histories, incorporating individual and group transactions, networks, and brokers, are invaluable in checking whether a participant observer ethnographer's experience marks an unusual situation or a more general pattern.

Categories of Political Structure

American anthropologist Morton Fried arranged societal structures along a continuum from the smallest known human communities to major modern nations. He divided societies into four general categories according to public relationships within them. These are:

1. *Egalitarian societies.* The principal economic unit is the household, usually a married couple, their young children, and unmarried relatives such as a widowed parent. Each household is autonomous (independent), but several households normally cooperate in food-getting and other activities. Relationships are face-to-face rather than impersonal, and usually appear informal. The "egality" in egalitarian societies refers to the economic status of member families; some persons in the community may be given more respect than others.

Egalitarian relationships are found not only among the Ju/'hoansi and Mbuti and similar small hunting-gathering communities, but also in many peasant villages. Anthropologist Dorothy Keur, for example, lived in a Dutch village that strongly discouraged any family living in a richer manner than the rest. The few farmers who had more money than the average hid the money until it could be invested in setting up a newly married child. A representative from each household attended an annual public meeting to discuss allocating use of communal land and other business of the community as a group. Next-door neighbors regularly assisted one another, linking the entire village in mutual-aid sets. When someone was required to openly organize an activity, villagers tried to get "outsiders," the schoolteacher or minister, to take the "boss" role, preserving the egalitarian relationships of the village households. The same device was observed by English anthropologist Ronald Frankenberg in a Welsh village. Frankenberg, a young man when he lived as participant observer in the community, concentrated on the local soccer team, noticing how "outsiders" were recruited to be coach, who of course had to order the players about. All losses could be blamed on the coach, and because he was an outsider, it was easy to fire him. The insights of these two anthropologists, among the first to apply anthropological research methods to contemporary European communities, clarify the means by which egalitarian societies maintain the political relationship: No community is entirely isolated, and it is usually when the people have to take account of the outside world that organized leadership becomes necessary. Recruiting "outsiders" to deal with "outside" matters saves the precious egalitarianism of the small community.

egalitarian: equal. The spelling is changed from "-qu-" to "-g-"

Mombasa, Kenya, 1928. An annual carnival allows all classes of society to mingle, dance, feast, and express ribald opinions of "high-hatted gents" and "fancy-haired ladies."
Photo credit: Milwaukee Public Museum.

2. *Rank societies.* Societies with hundreds of people living together cannot rely on informal face-to-face discussion to maintain cooperative relationships. A manager is needed. Rank societies acknowledge the social *status* of leader; this is more than the *role* of leader that may be activated occasionally in egalitarian societies. Rank societies have a permanent office of leader-manager, an office that may be called chief, headman or headwoman, *cacique* (term used in Latin America), Beloved Man or Woman (Cherokee Indian terms), *sachem* (Algonkian Indian), and so on. This official has the full-time duty to oversee the welfare of the community, to lead, and to represent it. He or she directs others. Chiefs in rank societies generally are chosen by a council from among adult members of a "leading family." There is no large class of aristocrats in the community, only an extended family that expects and trains its children to be leaders. When a chief dies or becomes incapacitated, a council—of the family, or drawn from the community—considers who in the leading family seems most capable of assuming the office. There may be a custom of selecting the chief's brother or son, or his eldest sister's son, but there is no absolute hereditary right of succession that would put an imbecile in the office. Likely candidates

Upper class: the captain of a British ocean liner, 1928.
Photo credit: Milwaukee Public Museum.

for chief frequently marry into chiefly families in neighboring regions, creating strong alliances between their communities and, by being backed by the alliances, strengthening the politically shrewd individual's likelihood of being selected for the office. Marriages between noble families set up an aristocratic class in the region, but rank societies cannot be termed true class-based societies because there is regularly also marriage between some members of the chiefly families and respectable commoners in their own communities. Rank societies have the rank of noble but do not separate noble families as a class from the commoners in the community.

Morton Fried added that rank societies have *redistributive economies,* that is, the chiefs take surplus production from the commoners and redistribute it— to them in feasts and aid, and to visitors from outside. Chiefs live in houses larger than those of commoners, partly to symbolize their "larger" status in the community, partly to give room to host visitors (dignitaries of other communities, traders) and to prepare feasts. There is usually an open space or plaza in front of the chief's house so the people can gather together to attend the feasts, trade, witness legal proceedings (chaired or attended by the chief), or petition the chief. The chief is responsible for seeing that those unable to provide for themselves, whether visitors from outside or widowed, orphaned, or handicapped members of the community, are taken care of. Since rank societies usually are agricultural or specialized producers for a market (for example, fishermen), the chief's redistributive duties include managing exchanges of surplus production as well as feasting the community.

3. *Stratified societies.* Societies with populations in the thousands sustain *classes* of people in different social ranks. Nobles are sufficiently numerous that they can find eligible mates within their own polity (civic government), although kings will seek alliances through marriage with royalty of other polities. The classes in stratified societies are ranked, perhaps with three recognized levels as in America—upper class, middle class, lower class—perhaps with five as among

> Social classes are ranks in society. In a rank society, an individual family occupies higher rank in a community. In class-stratified societies, hundreds occupy the higher class, thousands are in the lower classes.

the Patwin Indians of California—nobility, professional people, commoners, slaves, and "no-account trash" (drifters, beggars). People expect to marry within their own class, though they tell stories about marriages across classes, whether about the poor but hardworking youth who wins the chief's daughter, or about weak, upper-class people who let foolish love for a callous ne'er-do-well drag them down into poverty and contempt.

Stratified societies have enough surplus production to support hundreds of upper-class members. These include the leisured class who not only do not work in production themselves but also usually employ managers to supervise workers. The existence of leisured classes has baffled many analysts. Why do the commoners, who always outnumber them, allow this class to enjoy leisure and luxuries at commoners' expense? Why do British taxpayers pay the royal family, even the younger sisters and brothers of the monarch, the equivalent of millions

Lower class: crew members of a British ocean liner, 1928.
Photo credit: Milwaukee Public Museum.

Social classes, stratified: well-to-do passengers enjoy a deck game on a British ocean liner, 1928, assisted by a middle-class steward and a lower-class sailor.
Photo credit: Milwaukee Public Museum.

of dollars? All the "royals" seem required to do is cut ribbons at ceremonies opening new facilities. The answer seems to lie in the importance of symbols. The monarch represents the nation, on coins and stamps and wherever public contributions have built a facility. British taxpayers support Buckingham and Windsor palaces, with their occupants, as U.S. taxpayers support the cost of the White House: These are physical, tangible signs of the grandeur of the nation. Ostentatious luxury symbolizes power. Power can be frightening, but it is good when it's on your side. A powerful nation or, in feudal societies, a powerful lord protects its citizens. Being able to pay for ostentatious luxuries for the head of state demonstrates the nation's economy can pay, also, for armed forces and social services. In stratified societies, the upper class controls a great deal of surplus production. Ideally, it invests in maintenance and development for commoner needs as well as in ostentatious luxury. When an avaricious dictator displays personal wealth while the public standard of living is falling, people plot rebellion.

4. *The Nation-State* is the somewhat awkward term for societies with hundreds of thousands, or millions, of people. States (the more common term) are class stratified; they differ from smaller stratified societies in having a formal bureaucracy of civil servants to run the nation. The civil bureaucracy is not a class but a political structure containing people from several social classes. In the bureaucracy are the faceless clerks who keep the records, construct the office staffs and procedures for spending public money, make the little operating decisions such as the time when street lights are turned on each night. States have market economies and territorial boundaries. Officially they operate under rules of law, not face-to-face relationships. The hyphenated term *nation-state* notes that, ideally, the state coincides with a territory within which people share a common language and cultural traditions (the citizens of the state are "born into"—*nation* is from the Latin word for birth—the culture maintained by the state government). In fact, states almost always incorporate cultural diversity and impose an official language and often an official religion upon all citizens. The United States and Canadian federal governments wrestle with the problem of acknowledging demands for self-rule from American Indian, French Canadian, and Hispanic nations that were incorporated into the two dominantly English states. Political factions within a nation-state may label themselves by an ethnic name and claim they were "born into" a suppressed group fighting for its right of self-determination.

Agra, India, the elegant, massive, state-supported Pearl Mosque.
Photo credit: Milwaukee Public Museum.

Pisa, Italy, cloistered courtyard of the officially recognized church (Campo Santo). State power is communicated through buildings leading visitors' eyes along vast vistas to guarded doorways.
Photo credit: Milwaukee Public Museum.

Cautions about Categories of Political Structure

Morton Fried's categories are to be understood as marking rather arbitrary sections of a continuum. His scheme has the virtue of highlighting political structure while bringing in rough correlations with population size and economic features. Fried's scheme has a historical dimension, in that the archaeological record shows a broad trend from early hominids who presumably, like apes and monkeys, were basically egalitarian although allowing limited leadership, through Upper Paleolithic and Neolithic village communities that look like rank societies, to the early stratified city-states and eventually the large nation-states.

Other anthropologists have published schemes similar to Morton Fried's. Elman Service suggested, in a 1962 book, that early hominids and existing hunter-gatherer communities can be termed "bands," and that as populations grew bands allied into "tribes" and then into "chiefdoms" and finally state organization emerged. Fried criticized Service's category "tribe," arguing that historical records suggest that "tribes" are alliances of small nations resisting domination by expanding empires. Examples can be found in the histories of U.S. expansion resisted by American Indian nations and of China resisted by Central Asian nations. Service accepted Fried's historically grounded critique, dropping "tribe" from his scheme. The discussion between these colleagues, Fried and Service, illustrates the importance anthropologists place on empirical data—actual observations, by participant observation today or by examining historical documents preserving descriptions and through archaeological data.

Schemes such as Fried's and Service's are designed to reveal universal characteristics of human societies, in this case the need to devise social organizations that will maintain communities and groups of communities. Natural selection favored gregariousness in our ancestors. Our large and complex brains, another feature selected for among our ancestors, amassed know-how and skills in harvesting food and compensating for adverse climate so that, eventually, populations in many regions grew large and densely settled. Similar management challenges resulted in roughly similar forms of social organization in various regions of the world. These rough similarities constitute the categories devised by Fried, Service, and others. It is essential to keep in mind that contemporary, small, egalitarian communities are *not* survivals from the Paleolithic, but modern political groups who have resisted assimilation into nation-states at the cost of foregoing some material benefits. Contemporary ranked societies are *not* survivals from the Neolithic: some (e.g., Trobrianders of Papua New Guinea) occupy areas that will not support dense populations, others (e.g., a number of North American Indian nations) have retrenched social organization after suffering heavy population losses due to epidemics and European invaders' unremitting wars against them. Contemporary societies that exemplify these categories of social organization give us only a rough idea of possible Upper Paleolithic and Neolithic societies. Every contemporary or historic human society is as evolved in its adaptation to its ecological niche as any and every other modern society.

Law and Custom

Political systems must structure the cooperation necessary for human survival. Written laws, like written rules in general, are part of bureaucracies governing states with many thousands, or millions, of residents. To manage such numbers, procedures are standardized and recorded. Small societies, where everybody knows, if not quite everybody else, at least some cousin or neighbor of everybody else, can operate without such repositories of rules accessible to thousands of officials. In societies without marked class stratification, separation between public and private, government and family is not an ideal. Anthropologists who have been participant observers in small nonwestern communities describe how people call back and forth from their houses, discussing public business. Even if there is a formal council of senior men representing the families, women listen and the opinions of the older women are influential.

Our society contrasts government with family, public with private spheres. Opposition between public and private in community life is widespread in Western Asia, Europe, and North Africa. This also goes back to Classical Greece. Men were supposed to work and socialize outside the home, women to remain inside. Greek freemen met in the agora, a plaza where markets, public discussions, and elections were held. Their wives were expected to stay in the house, spinning and weaving. (Household chores were done by slaves.) This ideal separation between public and private, government and family, lessened during the Roman Empire following Classical Greece but remained part of the European cultural tradition, becoming strong again in the nineteenth century. Women were to have no part in government, not even a citizen's vote, for it was said that if they participated in public affairs, family life would be harmed. Doctors claimed that girls who studied and thought were diverting energy from the growth of their reproductive organs and would be unable to bear healthy children. Girls should devote themselves to learning sweet manners and how to dress attractively—this included wearing excessively tight corsets that did harm the reproductive organs of many young women—while boys went to school, played hard, and roamed about with buddies. In Classical Greece and in nineteenth-century Europe and America, the ideal separation between public and private, government and family, men and women had a hidden second separation between upper and lower social classes. Only in well-to-do families could men devote time to public affairs and ladies remain home, while employees performed the daily grind of factory, farm, and household work. In these societies, government was by and for upper-class men, with lower-class working men as well as all women prohibited from voting or taking office. Classical Greece's famous democracy applied only to Greek men who did not have to work as employees or slaves.

Contrasting custom with law is misleading. Small societies seldom possess written codes of law, relying instead on the memories of the mature members, some of whom may be rigorously trained in accurate recall. Anthropologists have occasionally been able to check orally transmitted history against documents, and generally found a high degree of accuracy. Oral tradition does allow changes to slip in unnoticed (this too has been demonstrated), but so can written laws, their interpretation or application shifting as time goes on. Some scholars say that "custom" applies only to a particular group, while "laws" are written as if they would be of universal application, but the concept that laws should apply universally without regard to individuals' social status would be rejected even by many European and American governments. "Jim Crow" laws in many southern U.S. jurisdictions included parallel laws, one for blacks and the other for whites. Europe and China used to have sumptuary laws stipulating what classes of people were entitled to wear and to eat particular items: Peasants, for example, might be forbidden to wear silk or eat white bread, reserved for upper-class people. These were written laws; in other areas, similar rules are only unwritten "custom."

An African diplomat to the United Nations thoughtfully compared his experiences in his home country with his work at the UN. West African political systems assume that conflict *will* be resolved by discussion, each party clarifying their position and reasons until it becomes clear where mutual interests lie, and the parties can construct a procedure or settlement meeting these common interests. *Palaver* is the West African trade jargon term used for this process. European political processes, in contrast, he felt were based on an assumption that conflict will *not* be resolved but disputing parties will compromise to avoid more damaging outcomes. European systems tend to pose involved parties as adversaries, opposing one another until one side "wins." Outwardly, palaver and European political-legal processes look similar, people sitting together presenting their arguments as forcefully as they can, but the diplomat felt that the difference in underlying assumptions is critical: European political and legal systems tend to be run as zero-sum games, while West African systems aim for a draw. The diplomat thought the U.N. should more consciously use a palaver system, since its members are there to find agreement.

> Zero-sum games take away from the loser to give the gain to the winner. Alternately, games may be structured so that everyone ends up sharing the pot or selecting a prize. In real life, competition need not end in somebody's loss.

Either palaver or adversarial systems can be used in any size society, and both are likely to be used, with the choice depending upon the situation. Australian desert Aborigines (indigenous nations' descendants) usually resolve disagreements by palaver, but people can reject the wisdom of palaver and jump up, physically threatening those who oppose them. Two bands might find each other so opposed that the men line up as adversaries for a spear-throwing battle. Afterward, when anger has cooled, the bands could restore fellowship through ritual gestures of intimacy. At the other extreme of national size, in the United States the adversarial system of two opposed political parties competing for votes, or opposed lawyers in the courtrooms, is not the only process. Mediation or arbitration, based on the palaver idea that the parties involved do have mutual interests, often is used in settling disputes and setting up contracts. The European worldview, drawn in part from the Bible, presents opposition as the common situation and glorifies the winner, but unheroic cooperation is more typical of everyday life.

British anthropologist Max Gluckman studied the legal systems of the African kingdoms of Zulu and Barotse. Gluckman's own family contained several lawyers, giving him intimate knowledge of how British law really worked. As he compared the processes of law in these three systems, two African and the British, Gluckman realized that formal legal rules and procedures are only part of societies' maintenance of law and order. What tended to be overlooked is the function of gossip. Neighbors chatting, citizens relaxing in coffeehouses, students whispering in class about the kids who . . .—all are articulating community standards and defining unacceptable conduct. Informal face-to-face evaluation of behavior is the other side of law enforcement. Community standards are explicitly discussed in one area of American law, the question of what constitutes pornography. Gossip condones posters of naked young women in men's locker rooms, yet demands jail for a man who entices young children to look at such posters. A great deal of behavior is constantly discussed as people decide what will earn them approbation from their peers and what will be condemned. Modern, literate societies use news media to assist in articulating community standards for millions. "Ann Landers" and "Dear Abby" daily present situations for newspaper readers throughout the country to ponder, with Ann or Abby suggesting what she feels would be majority opinion on the case. When Ann or Abby miscall the case, letters flood in and are printed, clarifying actual community standards. Gluckman assumed gossip works only in small communities, but "Ann Landers" and her sister "Abby," plus the letters-to-the-editor and op-ed features in newspapers and magazines, call-in shows on radio, and cable television shows enable millions to hear and thousands to respond actively to form community opinion on behavior.

> A reader of advice columns wrote in to confess that as a teenager, she and her friends thumbed their noses at parents' and teachers' warnings about the consequences of misconduct. "We studied your column," she said, took to heart its direful stories, and let it guide them round the pitfalls of contemporary life.

World-Systems

In 1974, Immanuel Wallerstein, a sociologist, published a historical study of the development of the modern multinational political economy. He showed the inadequacy of limiting political or economic analyses to national boundaries. Anthropologists were excited by Wallerstein's perspective, for it related "tribal" groups to the big picture. With Morton Fried's argument that tribes are a

A tea plantation in Sri Lanka, 1930. Local laborers producing a beverage for a world market.

Photo credit: Milwaukee Public Museum.

Laborers bring the tea leaves to the processing factory, Sri Lanka, 1930. Note that the local headquarters of this world-system enterprise is built in the style of the owners' English homeland houses.

Photo credit: Milwaukee Public Museum.

1932, Rotonia, New Zealand. Surrounding a woodcarver creating a traditional design, Maori in contemporary versions of indigenous dress recreate Maori heritage for the world tourist market.

Photo credit: Milwaukee Public Museum.

response to—now we have a term—world-system encroachment, political anthropology turned from neat categorizations toward the complex effects of expanding businesses. There was a new frame for interpretation.

A 1982 book by American anthropologist Eric Wolf, *Europe and the People Without History,* strengthened the impact of Wallerstein's work by championing the worth of the colonized nations whose earlier histories had been ignored. Sixteenth-century Spanish conquerors literally destroyed Mexican history by burning all the native books they could find—only four out of many thousands survived the bonfires. Three centuries later, anthropologists had contrasted "primitive," "static" "tribes" without (known) history to "civilized," "dynamic," historically documented western nations. Major John Wesley Powell, founder and director of the Smithsonian's Bureau of American Ethnology after the Civil War, told Congress that American Indians are primitive people whose minds cannot think like those of civilized citizens of European descent; the U.S. government would have to administer Indian tribes like a father supervising children. Powell assumed Indian cultures had hardly changed over thousands of years. He read the statement of Lewis Henry Morgan, a businessman of the time who interviewed American Indians, that no American Indian society had ever "progressed" beyond a simple tribal organization; Morgan insisted, without any evidence, that the chroniclers of the Spanish conquests of Mexico and Peru must have lied about the splendor of those empires. Morgan and Powell let their enthusiasm for what their generation believed was America's Manifest Destiny override reasonable judgment. Abundant data on the complexities of nonwestern societies, on the intelligence with which they adapted to different environments, and on their readiness to change when change seemed the sensible course, had been systematically denied by conventional anthropologists. Wallerstein and Eric Wolf, a century after Powell and Morgan, pointed out that the so-called primitives were the less powerful nations on the "periphery" of a world-system, nations conquered and exploited for their labor and resources. Western industrial empires squared these actions with their avowed moral precepts by claiming the conquered nations were "backward."

Ethnohistory is a growing subfield bridging history and anthropology. Scholars researching the histories of nonwestern nations, and of ethnic groups within the major modern nations, are contributing much new data to political anthropology. An actual world-system may be a modern development, but continental economic systems can be traced archaeologically back to the Upper Paleolithic. Historically, in the St. Lawrence River region between New York State and Ontario, the "rank society" Iroquois nations raised corn to trade for meat and leather with the "egalitarian band societies" of the Algonkians. This was a complex economic and political system that sustained yields for generations. It wasn't idyllic—the Iroquois nations warred against each other and tried to dominate the Algonkians—but it, and the internal political structures of the Indian nations, demonstrate the dynamic interactions of indigenous nations within large sections of a continent. When first Norse, around A.D. 1000, and then European fishermen beginning in the 1490s entered the Gulf of St.

Lawrence, the Indian nations extended their indigenous trading system to include the newcomers. Norse colonists (Leif Eriksson and his brother Thorvald) were hostile toward the First Americans, dooming the small colony. The fishermen were less aggressive; from their barter, the international fur trade developed that linked northern American Indians directly into the Eurasian world-system. Ethnohistoric research strongly contradicts the racist notions about so-called primitives in America and other continents. This contemporary research adds greatly to our information on the range and variety of systems of social organization.

PART II:
KINSHIP

All political systems include the basic unit structured to promote reproduction and the care of children. This basic unit Americans call the family. *Nuclear family* consists of parents and their children living together, *extended family* includes relatives of the couple and children. Americans also use the word "family" to indicate a group whose members support each other unstintingly, for example a loyal varsity sports team or—famous example—Mafia gangsters. Conversely, when relatives refuse to support each other unstintingly, we may speak of a broken family. Remembering that we emphasize the characteristic of unstinting support marking families, we can more easily see how societies may structure a residential group as the basic "familial" unit, regardless of genetic relationships. We can also see how kinship terms may be applied quite differently than in English usage, according to the roles people play toward one another.

> *kin*: relatives (Old English word)
> *kinship*: family relationships

Nineteenth-century anthropologists began with kinship terms accepted in English law. "Blood" relatives (*consanguines,* from the Latin words for "together" and "blood") were biologically—that is, genetically—related and because no action can change genetic relationships once a child is conceived, consanguineous relationships were held to be unbreakable. People learned to think of these as their "real" relatives. *Affinal* relationships were set up by marriages; these are one's in-laws. Consanguines, especially the closest consanguines in the nuclear family, had legal obligations to support one another. Close consanguines are not permitted to marry one another. (If they did they would commit incest, a sin or crime.) Why members of a nuclear family are not permitted to marry one another has never been well understood; in-breeding doesn't necessarily promote genetic abnormalities. The usual anthropological explanation is that marriage allies families, widening the net of unstinting support on which survival may depend. Another explanation is that boys and girls who grow up together don't readily see each other as sexually attractive, since they learned nonsexual roles toward one another before puberty awakened sexual feelings. This explanation is supported by observation that other primates seldom seem to mate with the parents or siblings they grew up with. The two explanations may both be true.

Lewis Henry Morgan, one of the pioneer American anthropologists, was astounded to discover, as he came to know Seneca Iroquois Indians who lived on a reservation near his upstate New York home, that Iroquois inherit surname and property from their mothers' families, i.e., matrilineally. This was the mirror image of English law in which, especially in Morgan's nineteenth century, a woman was obliged to drop her family surname and take that of her husband upon marriage, children had their father's name, and inheritance was normally patrilineal, from the father's family. In Morgan's time, custody of children in a divorce was awarded

> matrilineal: mother's line (Latin *mater* "mother")
> patrilineal: father's line (Latin *pater* "father")
> bilateral: both (Latin *bi-*) sides (Latin *latus* "side")

to the father even if the children were very small (a custom that Morgan's feminist neighbor Elizabeth Cady Stanton claimed caused unbearable distress to wronged wives).

Wondering whether Iroquois matrilineal customs are unique, Morgan traveled to the Midwestern frontier to interview Indians from a number of other nations, and sent questionnaires to missionaries and agents in nonwestern countries. He found many variations on kinship terms and customs, enough to make a thick volume published in 1871 by the Smithsonian Institution. Morgan identified several contrasting systems, naming them from the Indian nations where he had learned of them: the Iroquoian matrilineal system, the Omaha patrilineal system, the Eskimo bilateral (both parents equally acknowledged). It took half a century before anthropologists could understand that some societies, for example the Mandan and Hidatsa in North Dakota and the Ashanti in Ghana (West Africa), divided familial responsibility so that children inherited such goods as residence rights and farmland from the mother's family and religious training and offices from the father's family. (This is called "double descent.") Morgan, being a lawyer by profession, was most concerned with inheritance, frequently disputed and brought to law among his associates. It is better to look at relationships as *responsibilities,* so that Hidatsa, for example, place the responsibility for spiritual nurturance upon the father's family and for physical nurturance upon the mother's. For a grown child, this becomes a claim to religious office and to land for house and farm. To put it bluntly, children who don't survive can't inherit anything, so responsibility for nurturing children is more basic than inheritance rules.

Again from the basic perspective of survival, the fact that families may include members who are not genetically related makes sense. The older notion that kinship terms describe actual blood relationships left adoption a puzzle, but if kinship terminology names social roles, and families are instruments for children's survival, then adoption is an obvious way to maximize the number of children who survive in a society. What matters is that some adult take the *role* of parent to an orphaned or neglected child and, if they act the role, they ought to be called by the term for that role. It also makes sense that societies may make little distinction between biological parents and other caretakers. Morgan was shocked that in Hawai'i, he was told, Polynesian children addressed any man in a household as "Father," any woman as "Mother," and the adults used the same word for their biological children and for other children in an extended-family household. This was not, as Morgan thought, because Hawai'ian men and women had sex indiscriminately within a household and couldn't tell which child was theirs (obviously, a child's birth mother could be definitely identified, a fact he elsewhere suggested as the reason for Iroquois preference for matrilineality). The terms reported to him by the missionary actually referred to the roles of "adult man in one's household" and "adult woman in one's household," all the men sharing the male householders' duties and all the women sharing the women's. As for the term Morgan was told meant "child," it meant "little one," and could be used to refer to a little coconut as well as to a child.

KINSHIP

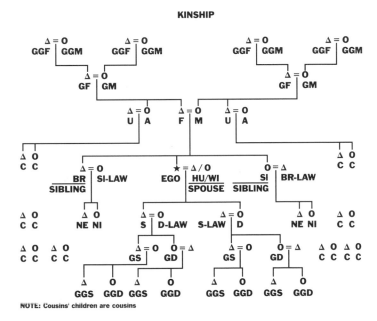

NOTE: Cousins' children are cousins

AMERICAN KINSHIP
CONSANGUINES ("Blood Relations")

GGF-GREATGRANDFATHER
GGM-GREATGRANDMOTHER
GF-GRANDFATHER
GM-GRANDMOTHER
F-FATHER
M-MOTHER
U-UNCLE
A-AUNT
EGO-SELF (Latin="I")
BR-BROTHER ⎫
                    ⎬ SIBLINGS
SI-SISTER ⎭

NE-NEPHEW
NI-NIECE
C-COUSIN
S-SON
D-DAUGHTER
GS-GRANDSON
GD-GRANDDAUGHER
GGS-GREATGRANDSON
GGD-GREATGRANDDAUGHTER

AFFINES ("In-laws")
HU-HUSBAND ⎫
                     ⎬ SPOUSE
WI-WIFE ⎭

NOTE: SPOUSES OF UNCLE AND AUNT ARE AFFINES BUT
ARE COMMONLY ADDRESSED AS "AUNT" AND "UNCLE"

The American kinship system is a kindred: Note that the same terms are applied to relatives on the father's and on the mother's side (that is, bilateral). Note that the differentiating principles in American kinship are (1) generation—people of the same generation are differentiated from those of older and younger generations, and (2) sex—males and females receive different terms, except for people more than two linking relations away ("cousins"). To see what a diagram of a unilineal system looks like, copy the diagram and color in the symbols that would represent people, including you (EGO, "I") with your father's last name: That will give you a patrilineage.

Kinship systems are one form of political structure. They name social roles involved in the reproduction of the society through the reproduction of members. "Fictive kinship"—adoption, and also the institution of godparents— broadens the family beyond what biological reproduction may provide, and adjusts the number of supportive adults to the number of children. The "rhetoric of kinship" describes political responsibilities as if they were familial. Where there are formal governments, their officers are often said to be like parents, watching over citizens as parents do for children. U.S. government representatives to American Indian nations liked to say that the president would be a "Great Father" to the Indians if they would sign a treaty. That term was as much from European philosophy as from any Indian custom: 2,000 years ago in Classical Greece and Rome, politicians promised voters they would be like fathers to the populace, if elected. We've all heard that President George Washington was the father of his country.

Americans contrast families with government. Families are what you're born into, families are warm and loving, they give unstinting support. Governments are organizations constructed by people to manage public affairs; government agents are appointed or elected by other adults; governments are rule governed, impersonal, and cold. Political systems are not that simple. Families are the basic political unit, their role set by law. Nuclear families are organized into larger units with economic and political obligations: anthropologists categorize these as *lineages* or *kindreds,* depending on whether membership is exclusive (lineages) or may overlap (kindreds). In societies without centralized government, kindreds or clans (sets of lineages) protect their members by demanding justice when one has been harmed. Kindreds or clans are present in modern nations,

---

kindred: relatives including both those of one's father and of one's mother, considered equivalent; kindreds are what you see at family reunions; kindreds don't own property but members assist one another, economically and politically.
lineage: people who trace descent from an ancestor in common; lineages may be grouped into *clans*; clans are like corporations, holding property in common, transacting business, and held liable for fines if their members disobey laws; clan members cannot marry one another because they are held to be related. Societies may be divided into two complementary parts, or *moieties*, that exchange services and marry each other.

An extended family gathers in an American living room to enjoy holiday festivities.
Affines are merged with consanguines in this bilateral kindred.
Photo credit: Aldis Strazdins

informally assisting members with economic and political support while leaving administration of justice to the formal government.

Some societies rely strongly on clans. The word "clan" is Gaelic from Scotland, where territory was held by groups of families said to be related through their fathers (patrilineally)—hence the names beginning with Mac, "son of"—and organized through clan chiefs from noble lineages within the clan. Members of Scots clans have been permitted to marry one another, so strictly speaking these clans are "ambilineal" rather than patrilineal. Clans, like the Scots', that are primarily territorial rather than strictly lineages are more common than earlier anthropologists assumed. China before its 1949 Communist Revolution had a highly bureaucratized government centered in its emperor and court, yet it also operated through patrilineal clans, in this case house compounds sheltering families related through the husbands.

Iroquois Indians obtained rights to house and the produce of farm land through matrilineally inherited membership in clans. Iroquois government operates through officers, called "chiefs" in English, who are appointed by the senior women of each clan in a community. Chiefs are expected to convey their clans' opinions to the community and League of the Iroquois councils; if a chief fails to present his clan's concerns and opinions, the senior clanswomen depose him and appoint another. The women can veto council decisions. Young men are appointed by the clan to assist their chief in carrying out the wishes of the clan. Iroquois nations are structured as representative democracies, with town councils functioning as federations of the clans, and the League as a confederation of small states. (Benjamin Franklin was familiar with Iroquois government through serving at treaty councils, and pointed out at the U.S. Constitutional Convention that the viability of Iroquois government proved a U.S. federal government could be a success, too.)

Hopi and Zuni, two Pueblo Indian nations in Arizona, tie their matrilineal clans to religious priestly offices, each clan carrying out its special ritual for the welfare of the village. Government is exercised through the organization of senior priests, in this manner coordinating the interests of the several clans. Eastern Pueblos, in New Mexico, don't have clans but instead divide villages into moieties such as Summer and Winter, half the people in one, half in the other. Summer moiety is in charge of rituals and governance during that half the year, Winter during the other half. Several Pueblos, between the west and east groups, have both clans and moieties, showing a gradation from one structure to the other. Careful study of societies governing through clans reveals their property ownership to be a highly significant aspect of their function, so much so that people who live on the land of a certain clan are usually assumed to be members of that clan even when villagers remember that particular individuals were immigrants from elsewhere known not to be biologically descended from the clan ancestor. Clans and moieties often operate much like neighborhood property-owners' organizations.

Kindreds seem a more flexible type of organization because they overlap, giving people more choice of affiliation. Kindreds are bilateral, recognizing the father's and mother's families as equally important, reflected in applying the same kin terms to each side. American society is based on kindreds, with both parents' parents called grandfather or grandmother, brothers of both parents called uncles, sisters of both parents called aunts, uncles' and aunts' children called cousins (note that although the gender of the linking person is ignored, gender of the person referred to determines which of two terms will be applied, except for the more distant relatives called cousins, who are lumped under a single term regardless of gender). Rich and powerful people like the Kennedys and Rockefellers have big kindreds because it is advantageous to be seen as related to prestigious people. Poor but decent people are also likely to have large kindreds, because poor people need to help each other out. In northern Europe during the time of the Roman Empire and several following centuries, fighting men were recruited from leaders' kindreds. Today, fishing boats, unions with apprenticeship programs, and many businesses often recruit young workers from bosses' kindreds. Kindreds are a kind of network enabling people seeking opportunities or assistance to find offers. Next time you go to a family reunion, notice how your kindred is good fellowship and more, how the relatives tell one another who might have a job for Cousin Jan, where you could get a good car from Pat's brother's wife's nephew, what courses Kim recommends at the college. The socially designated tie of kinship brought all these people together and tells them they ought to like and help one another.

Summary

Societies are regulated by many simultaneous means. Analysis of societies from the perspective of politics focuses on power: how power is delegated, what marks the offices and persons to whom power is delegated, how the existence and delegation of power is explained within the worldview. From a broader anthropological perspective, we see that power in a society is enmeshed in its economic structure, reflected in its religion, expressed in its arts and games, and tied into larger regional or even world systems. Anthropologists have set up categories of social organization based upon number of people in polities, ranging from a few cooperating households, through villages administering their affairs through a chief, to class-stratified polities, and, at one extreme, large bureaucratic nation-states. People act the roles assigned them by their social group more thoroughly than most of us realize, taking on particular speech forms as well as dress and mannerisms, occupation, and recreation preferences. The way a social role pervades a person's behavior, directing their choices, makes it part of society's regulation of its members. It is characteristic of all societies to believe, and teach, that some political structures are "natural" to humans, rather than social constructions that could be changed. Kinship roles and family structures are particularly likely to be assumed to be natural; the variety of these seen cross-culturally shows that kinship is social organization more than genetics.

RECOMMENDED READINGS

In the Case Studies in Cultural Anthropology Series (Harcourt Brace)

Chance, Norman A. *China's Urban Villagers.* 1991. Contemporary China is highly conscious of its political structures and philosophy. Chance personalizes this with his focus on Red Flag commune and adjacent Half Moon village.

Keesing, Roger M. *'Elota's Story.* 1983. The biography of a leader in a Melanesian community in the Solomon Islands, largely told in a translation of his own lively reminiscences.

Kuper, Hilda. *The Swazi: A South African Kingdom.* 1986. The Swazi kingdom was gradually overcome in the nineteenth century by the Union of South Africa, and since the 1960s has been contesting that nation's dominance. Kuper describes the traditional kingdom and its contemporary politics.

O'Meara, Tim. *Samoan Planters.* 1990. An interesting contrast to 'Elota, the Samoans in this study live in a stratified society adapting to incorporation in the contemporary world-system.

Trigger, Bruce G. *The Huron.* 1990. An account of one of the Iroquois nations in the early seventeenth century. This is one of the more accessible descriptions of the Iroquois for students.

REFERENCES

Ardener, Edwin and Shirley. *Perceiving Women* (edited by Shirley Ardener). London: Malaby, 1975. See also Shirley Ardener's Introduction to *Defining Females*, edited by her (New York: John Wiley).

Arnold, Arnold. *Winners . . . and Other Losers in War and Peace*. London: Paladin Grafton Books (Collins), 1989.

Frankenberg, Ronald. *Village on the Border*. Prospect Heights; Il.: Waveland Press, 1957; reprinted 1990.

Fried, Morton H. *The Evolution of Political Society*. New York: Random House, 1967.

Gluckman, Max. "Gossip and Scandal." *Current Anthropology* 4:(1963) 307–316.

Goffman, Erving. *The Presentation of Self in Everyday Life*. New York: Doubleday, 1959.

Gubrium, Jaber F., and James A. Holstein. *What is Family?* Mountain View, Cal: Mayfield, 1990.

Keur, Dorothy, and John Y. Keur. *The Deeply Rooted: A Study of a Drents Community in the Netherlands*. American Ethnological Society Monograph No. 25, 1955.

Underhill, Ruth M. *Papago Woman*. New York: Holt Rinehart Winston, 1979.

Wallerstein, Immanuel. *The Modern World-System: Capitalist Agriculture and the Origins of the European World Economy in the Sixteenth Century*. New York: Academic Press, 1974.

Wolf, Eric R. *Europe and the People Without History*. Berkeley: University of California Press, 1982.

12

Analyzing Societies (IV): Religion

In this chapter, we focus on the upper sections of our chart:

```
                            D       V
                    L               I
                R                           E
        O                                       W
W                                                   W
e x p r e s s i o n        a n d        r e c r e a t i o n
                V A L U E S
                    SOCIALIZING
            A R T S     (visual, musical, dramatic, literary)
                    N   O
                O       F
            I
        T               S
    A                       O
    L                           C
G   U                               I
E                                       E
R                                           T
                                                Y
            r e l i g i o n
```

Religion, like families, is said to be universal in human societies. The family we can understand, since our species would become extinct if men and women did not copulate and then cooperate in nurturing the resulting baby. Religion, unlike the family, does not appear to answer what Malinowski called a "biological imperative." Why should it be universal?

What *is* religion? The term applies to humans' conviction that there is something greater than they, something beyond the everyday world: transcendental. Every sensible person realizes that our senses are too limited to take in all the world, our intelligence too limited to fully understand the world. Faced with the vast unknown, people fear they will be overwhelmed. "Whence cometh my help?" is an ancient cry. Many philosophers, over hundreds of generations, have offered answers, building cultural traditions that teach members of human societies what seems to them a reasonable and practical understanding of the mystery of life.

> Religious leaders may assert that they teach knowledge revealed by a transcendental power. If this is so, it cannot be tested by scientific methods because science *by definition* limits itself to phenomena observable *in this world*.

The anthropological study of religions makes no attempt to discover which, if any, is the ultimate Truth. As social scientists, anthropologists focus on observable human behavior. What anthropologists discover is how religions function to maintain human societies, and how religious beliefs relate to the experiences of the people who hold them. Religion is part of the habitus, to use Bourdieu's term, that emphasizes how much more than formal articulated knowledge is comprised in an individual's, or social group's, "way of being." That habitual interpretation of the nature of the world and its people (worldview), shaped by the society's environment and its interaction with that environment, is expressed through everyday arrangement of homes, communities, workplaces,

> *ritual:* strongly patterned actions believed to be necessarily exactly repeated; usually refers to religious actions
> *myth:* narrative of supernatural beings and events

and interpersonal activities. Additionally, critical aspects of the habitus are reinforced through *ritual*—highly patterned behavior. People often say they perform certain rituals because these were taught in an ancient time by a transcendental being; such explanations are said to be *myth*. Some anthropologists have approached the study of religion by focusing on rituals (the action side), others by focusing on myths (the intellectual side of religion). The two approaches are like looking at the two sides of a coin: They may appear quite different but they are not separable.

Explanations of Religion

When anthropology, as a formal field of research, began in the mid-nineteenth century, heated debates over the relative value of scientific versus religious explanations were popular. During the previous two centuries, a number of scientifically minded thinkers such as Thomas Jefferson had rejected the quarrels between various churches over details of doctrine. Instead, these Enlightenment thinkers assumed that the Deity (God, but not necessarily God as described in the Christian Bible) had created the world so that it ran like a well-engineered machine without need of an operator. (They suggested this world machine was like a finely crafted clock. Wealthy people enjoyed the godlike feeling of winding up clockwork figures that imitated live beings—one figurine, for example, would drop a dish of carved food in its mouth, then a little, turd-shaped carving would drop out of the opposite end of its torso.) "Natural philosophers" should carefully observe the world and deduce how the world machine and its principles of operation are constructed. God gave us a "Book of Nature"—a technical manual—to read beside the Bible, it was said.

By the mid-nineteenth century, a couple hundred years of experiments using increasingly elaborate apparatus, from telescopes to microscopes, static electricity machines to the classification of hundreds of thousands of fossils, all had produced data and explanatory hypotheses that made the Bible seem inadequate or even downright erroneous in places. Some clergymen insisted that nothing should contradict the Bible even in details, that such mythlike passages as the stories of Noah's Ark or the Tower of Babel must be historically true. Scientific data are illustrations of these events, they asserted. The fact that mammal fossils are found only in the higher strata of the earth does not mean, they said, that mammals had not evolved until more recent times; no, the explanation was that during Noah's flood, mammals had run for the higher mountains and finally died there as the waters rose. The Tower of Babel supposedly accounted for the diversity of languages in the world and, along with the dispersal of Noah's sons after the Flood, for the differences in human populations ("races"). "Savages," these believers proclaimed, had degenerated from the higher civilization at the time of Babel, losing technical knowledge and also morality. Europeans had somehow retained more of the primeval civilization.

Countering the literalist interpretation of the Christian Bible was the position that the Bible might be divinely inspired but that the copies we actually have were written by human hands and therefore liable to copyists' errors and mistranslations. Two thousand and more years have elapsed since the Bible was written; surely knowledge accumulated over so many generations should enrich humankind rather than be forced into the mold of ancient belief, said adherents of a liberal view. The rocks' sequence of fossils from ancient, simple shellfish, fish, and reptiles to mammals, higher primates, and at last humans, represents evolutionary development. This is perfectly compatible with the Bible, liberals noted, provided one understands the writers of Genesis to be using a poetic, mythic mode of communication. "And God rested on the seventh day" should not be interpreted to mean the white-bearded old guy flopped into a hammock in the backyard on Saturday and reached for a cool one. The Deity—whatever It is, It is beyond human ken—caused planets to coalesce, organic life to be sparked, eventually the human species to evolve, but not in six workdays like Grandpa down at the machine shop. The Bible is indeed an inspired guide to moral behavior and a compendium of the work of some of the greatest literary geniuses our species has known, but it was never meant to be a science textbook. "Progressive" thinkers advocated studying all the phenomena of the world with the methods of science, free of preconceived explanations. That included studying humans.

Nineteenth-century anthropologists collected data on the diversity of human attributes and behavior the way zoologists and botanists collected data on the diversity of plants and other animals. They went so far as to collect skeletons from graveyards, sometimes over the protests of the deceased's loved ones, and to bring people from other continents to museums and zoos in Europe to be measured and observed by scientists there. (The "specimens" often were eager to get a free trip to exotic Europe, making it a two-way exchange of observations.) Travelers' and missionaries' accounts were added to the store of observations. A great pile of "facts" became available, unhappily without the insistence on full context that later anthropologists have found to be absolutely necessary. Pioneer English anthropologist Edward Tylor arranged his collection of others' observations to illustrate the logical progression from an "animistic" stage of religion, in which "savages" confused dreams with spirit journeys, through a "polytheistic" stage in ancient civilizations believing in many gods, to modern monotheism (one god). Tylor predicted that eventually we should progress to a purely scientific understanding which would be atheistic. (Can you figure out the word? "a-": "without"). Lewis Henry Morgan, Tylor's American contemporary, suggested much the same logical scheme. James G. Frazer, a Scot, and his teacher W. Robertson Smith tried a different tack, fitting a mass of historical and contemporary travelers' observations into the premise that the Classical Greeks and Romans had a basic human religion and other religions are variations. One common failing marked all these armchair scholars: None had lived in a nonwestern community for any length of time, none had directly experienced life in a non-Christian community.

Bronislaw Malinowski, living for two years in a Trobriand Island community, 1916–1918, is credited with breaking this armchair convention. His classic study, *Argonauts of the Western Pacific,* is crammed with vivid details of real life in this Melanesian society. Though brought up in Poland as an upper-class scholar, Malinowski realized a real scientist has to get down and get dirty, gather data directly from the field. Malinowski got hot, sweaty, pushed around in the crowd of Trobrianders, recorded in his private journal his feelings aroused by the young Trobriand women around him, his struggles writing his notes with moths fluttering around his tent lantern—he dreamed of the cool clean comfort back home, but he knew he could never understand the Trobriand habitus without living it. Living it, he realized that much of Trobriand religion consisted of ritual actions designed to extend human capacity to control their world. Trobrianders are superb boatbuilders and highly knowledgeable navigators, but to avert dangerous storms at sea, they use rituals and prayers. These ritual actions were, to Malinowski, "skills" like woodworking in the sense that the religious actions were designed to accomplish practical ends. Maybe they didn't always work, but even the best woodworkers may sometimes encounter a knot in the wood that makes the knife slip. No human action is invariably totally successful. Often after the proper rituals, Trobriand sailors did enjoy calm seas and safe voyages. Rituals gave the Trobrianders confidence to try what might be dangerous undertakings.

Myths

Living on the island, Malinowski discovered another aspect of Trobriand religion. People in one village told him they were descended from the elder of a pair of sisters who had quarreled in ancient times. The elder sister had announced she would remain in the village, strictly obeying all their religious laws, and exiled the younger woman to live among low-class people who didn't properly maintain religious strictures. In the village claiming to be descended from the younger sister, he heard a different version: There, the younger sister had ordered the elder one to stay in the puritanical village while the younger woman happily moved to the enlightened community. Quite possibly, the chiefly families of the two villages were descended from a pair of high-ranking sisters who had quarreled; what fascinated Malinowski was how the legend was used in each village to explain and justify its own customs. Kiriwinans said their conservative values resulted from the elder sister's commitment to such values, while the western coastal villagers said their more liberal behavior reflected the younger sister's willingness to change. Each claimed its point of view, identified with a revered, legendary ancestor, was admirable. Malinowski concluded that legends, and myths, are often *social charters* spelling out proper behavior. They function like the charters of corporations in western nations that spell out the officers of the corporation and its proper business activities. The legend of the two sisters "chartered" Kiriwina to have a chief who scrupulously maintained traditional religious observances, and "chartered" the western coastal village to innovate change.

Legends provide "social charters" for societies with long written histories, such as the United States, as well as for small, nonliterate communities. Sociologist Robert Bellah called attention to the "civil religion" of the United States, carried on in civic observances and taught in public schools. George Washington chopping down the cherry tree, Abe Lincoln walking miles to return a penny, Indian chief Tecumseh refusing to sit on a chair instead of on Mother Earth, are myths that "charter" admirable behavior for American children. These popular myths are invented; facts are not allowed to spoil the preaching. The star-spangled banner that Francis Scott Key saw in the dawn's early light was a new flag just run up, but American civil religion uses the myth that the old one was still there to "charter" the virtue of persistence against the country's enemies. American civil religion glorifies the United States as the "redeemer nation" chosen by God to lead the world to salvation. The Thanksgiving holiday teaches Americans to be grateful for living in God's country. Fourth-of-July celebrations intertwine war with the founding of the country, "chartering" the wars of aggression that won the United States its territory from sea to shining sea. Christmas exalts shopping, "chartering" America's capitalist economy by associating it with a blessed birth at the turning of the year from darkness toward spring. Though the Deist founders of the United States took pains to write a clause separating churches from the government, they

Ikoma, Tanzania (Africa), 1928. Men dance in military formation behind their flag, carrying spears, ritually "chartering" their role as defenders of the nation.
Photo credit: Milwaukee Public Museum.

could not forestall American society developing a set of symbols, myths, and rituals inculcating a faith in our country. The human urge to cooperate, part of our nature as gregarious mammals, is expressed as shared faith.

Though people within a community are taught moral imperatives to cooperate, it's only too common that at the same time they're taught to oppose other communities. Ugly propaganda in wartime is familiar; racist stereotyping can be as ugly, directed at keeping disadvantaged groups in low status, easily exploited by upper status groups who are taught to avoid familiarity with the disadvantaged. Scapegoating is common, blaming an outsider for the ills of the community. Anthropological studies of villages, in Europe and elsewhere, where the members must cooperate to manage resources, show that frequently an outsider such as a schoolteacher, government agent, or the local wealthy landowner, is blamed for mismanaging when an enterprise fails. This allows the villagers to vent their disappointment while remaining on good terms with one another. On a larger scale, a nation can blame its ills on another country's supposed schemes against it.

French anthropologist Claude Lévi-Strauss believes that the human mind operates by setting up oppositions, then figuring out how to resolve them. Lévi-Strauss was associated during the 1940s with a group developing computers. They succeeded in programing computers by using a binary code (*bi-:* "2,":

Natal, South Africa, 1928. Before a chorus of men and women, Zulu young women dance with a male leader wearing the leopard-skin sash of office. The unity of the community, its valuation of both its mature leaders and its lively young women, is ritually "chartered" in this dance.

Photo credit: Milwaukee Public Museum.

on/off is a binary, or two-part, set). He reasoned that if computers can work with binary coding and apparently simulate human thinking, then it may be that humans think through paired concepts in the process termed the *dialectic* of thesis, *anti*thesis, and finally *syn*thesis. Lévi-Strauss analyzed the structure of hundreds of myths, beginning with many he had heard from Brazilian Indians with whom he had lived in the 1930s, and concluded that myths are usually set in the form of a dialectic: A situation such as a Garden of Eden paradise is described, then its antithesis—a place of dirt, suffering, and evil—is disclosed, finally the myth resolves the opposition by indicating a middle ground or synthesis, for example promising eternal life in heaven after death on earth. Thus, according to Lévi-Strauss, people are able to accept suffering by reasoning out both its causes and possible alleviation.

Malinowski's concept of myths and legends as social charters and Lévi-Strauss's focus on the philosophical content of myths are closely related. Whether purportedly history, or "once upon a time," myths begin with conditions quite different from what people are now experiencing. Then an event is retold that disrupts the conditions, allowing a new situation to develop, the pre-

Bali, 1930. In contrast to the Zulu community pictured on previous page, Bali "chartered" its young women to be demure, singing hymns from a still posture in their temple enclosure.

Photo credit: Milwaukee Public Museum.

sent. Do women suffer in childbirth? That's because Eve displeased God, who caused her daughters to inherit her sin. Are women forbidden to participate in secret rituals where men commune with the Almighty? That's because once upon a time, women had owned the sacred instruments and hidden them from men, who stole them and now must guard them lest women selfishly try to monopolize them again. Are men forbidden to unwrap the holy objects kept in containers out of the way of daily life? That's because the holy objects were entrusted once upon a time to a worthy woman by a powerful spirit taking pity upon a wretched people. And so on; myths give a more or less plausible explanation for how things came to be, and that's how it is and ought to be.

Must things always be so? Reforms can change conditions. Anthony F. C. Wallace's model of revitalization (page 159, Regulating Societies) shows how a reformer can believe he or she has been commissioned by God to do away with evil practices and institute or reinforce good ones. The prophet's revelation becomes the chartering myth for the reform. God doesn't have to come into it: Benjamin Franklin carefully made the Declaration of Independence say that human rights to "life, liberty, and the pursuit of happiness" are "*self-evident.*" American civil religion mythologizes the Founding Fathers (noble

George Washington, brilliant Thomas Jefferson, wise Benjamin Franklin), sets them against "mad King George," and out of that antithesis brings forth American democracy carrying the ancient spirit of the Magna Carta to fruition in the New World. If you think this is straightforward history, not myth, try reading the actual records of the 1787 Constitutional Convention.

Functions of Religion

Underlying the propositions that myth acts as social charter and explains the conditions of human life is the basic postulate that religions have social function. This was claimed early in the twentieth century by the French social

Roman Catholic Mass for college students. To build and symbolize the cooperating social group of students of this college, the priest has the young people face one another in a circle; to make them feel comfortable with the church, he has them attend in casual clothes and sit at ease on the floor. He maintains his superior position as leader and instructor by standing above them, separated, on a raised platform, wearing heavy formal vestments of rich cloth. The formal authority of the church is symbolized by the Bible open in front of him—note that only he can see this sacred book. Émile Durkheim would have understood how the priest seeks to build the congregation into a community; Van Gennep would note how the role of ordained leader is marked off from the role of layperson by empty space. Ralph Linton might suggest that the small statue of a praying saint, on the wall middle left, functions as a "totem" for the congregation-community, identifying and symbolizing its common activity.

Credit: Gary G. Dineen, Marquette University

anthropologist Émile Durkheim. The *practice* of a religion, he emphasized, is a means of maintaining the cooperating social group. Coming together to worship, members of the group can see who belongs, whom they are morally obliged to help, and from whom they can expect help. Worshipping together, the members express in their common prayers their mutual desire for prosperity, health, and goodwill. Durkheim suggested that social groups create a visible identifying symbol in the form of a founding ancestor or a "totem." George Washington, the father of our country, pictured on our most often used currency, is such a founding ancestor and symbol for the United States. The fictive kin relationship, Washington as "father," symbolizes the familylike mutual support that citizens should give one another. "Totems" are nonhuman symbols of the social group bound together in religious worship. (The word "totem" is from the Ojibwe *dodem,* meaning a spirit partner or protector.) Generally, the totem embodies qualities admired by the social group. The United States uses the bald eagle as its totem, seeing itself as soaring highest, proud, powerful, and fierce. Although Durkheim had thought, based on his readings, that "primitive" societies believed their totems were gods, a half-century later Lévi-Strauss, sensitized by actual fieldwork experience, emphasized that the totem creature is seen as *connected with* the members of the group, not itself the object of worship. Symbolizing a cooperating group by a single creature communicates the unity of the group.

> Ralph Linton, American anthropologist, pointed out that team mascots and advertising symbols such as the Campbell's Soup Kids or Betty Crocker, function like totems to communicate an appealing identity.

At the same time, early in the twentieth century, that Durkheim focused on the congregation as a social group, a Belgian social anthropologist, Arnold Van Gennep, analyzed individuals' places in social groups. Van Gennep wrote of *rites de passage,* rituals of passing from one social status to another. He identified three fundamental changes in a person's social status: from nonexistence to being a person, marked by a ritual bringing a baby into the social group; from childhood to responsible adulthood; and from living to deceased member of the social group, marked by a funeral ritual. This focus emphasizes the dominance of social roles and statuses over individual lives, and the critical importance of the social group's recognition of its members and their roles.

> Every society recognizes 3 basic social transitions, marked by rites of passage:
> - birth, from nonbeing to social person
> - maturity, from child to responsible adult
> - death, from society member to nonmember.

Particular rites of passage vary from society to society. "Birth" rites can be held for a newborn baby, or postponed for a year or more if infant mortality is high and a baby's chance of survival not good. When a birth ritual is held, the child is given a name so it can be addressed and referred to in its social roles. Often, as in Judaism and Christianity, the birth ritual also brings the child (or convert) into its social group's religious congregation. Adults adopted into a society, or newly into a church, are said to be "born into" their new group through a ritual of incorporation very similar to the birth ritual for babies. When a child becomes sexually mature, able to become a parent, he or she usually passes through a ritual marking a new social role of

*Angola, a village primary school, 1930. School classes function as age-sets, their members
passing through a series of grades that function as a prolonged rite of passage.*
Photo credit: Milwaukee Public Museum.

responsible adulthood. Since the real passage is to adulthood, not merely sexual capacity, the "puberty" ritual may be held for youngsters just barely beginning puberty or for young adults, depending upon when the society will be giving them adult roles. In our society, we mask puberty rituals as "graduations," asking for completion of schooling before adult responsibilities are undertaken. This has created much confusion as American society encourages teenagers to seek sexual relationships but denies them jobs that will support a family. Weddings are another version of puberty ritual, solemnly yet joyously marking a young couple's entry into full adult roles. The final rite of passage is the funeral marking a person's removal from living activity in the social group. American society often marks also the passage from wage-earning to retirement, a stage of physical capability without full adult social responsibilities that balances the similar, earlier stage of adolescence. Because American society stresses a finely detailed series of social roles through life, Americans mark their birthdays every year as a rite of passage.

Religious Practitioners

One final aspect of the anthropological study of religions is the contrast frequently made between shaman and priest. Since small societies don't maintain formal seminaries for training priests, it was assumed that their religious practitioners don't receive training but are simply inspired by a call to a spiritual vocation. Fieldwork in such societies reveals that people who feel such a call then seek out an experienced practitioner to train them by apprenticeship. Only after years of close association, learning rituals, and gradually assuming

> *shaman:* feels a *call to practice* spiritual leadership and healing. *priest:* is formally trained to religious leadership by an organized group of recognized practitioners. (In actuality, shamans are trained and priests usually feel a call.)

leadership, does the novice begin practice. Most societies combine psychological therapy with physical healing, though perhaps dividing practitioners much like western societies do, into full-time, highly respected doctors and priests, and part-time healers who receive less lengthy training. (Women's child-care responsibilities may make it difficult for younger women to apprentice to doctors, channeling women into part-time herbalist and therapist roles. This practical conflict may be legitimized by a myth that women's reproductive power conflicts with "male" healing or spiritual leadership power.)

In urban states, there is likely to be a stronger contrast between shamans and priests. States, like smaller societies, claim transcendental origin or blessing and employ theologians to teach rulers and populace their God-given roles. Even the United States with its Constitutional separation of church and state indirectly supports theologians by exempting churches from taxes. Recognized priests are trained to read and interpret a written text believed to be divinely revealed for human guidance. This holy book is the core of what American anthropologist Robert Redfield, in the mid-twentieth century, termed a Great Tradition. Training to read separated the elite class, the leaders, from ordinary people who remained uneducated. Those ordinary, "ignorant" people found their own spiritual revelations in local prophets and shamans, members of their communities who covertly challenged the elite priests' domination. Sometimes, as with the Shawnee Indian brothers Tecumseh and Tenkswatawa at the beginning of the nineteenth century, the local prophet ended up leading a political battle. Sometimes, as Anthony Wallace described for the Iroquois, the prophet leads a revitalizing reform. Generally, the officially unrecognized village healers and ritual leaders maintain ethnic cultural traditions—Redfield's Little Traditions—outside official state culture. Sharing such a Little Tradition reinforces community cooperation and may materially aid the members of the group attempting to survive in the face of heavy taxes and restricted economic opportunities.

Poverty may keep whole communities precariously near malnutrition, producing occasional convulsions and mental dissociation in the least well fed, and Little Traditions may label such fits to be occasions when a spirit takes possession of the sufferer. "Spirit possession" is more dignified than "having a fit,"

BLESSING OF THE BOCK BEER.
March 19, 1993 (St. Joseph's Day)
St. Casimir Roman Catholic Church, Milwaukee, Wisconsin

In "First Fruits" ceremonies, a community led by their priest offers thanks for harvests.
First-fruits ceremonies bond the members of the community and communicate the eco-
nomic importance of the selected food to the community. Here, in a neighborhood of mostly
young adults, people gather in their parish church and their priest formally blesses the
product of a small local brewery.
Photo credit: Aldis Strazdins

and usually calls for gifts of food to the spirit, thereby aiding the possessed person's nutrition and restoring health, at least for a while. Involuntarily being
"possessed" by a spirit is farily common in many regions of chronic malnourishment, where the sufferers gather into congregations ritually celebrating their
relationship with spirits and counseling one another, an important function of
religious groups. This general correlation between institutionalized spirit possession "cults" (i.e., congregations) and chronic malnourishment, particularly
of lower-class men or of women (whose nutrition needs differ from men's, and
are less likely to be well fulfilled), illustrates the social function of religion
through reducing anxiety by counseling and good fellowship, and possibly ame-
liorating adverse social conditions.

Possession is usually distinguished from trance, a condition deliberately produced by hallucinogens or sensory-manipulation techniques (rhythmic drumming, movement, darkness, intense concentration). The distinction is blurred by practices: People who have suffered possession may induce the mental dissociation by intently concentrating on music and movement, inviting their spirit to return to them so they can ritually dance with their fellow worshippers. It is useful to note that trance is much more common than belief in spirit possession. Practicing trance does not correlate with physical conditions, such as malnourishment, that might induce involuntary dissociation. Trance may reduce anxiety through relaxation. Societies that believe people's souls can travel independently of their bodies, for example many of the indigenous nations of Siberia, may ask shamans to concentrate—which has been often observed—and send their souls out flying to seek information or ordinary people's lost and wandering souls, to return them and thus restore bodily wholeness and health. Being told one's wandering soul has been restored and all will be well does usually improve believers' hormonal capability to regain health, sometimes resulting in cures—this too has been observed—but whether a shaman's soul has flown out and retrieved another's is not within a scientist's capacity to observe. Anthropologists as scientists record what they observe, how people in a society explain the occurrence, and—from our knowledge of biology, social behavior, and so on—suggest actual functions of the observed behavior.

Symbols and Religions

In American communities, a great number of religious traditions express ethnic origins and class and regional cultures. Some, such as the Old Order Amish, physically separate their villages from the dominant society. Others may populate districts, for example, Irish Catholic neighborhoods in Boston or Southern Baptist regions in Oklahoma. Still others, such as many Episcopalian and, at the other end of the social ranking, Black storefront churches, mark class affiliations. Because public schools pass on American mainstream beliefs and civil religion, adherents of some religions may school their children separately, not only Roman Catholics but also Fundamentalist Christians who find public education accepts principles at variance with their doctrines. The diversity of religions practiced in American cities, almost always each with its regular meetings of a congregation-community, offers anthropologists interesting studies of the interplay between traditions of worldview and rituals, politically charged "ethnic" or "racial" groupings, social class symbols, and personal quests for satisfying ways of being.

America is interesting, too, for its efforts to distinguish and regulate spiritual and therapeutic practitioners. In line with the view of the natural world as a complex, fine-tuned, clock mechanism, American culture has assumed the human body is best understood as a physical mechanism. Only recently have the effects of emotions upon hormones (and vice versa) been seriously studied. Other societies have trained their doctors to administer plant pharmaceuticals ("herb remedies") and/or manipulate sensory stimuli, as in hypnosis, to affect patients' emotional states. Shamans' training often includes learning sleight-of-hand magic tricks to impress patients (and their friends and relatives, attending) with the practitioner's great power, an impression that raises the patient's confidence in the cure, reducing depression and stimulating beneficial hormones. Both shamans and local priests usually hear confessions, offer advice on allaying anxiety, and monitor local gossip to be able to effectively counsel clients in their particular social predicaments. On some American Indian reservations, including the Navajo Nation, the realization of the value of indigenous therapies has led to native doctors—"medicine men"—attending patients alongside a licensed M.D. Among Euro-Americans, faith healers offer treatment for afflictions not amenable to standard medical practice. Some faith healers are unscrupulous frauds, but a great many are sincere carriers of Little Traditions overlooked by the dominant society. The line between faith healing and "legitimate religion" in America is thin when ordained ministers offer avowedly blessed Bibles or holy oil. For an anthropologist, trying to draw a line between spiritual and physical ministering would negate the holistic perspective from which we work. Humans' naturally selected-for need for social community creates a role for leaders who bind people into a supportive cooperating group, placed beyond casual manipulation by claimed spiritual empowerment.

Symbols are a major aspect of religions. Rituals incorporate symbols, both openly as when a Christian priest holds up a crucifix or chalice during a service, or a rabbi holds up the Torah, and also covertly as can be seen in the silk vestments of officiants, expensive beautiful clothing that silently communicates to the congregation the high status of the servant of their deity. (If the *servant* of the deity is of such high status, if the deity can command a person of such status, how very high indeed is the status of the deity!) Conversely, religious groups who do not ornament their meeting places and officiants communicate the importance they place on plain moral action as contrasted with rich show. American civil religion has its places where mainstream American values are symbolically communicated—in the department store and public lawn displays at Christmas, showing people coming together giving gifts as symbols of social bonds; in the fireworks at Fourth of July, symbolizing the blazing heavenly glory of our nation.

Among the activities associated with religions are the creative arts. Around the world, societies provide arenas for performance and display of the arts within religious ceremonies. Many societies encourage craftsworkers to make objects as beautiful as they can, to please deities or express humans' joy in the gift of life. If religions through their myths provide social charters, through their ritual actions and objects they provide media to express, via tangible symbols, the worldview and principles of that social charter.

Symbols associated with particular religions—such as the turban worn by Sikh men, the head covering worn by many Muslim women, the necklace with a cross, Star of David, or crescent communicating the wearer is Christian, Jewish, or Muslim—identify at a glance the person's membership in one or another of groups playing major roles in world affairs. Sadly, symbols can elicit

Darjeeling, India, 1930. A refugee Tibetan lama holds up his prayer wheel and rosary as he leads religious worship.

Photo credit: Milwaukee Public Museum.

hate and killing, too, under social charters that prescribe the annihilation of opposing groups. It is the functioning of religious affiliation in prescribing codes of behavior, within and across social groups, that demonstrates that, from an anthropological perspective, religions are among the means of regulating societies.

Summary

Religion is the label we give to socially patterned behavior said to be prescribed by spiritual beliefs—belief in powerful beings or force transcending the physical world we live in. Anthropologists work with observed behavior (including expressed beliefs), and have concluded that religions serve important social functions: Worshipping together molds people into communities, facilitating cooperation, and religious leaders and rituals may allay anxiety, helping people to act with confidence. Myths explain how things came to be as they are, and are, in Malinowski's words, "social charters" describing and validating advocated social behavior. Rituals, because they are so highly patterned, strongly impress symbols of prescribed social behavior on people's consciousness; they communicate values through several media (visual, aural, movement). Rites of passage are rituals that mark major transitions in the lives of members of societies: Birth or naming rituals mark the inclusion of a new person in the community, puberty or marriage rituals (and in our society, graduations) mark the change from childhood to adult responsibilities, and funerals mark the loss of a person from their community.

RECOMMENDED READING

Malinowski, Bronislaw. *Magic, Science and Religion*. Prospect Heights Il: Waveland Press, 1954 (1992 reprint). A collection of his papers including the classic "Myth in Primitive Psychology"—his discussion of "social charters"—of 1926.

Case Studies in Cultural Anthropology Series (Holt Rinehart Winston/Harcourt Brace, Fort Worth)

Herdt, Gilbert. *The Sambia: Ritual and Gender in New Guinea*. 1986. Herdt was interested in the Sambia belief (superficially like that of the Greeks of Classical Athens) that homosexual experience with older men is valuable for youths' development; he describes this as part of Sambia culture.

Hostetler, John A., and Gertrude Enders Huntington. *The Hutterites in North America*. 1996. Hutterites follow a radical, conservative, communal way of life they believe to be the only true Christianity; they also carry on highly successful modern agribusinesses in Montana and western Canada. Hostetler and Huntington have published a comparable study of the Amish, less radical than the Hutterites but similarly devoted to a conservative devoutly Christian way of life: *Amish Children: Education in the Family, School, and Community*, 2d ed., 1992.

Kehoe, Alice Beck. *The Ghost Dance: Ethnohistory and Revitalization*. 1989. Well-known American Indian religious movements—the Ghost Dance, Black Elk of the Lakota Sioux, Navaho peyotism, and Handsome Lake's Iroquois religious reforms—presented in the context of American Indian ethnohistory.

Kintz, Ellen. *Life Under the Tropical Canopy: Tradition and Change Among the Yucatec Maya*. 1990. Kintz connects the present Maya in lowland eastern Mexico with their preconquest ancestors.

Tonkinson, Robert. *The Mardu Aborigines: Living the Dream in Australia's Desert*. 1991 (2d ed.). Australian aborigines are often assumed to be enmeshed in a nature religion that interferes with modernization; Tonkinson's study of Mardu religion shows it as part of the community's means of preserving their identity and heritage.

Vogt, Evon Z. *The Zinacantecos of Mexico: A Modern Maya Way of Life*. 1990 (2d ed.). The highland Maya have meshed their preconquest religion with Catholicism, and order their activities by a religious calendar. These Maya can be compared with the lowland Maya of Kintz's book, to see some effects of ecological and historical differences.

Weiner, Annette. *The Trobrianders of Papua New Guinea*. Fort Worth: Harcourt Brace, 1988. Update of Malinowski's classic work in the islands.

Case Study Reprinted by Waveland Press

Deng, Francis Mading. *The Dinka of the Sudan*. Prospect Heights, Il: Waveland Press, 1986 (reprinted). Deng describes his own people, close neighbors of the famous Nuer cattle-herders presented in classic studies by E. E. Evans-Pritchard.

Conclusion: Looking Us Over

Anthropology aims, above all, to look at humans as we exist, not broken apart into psychology, biology, political science, religious studies, and so on. Our true history through millions of years of primate species followed by the development of hominids made us what we are. What we humans share, our physical needs and the societal relationships through which they are met, are far more important than the variations in behavior and beliefs our large and complex, fertile brains have devised. Particularly in the twenty-first-century world of instant global communications and supranational economic and political structures, we humans must look beyond the flags to the reality of one species spread throughout Planet Earth.

Let us look again over the holistic perspective we have emphasized in this textbook. From this broad perspective, anthropologists integrate the biological and social facets of human experience. Anything less is an incomplete view of human life. This book sketches the essential features of the contemporary anthropological perspective. We have deliberately kept it concise and short so it doesn't compete for your time with the case studies that give you the real taste of anthropology. This text is the foundation upon which you, through your reading and your actual experience, build an understanding of yourself and your fellow humans.

Like the playwright Moliere's character who was delighted to discover he was speaking prose, not just talking, you have been making ethnographic observations all your life. Between this short text and the anthropological studies you've read, you can take our generalizations on human life and test them against your own life as a human. We are each a *participant observer* in whatever society we find ourselves.

It is through reading the case studies and perhaps carrying out an ethnographic observation project yourself that you can understand the *anthropological method.* Simply defining the anthropological method as participant observation followed by cross-cultural comparisons doesn't convey the feel of anthropology; reading actual descriptions by anthropologists brings out the unusual situation of the anthropologist in the field, a person who, in the words of American anthropologist Hortense Powdermaker, is both "stranger" and "friend" in a community. Perhaps "stranger *and* friend" is another way of saying "participant observer," one who participates in the everyday life of a community while observing in a scientific manner. It's not always a comfortable dual role, doing your fair share of work or joking while simultaneously taking mental note of what's going on. Unlike the laboratory scientist or experimental psychologist who can control a situation to allow for record-keeping, anthropologists must sharpen their memory to recall accurately when there's a natural break permitting recording notes. We find the participant observer situation keys us up, so we do in fact recall a great deal as we scribble madly back in the car or house right after an event. Then later we transcribe our notes, add some notions of possible significance or explanation, and cross-reference to other sets of observations. Our precious field notebooks, small enough to be inconspicuous, stained and soiled, are our data banks from which we build our cross-cultural comparisons that highlight basic human needs and particular societies' adaptations.

Biological anthropologists, archaeologists, anthropological linguists, and anthropologists who practice in business or agency settings share much of the basic methodology of participant observation and cross-cultural comparison. Many biological anthropologists spend time in communities to observe behavior that may affect biological characteristics of the population. Archaeologists may use ethnographic participant observation to figure out how archaeological features may have been constructed and used. Linguists depend upon recording dictated texts in order to get phonemes and syntax correctly, but amplify these with notes on natural speech. Applied anthropologists of course must take ethnographic notes of the work situations they are paid to analyze. Participant observation, being simultaneously friend and stranger in real-life activities, is a common thread in much of anthropology.

Schools of Anthropology

Some anthropologists glory in being *eclectic,* using whatever ideas or methods seem to produce insights. Others insist that their preferred techniques or basic postulates are more valid than others. It is often the case that a bright, ambitious, young anthropologist loudly trumpets his or her breakthrough, hoping to be offered a job in a prestigious institution. Once well known for a much-discussed idea, the innovator sometimes sticks to it, disregarding criticism. The conviction of many anthropologists that there is no one sure way to knowledge—a by-product of understanding *cultural relativism*—tends to discourage exclusive claims to truth, and it is perhaps more common in anthropology than in other disciplines for a mature professional to become more eclectic and tolerant. The history of anthropology has come to show a succession of approaches and explanations that have proven inadequate or misguided, prompting the thoughtful anthropologist to be modest in claiming great ideas.

Anthropology began, as a profession and scholarly discipline, in the 1840s, the decade when the traditional landed aristocracies of Europe and colonial America lost power to the expanding middle classes of business owners and professionals. As the Industrial Revolution of the early nineteenth century shifted economic weight away from agricultural estates to manufacturing and distribution, the disciplines of history and the natural sciences developed to rationally answer the question of why societies were changing so noticeably. Anthropology was added to these studies as the expansion of European and American economic empires raised the question of why foreign societies are so different. The old explanation that God made them so seemed too simplistic, once social change was so publicly discussed. For nineteenth-century middle-class scholars in Europe and America, the evident answer to the Big Question was Evolutionary Progress, that God or Nature (or God working through Nature, you can have both together) had set up the universe so that there would be Progress from small and simple to large and complex. Fossils in the geological record seemed to demonstrate this Progress through time. It was also supposed that the growth of embryos from single-celled eggs to larger and more complex organisms "recapitulated" (repeated) evolution of species. Pioneer anthropologists—Daniel Wilson of Scotland and then Canada, Edward Tylor of England, Lewis Henry Morgan in America—arranged "races" and cultures into series supposedly revealing the Evolutionary Progress of humanity.

As we have mentioned in earlier chapters, the next generation of anthropologists, at the end of the nineteenth century and beginning of the twentieth, challenged the validity of these series that invariably put conquered nonwestern nations lower than the then-dominant conquering nations. Franz Boas, deeply impressed by the culture as well as survival technology of the Baffinland Inuit he lived with for a year, and the French scholar Émile Durkheim could not accept any scheme that separated nonwestern peoples from their own. Durkheim lacked Boas's gut experience of life in a nonwestern society, but he realized that it was, in the end, a sterile exercise to study other societies and then say they were fundamentally different. If the Big Question remains why societies are changing so noticeably, we have to postulate (assume) that nonwestern peoples are basically similar to us, so that we can seek to explain *both* change in western societies *and* differences between societies: these are two aspects of the same Big Question. The bottom line, Durkheim understood, is "What is human nature?" Durkheim, like Boas, figured that the particular history of a society attempting to survive (i.e., adapting) in its particular environment should explain much difference. Underneath the

> Boas's search for the *particular* history of *particular* societies has been termed *historical particularism.*

differences are the characteristics of the human species, forcing us to live in groups, to find edible food and shelter. Durkheim argued that the totem animals respected by American Indian or Australian Aborigine communities were like the Eagle representing the United States, Austria, Germany, or Mexico, impressive creatures seen in the society's habitus (not the word he used, but the idea is there) and taken as symbol of the worth of the community. Projecting this symbol of worth, he said, the society identifies and respects itself, calling up its members' efforts to cooperate in survival and success. Durkheim thus developed a *functional* explanation for societal customs.

Malinowski, in the next generation, accepted Durkheim's emphasis on functional reasons for cultural behavior. He grouped activities by the function they served, for example, providing food. Malinowski's English colleague A. R. Radcliffe-Brown was more interested in the *structures* one could describe through grouping activities by function, thus casting his descriptions in what came to be called *structural-functionalist* terms. (These "structures" might be actual, such as a village divided into households, or a metaphor of analysis, such as the role of the mother's clan's male members in a matrilineal society.) Structural-functionalism was a popular mode of explanation in sociology as well as anthropology during the middle twentieth century. A parallel intellectual movement in France, *structuralism,* developed for anthropology by Claude Lévi-Strauss, emphasized the "mental" (that is, analytical, not visible) "structures" of various cultures' thinking. Lévi-Strauss was fascinated by the structures of myths, which he found similar over broad regions and believed reflected the human brain's tendency to conceptualize ideas in terms of opposites ("If this is like this, then something else must be different"). Structuralism is rooted in linguistics, using the linguists' method of comparison and contrast and seeing words functioning as "signs" for concepts.

In the 1960s, an extreme version of cultural ecology called *cultural materialism* became popular in America, although not so much elsewhere. This mode of explanation claimed factors in the environment so powerfully affected a society's behavior that the analyst need only identify the one or few environmental factors in order to explain cultural values and customs. The most famous effort to demonstrate cultural materialism was American anthropologist Marvin Harris's argument that the reason Hindus in India will not slaughter cattle is that allowing the animals to roam as best they can maximizes the amount of nutrition (milk) available to the greatest number of people over the long run. Harris listed figures in support of his argument, but it remains controversial. Harris's teacher Leslie White and his fellow student the archaeologist Lewis Binford helped develop the theory of cultural materialism, and Binford built it into what he called the "New Archaeology" of the 1970s. Somehow, cultural materialism got hooked into the nineteenth-century notion of one-directional evolution. White insisted that the harnessing of energy was the basis of human activity, the more energy a society harnessed the more evolved it was, and, well, with White writing in the 1950s, that meant the United States of America, the country with the most nuclear power, was the most evolved. This was not at all compatible with the concept of cultural relativism, and in fact Leslie White strongly disparaged the deceased Franz Boas.

As former colonies gained their independence and war-ravaged countries rebuilt competitive economies, the United States could no longer rest confident that it was the Biggest and Best, *period!* More and more anthropologists began questioning the assumptions of one-directional evolution. More and more saw it tends to be jingoistic, that is (as the Oxford Dictionary puts it), chosen by "vulgar, blustering patriots." Worse, to a serious scientist, one-directional evolution is bad science, contrary to our contemporary understanding of evolutionary biology. (We've insisted in this textbook that you've *got* to understand evolutionary biology if you want to understand human behavior.) Anthropologists engaged in "development" projects often saw that sensible sustainable practices were rejected in favor of building huge dams, clearing forests, and other very expensive plans profiting the owners of heavy machinery but destructive to the local environment and its human communities. Maybe it is time to look again at others' ways of life, to realize that most of these societies, such as the Inuit in the Arctic North, have learned over thousands of years how to live without destroying their resources.

The whole question of how cultures change has radically shifted from the assumption of "acculturation" discussed in the 1930s. The "ac-" of "acculturation" meant change *toward* (from the Latin prefix *ad-*, "to"); change toward modern western culture was considered inevitable, either because unidirectional evolution was believed to be true, or because most Westerners believed everybody must want the "superior" artifacts and government of western democracies. The obvious fact that conquered people in colonies saw no democracy, only foreign agents acting like totalitarian dictators, was glossed over—except by a courageous few anthropologists (for example, Godfrey and Monica Hunter Wilson in South Africa, and their friend Hortense Powdermaker) who might find themselves out of a job once their opinions became known. After World War II and its aftermath of political independence for colonies, a greater number of anthropologists realized societies, and cultures, changed through a diversity of causes ranging from force imposed by a ruler, through efforts to adjust production to meet changed resource availability, labor demands, or markets, to ideological shifts perhaps preached by a charismatic prophet (like Martin Luther King, Jr.). Most important, no one factor seems sufficient to explain societal change: Political, economic, and ideological "causes" interact. One illuminating case has been the movement for independence in India, where the British-educated lawyer Mohandas Gandhi rejected international style of dress and economic structure, organized thousands of followers for nonviolent protests against armed police, and seemed to have proved to the world the power of idealism, only to be assassinated by a political rival. One lesson from India has been the recognition of many subcultures within political nations, and the manner in which "cultural heritage" is often manipulated (even invented!) to identify political-economic factions. The complexities of cultural change defy any simplistic "laws" of development.

Most recently, a number of anthropologists have been directly criticizing standard anthropological notions. The emphasis on kinship as dominant in nonwestern societies has been shown to often be a preconception in the mind of the anthropologist, contradicted by observations and the words of the members of the observed communities. One anthropologist recently looked at the marginal notes of a nineteenth-century anthropologist who put down in his field notebook the frequent comments of a man named Two Crows who liked to hang around when the anthropologist was questioning elders of the community. From the field notes, it is apparent that the nineteenth-century anthropologist asked leading questions and insisted this American Indian society *had* to be organized according to Lewis Henry Morgan's theory. The recent analysis carefully included the information volunteered by Two Crows and others, and came up with a picture of a more dynamic, sophisticated society than Morgan's theory would allow.

Other anthropologists are attempting to rectify omissions stemming from earlier anthropologists' neglect of women and of lower social classes. (Annette Weiner's study of the Trobrianders of Papua New Guinea, discovering the many activities that Bronislaw Malinowski, as a man, was never invited to witness, is a striking example.) Another trend today is to be much more aware of how the form of our presentation affects the readers' understanding. Should anthropologists tell their participant observation experiences as a story, with themselves as the hero (brave or simple, as the case may appear)? Such a narrative form engages the readers' sympathy and promotes an understanding of cultural relativism, but it obscures variant behavior in the community since it must be told from one point of view. Or should the anthropologist appear detached, describing all the variant behavior in a cold distant manner as if the people in the community were so many prairie chickens. This may make it easier to develop cross-cultural comparisons and arrive at a more general understanding of human behavior, but at the expense of a humane feeling for others. Should an archaeologist excavate, to add to the store of human knowledge of the past, when the descendants of the inhabitants of a site object to disturbing their ancestors' home? Should a biological anthropologist study ancient bones when people in the locality believe that shows disrespect to souls? Our world today no longer lets the western anthropologist simply follow the flag of a conquering power: Anthropologists, including the many who now come from nonwestern societies themselves, find their commitment to cultural relativism demands they plan their research so as to clearly respect the communities in which they wish to participate. It turns out that, after all, most of the best anthropology in the past came from fieldworkers who did respect those to whom they came as stranger and friend.

As We Close,

If you feel more comfortable with yourself, your family, and the people you work with, if you can better see how you and your section of society live within the character of our species, then the purpose of this book will be accomplished.

Anthropology is not a set of facts to be memorized. It is the overview of the human species, the picture of us in our millions, through time and across the planet. We are us, we are human, and we can live only as humans. That's why we anthropologists have asked for your time, to sharpen your understanding of our world and all ourselves. Our species' survival depends upon an intelligent approach to live on earth.

RECOMMENDED READING

Powdermaker, Hortense. *Stranger and Friend*. Prospect Heights, Ill: Waveland. 1966. One of the first autobiographies of a field anthropologist, Powdermaker's story tells of her efforts to study Hollywood and the segregated communities of Mississippi in the 1930s, as well as a Pacific island and African laborers.

Finis

Looking at humans from the broad holistic perspective, anthropology connects biological and social factors that act upon our lives. To see the ecology of humans is to recognize how wide our gaze must be, taking in the environments, resources, physical nature, histories, and faiths of our fellows around the globe.

The method of anthropologists is to be human, to live amongst other people, observe their habitat and neighbors, listen to them, and highlight the particulars of their culture by comparison with many others, the remnants of past societies and even the behavior of other primates. Out of the comparisons comes knowledge of the basic needs and capacities of our species.

Recognizing our common humanity and respecting the diversity of cultural adaptations to challenges to survival are anthropology's goals. You and your classmates have this world to sustain, and to delight in.

Glossary

acculturation—changing toward another cultural pattern.

Acheulian—style of stone tools associated with *Homo erectus,* better designed and showing more skill in the making than Oldowan style tools.

actualism, principle of—scientists match evidence from the past to similar effects observed in the present, assuming processes similar to those of the present operated in the past.

adapt—adjust to.

affines—persons related by marriage, in-laws.

allele—one form of a gene that has alternative forms.

approbation—approval.

arboreal—living in trees.

archaeology—study of what remains of human activities in the past.

artifact—anything made by humans, not a natural object or feature.

Australopithecus—earliest genus of hominids. Several species developed through four million years, overlapping with early *Homo* around two million years ago.

bilateral—using both sides, for example accepting relatives of both mother and father as equally "grandparent," "uncle," "aunt."

bipedal—walks on two legs.

chromosome—long strands of DNA in the nucleus of cells; segments of chromosomes are called *genes.*

clan—a group of persons who believe themselves biologically related and who control territory or property as a group.

code-switch—change from one dialect or behavior pattern to another, as when bilingual people switch from the language they speak at home to the language they speak in school, or a person has an impersonal professional manner while at work but is warm, lively, and expressive after work.

consanguines—"blood" relatives, persons who are biologically related.

conspicuous consumption—ostentatious display of expensive goods, meant to signal the consumer's high social status.

cross-cultural comparison—basic method of anthropological analysis, comparing human behavior in one society with that in another to determine what is universally human and what varies by societies, in response to different environments or historical events.

cultural relativism—understanding that human behavior and values are affected by a society's geographical situation and history.

culture—behavior that is learned through being a member of a social group or community; includes beliefs, values, language, everyday behavior (both public and private), rituals, recreation.

culture area—a geographic region and the human societies within it. Societies sharing a geographic area will be similar because they have the same resources and climate to work with, plus they are in easy contact with one another and may have been affected by the same historical events.

Danubians—farming societies spreading across Europe around 4500 B.C. They represent the Neolithic in central and western Europe.

differential reproduction—organisms with bodies well adapted to survive, remain healthy, and mate in the environment in which they live will likely produce more offspring than others in their populations who are sickly, deformed, or poor at mating. Over the generations, the well-adapted organisms' alleles will predominate as their offspring outnumber those of the poorly adapted: the population will increasingly resemble the well adapted.

dimorphism—two body shapes or sizes, usually referring to differences in body size and shape between adult males and adult females (sexual dimorphism).

diurnal—active in the daytime.

eclectic—using whatever seems useful (rather than rigidly sticking to one school of thought or method).

ecological niche—a way of surviving in a particular environment. In any locality, there will be more than one ecological niche: animals in the locality eat different foods, may be active at night or only in the day, may stay on the ground or in trees, etc.

ecology—the interaction of organisms and their surroundings in an environment. Cultural ecology focuses on a human society's interactions with its environment.

egalitarian—persons are considered equal to one another.

ethnocentrism—the conviction that one's own society and culture is superior to any other.

ethnography—recording observations of people in communities.

evolution—change over time. Biological evolution is change in populations of organisms (plants or animals), due to changes in genes and chromosomes which affect organisms' survival and reproduction, and differential reproduction.

gender—in linguistics, an obligatory grammatical category. Indo-European languages such as English oblige speakers to identify males, females, or nonsexed in order to match pronouns (he, she, it) to nouns. The term "gender" has been extended to mean social roles and behavior expected of people because they are male or female.

gene—a segment of chromosomes (DNA strands) inside cells. Each segment of the long strands of DNA produces a biochemical effect on the organism in which the cell lies.

gene pool—a population reproducing through mating: the individuals in the population "pool" their genes as they mate and pass on genes to the next generation.

genetic drift—when a portion of a population becomes separated and no longer draws on the larger gene pool of the parent population, the separated population will lack some alleles in the parental population and will have a greater or lesser proportion of many alleles compared to the parental population. The result may be divergence, new phenotypes and eventually new species.

genotype—an organism's alleles (forms of genes). Genotypes are hidden in the cell nucleus, and because not all the alleles in a heterozygous individual may have distinct visible effects, an observer cannot be sure of the genotype just by seeing the phenotype (organism's appearance).

gregarious—social, living with others of its kind.

habitus—interaction of society and environment, forming the society's worldview and metaphors as well as its economy.

heterozygous—an organism that received different alleles of a gene from its parents is heterozygous for that gene.

holistic perspective—analyzing human behavior by taking into account a wide range of observations (data) including human biology, ecology, history, linguistics, societal values, beliefs.

Holocene—present geological period, which began 10,000 years ago.

hominid—bipedal primate, most recently evolved type of primate (last five million years), including australopithecines and humans.

Homo—*Homo,* the biological genus of humans.

  Homo habilis, earliest species of humans.

  Homo erectus, species of human for most of human existence, over a million years. Some anthropologists prefer not to label these fossils *erectus,* noting that they are not radically different from the succeeding *Homo sapiens.*

  Homo sapiens, present species of humans.

  Homo sapiens neandertalensis, race of humans living in Europe and Western Asia during later Pleistocene; some anthropologists consider these distinct enough to be named a species, *Homo neandertalensis.*

homozygous—an organism that received the same allele of a gene from each of its parents is homozygous for that gene.

hypothesize—making a supposition based on some evidence, which is to be tested by obtaining more evidence.

informal economy—off-the-record economic activities such as direct exchange of goods and services, helping relatives and friends, or holding yard sales.

kindred—persons considered related to one another because they are related to a married couple.

kula—in the Massim Islands off New Guinea, exchange of valuable ornaments made of shell. Men go on long canoe voyages to present prized ornaments to leaders on other islands; the exchange of these heirloom ornaments maintains political and economic alliances.

lineage—persons descended from one ancestor.

linguistics—study of languages.

mammal—warmblooded animal, the females carrying their fetus inside the body and nourishing the infant with milk from mammary glands.

matrilineal—the mother's line, referring to inheriting from the mother and/or being considered belonging to the mother's family line.

Mesolithic—period in the early Holocene when climate was similar to today but people had not yet developed an agricultural economy.

Mesopotamia—present-day Iran and Iraq.

millennium—a thousand years (ten centuries). "The first millennium B.C." would be the years 1000–1 B.C.

mode of discourse—customary form of discussion in a particular field such as a science, humanities, business, or sport. In anthropology, it is customary to illustrate a topic by describing an actual observed case (method of apt illustration).

moiety—half of something, such as a community divided into two sections.

morpheme—meaningful combination of phonemes. (A few morphemes consist of only one phoneme.) Morphemes are words.

Mousterian—style of stone tools associated with *Homo sapiens* and Neanderthals, often using carefully prepared stone cores to more efficiently flake off artifacts.

mutation—change in the chemical structure of DNA in a gene.

myth—narrative of more or less supernatural beings and events.

Neolithic—term means "new stone" but refers to relatively recent period of human prehistory when agriculture was developed.

nocturnal—active at night.

Oldowan—style of stone tools found in the older layers of Olduvai Gorge, Africa, likely to have been made by *Homo habilis* and *Homo erectus*.

omnivore—an animal that eats both plant foods and meat. Humans are omnivores (we have some teeth adapted to chewing plant foods and some teeth adapted to chewing meat).

palaver—discussion leading to a resolution of conflicts. Many societies reject the adversary structure of western courts in favor of their procedures of palaver and mediation.

Paleolithic—Old Stone Age: the cultural period lasting two million years, known through stone tools that have resisted decay.

participant observer—one who observes behavior by joining with the persons being observed, for example working with a farmer, mingling in a market, sitting with worshippers, residing within a village, in order to fully observe actual behavior.

patrilineal—the father's line, referring to inheriting from the father and/or being considered belonging to the father's family line.

phenotype—an organism's appearance.

phoneme—minimal sound or set of sounds used in a particular language to distinguish meanings.

Pleistocene—geological epoch preceding the present, lasting one million years and ending 10,000 years ago; called the Ice Age because several long periods of increased cold occurred during the Pleistocene.

polymorphic—in a population, different alleles for certain genes are passed on generation after generation, maintaining diversity in the population.

potlatch—Northwest Coast Indian (Chinook) term for a feast and gift-giving meant to impress guests with the hosts' importance and power.

practicing anthropologist—an anthropologist employed in a business, institution, or project to apply anthropological methods and knowledge to business or societal needs.

primates—biological order including prosimians, monkeys, apes, and hominids. Primates are characterized by grasping hands with flat nails, stereoscopic vision, relatively large brains, one or few young at a birth and relatively long juvenile stage, and teeth suited to a range of foods.

prosimians—earliest types of primates, surviving today only in a few tropical jungle regions as lemurs, lorises, and tarsiers.

quadripedal—walks on four legs.

race—a population that maintains some distinctive gene alleles through reproductive isolation. Generally, races are separated by geographic barriers such as seas, mountains, or deserts (geographic races). If reproductive isolation continues for many generations, a race is likely to become so different from ancestral populations that it is a new species. (This cannot happen with modern humans because individuals frequently cross between our geographic populations.)

reciprocity—exchange, giving back in return for a gift or assist.

reify—talking about abstract concepts as if they were actual things.

reproductive isolation—a population will not mate with any outside its own. Reproductive isolation usually results in genetic drift. Isolation may be due to geographic separation but can be due to other hindrances to mating.

revitalization—a social movement that gives participants a sense of renewed life.

rite of passage—a ritual marking a change in social status, for example, from childhood to adulthood or single to married.

ritual—strongly patterned action. The strict repetition of the pattern of action communicates that the event is important.

Sapir-Whorf hypothesis—a language's syntax affects its speakers' thinking. For example, Navajos more easily think of ongoing dynamic action without an actor causing it, because their syntax does not require a noun subject in every sentence, a verb without stated subject may be sufficient for a complete sentence. In contrast, English speakers must specify a noun subject and so may expect always to identify actors causing action.

shaman—a religious practitioner who is trained to make contact with spirits on behalf of ill and unfortunate members of a community.

simians—monkeys and apes, primates evolved after millions of years of prosimian evolution.

social charter—Bronislaw Malinowski's concept that myths and legends tell how people ought to behave, providing a charter or organization blueprint.

species—actually or potentially breeding populations, differing in some gene alleles from all other populations. Organisms can mate and produce fertile offspring only with others of their own species.

status—a person's (or group's) standing in their community.

stratified—(1) in archaeology, layers of soil one above the other.
(2) in societies, social classes ranked higher or lower.

subsistence—means of staying alive. In a subsistence economy, workers produce only the food, clothing, shelter, and artifacts necessary to support families, not producing extra for a market.

symbiosis—two organisms living together in such a way that each assists the other's survival.

terrestrial—living on the ground.

totem—an animal exemplifying characteristics attributed to the human group that honors it.

tribe—a political term denoting a less-complex nation fighting or conquered by a more powerful nation-state. Members of the conquered nations generally prefer to be recognized as nations.

world-system—international economic ties making each nation dependent, at least partly, on other nations' demand and supply.

worldview—a person's or society's beliefs about the universe and humankind.

zygote—new cell produced by union of sperm and egg cells.

To Follow up Your Interests: Further Readings

Helpful Background References

Bernard, H. Russell, and Pertti J. Pelto. *Technology and Social Change*. Prospect Heights. IL: Waveland, 1987.

Brettell, Caroline B., and Carolyn F. Sargent, eds. *Gender in Cross-Cultural Perspective*. Upper Saddle River, NJ: Prentice-Hall, 1997.

Bruhns, Karen Olsen. *Ancient South America*. Cambridge: Cambridge University Press, 1994.

Chambers, Erve. *Applied Anthropology: A Practical Guide*. Prospect Heights, IL: Waveland, 1985.

Fagan, Brian M. *Ancient North America*. New York: Thames and Hudson, 1995.

———*People of the Earth: An Introduction to World Prehistory*. New York: Harper Collins.

Godfrey, Laurie R. ed. *Scientists Confront Creationists*. New York: W. W. Norton, 1983.

Gubrium, Jaber F., and James A. Holstein. *What is Family?* Mountain View, CA: Mayfield, 1990.

Jolly, Alison. *The Evolution of Primate Behavior*. 2d edition. New York: Macmillan, 1985.

Linden, Eugene. *Apes, Men, and Language*. Baltimore: Penguin, 1974.

McGrew, W. C. *Chimpanzee Material Culture: Implications for Human Evolution*. Cambridge: Cambridge University Press, 1993.

Miller, Barbara Diane, ed. *Sex and Gender Hierarchies*. Cambridge: Cambridge University Press, 1993.

Netting, Robert M. *Cultural Ecology*. Prospect Heights, IL: Waveland, 1986.

Renfrew, Colin, and Paul Bahn. *Archaeology: Theories, Methods, and Practice*. New York: Thames and Hudson, 1996.

Schele, Linda, and David Freidel. *A Forest of Kings: The Untold Story of the Ancient Maya*. New York: Morrow, 1990.

Spindler, George, ed. *Education and Cultural Process: Anthropological Approaches*. Prospect Heights IL: Waveland, 1987.

Swann, Brian, ed. *Coming to Light: Contemporary Translations of the Native Literatures of North America*. New York: Vintage, 1994.

Tannen, Deborah. *You Just Don't Understand: Women and Men in Conversation*. New York: William Morris, 1990.

Walker, Alan, and Pat Shipman. *The Wisdom of the Bones: In Search of Human Origins*. New York: Knopf, 1996.

Case Studies in Ethnography and Cultural Anthropology

Chance, Norman A. *The Iñupiat and Arctic Alaska: An Ethnography of Development*. Fort Worth: Harcourt Brace, 1990.

Chavez, Leo R. *Shadowed Lives: Undocumented Immigrants in American Society*. Fort Worth: Harcourt Brace, 1992.

Deng, Francis Mading. *The Dinka of the Sudan*. Prospect Heights, IL: Waveland, 1986.

Dettwyler, Katherine A. *Dancing Skeletons* (Mali, Africa). Prospect Heights, IL: Waveland, 1994.

Esman, Marjorie R. *Henderson, Louisiana: Cultural Adaptation in a Cajun Community*. Fort Worth: Harcourt Brace, 1985.

Frankenberg, Ronald. *Village on the Border*. Prospect Heights, IL: Waveland, 1990 (1957).

Goldschmidt, Walter. *The Sebei: A Study in Cultural Adaptation* (Central Africa). Fort Worth: Harcourt Brace, 1987.

Hallowell, A. Irving, and Jennifer S.H. Brown. *The Ojibwa of Berens River, Manitoba: Ethnography Into History*. Fort Worth: Harcourt Brace, 1992.

Herdt, Gilbert. *The Sambia: Ritual and Gender in New Guinea*. Fort Worth: Harcourt Brace, 1986.

Hostetler, John A., and Gertrude Enders Huntington. *The Hutterites in North America*. Fort Worth: Harcourt Brace, 1996.

Kehoe, Alice Beck. *The Ghost Dance: Ethnohistory and Revitalization*. Fort Worth: Harcourt Brace, 1989.

Keur, Dorothy, and John Y. Keur. *The Deeply Rooted: A Study of a Drents Community in the Netherlands.* American Ethnological Society Monograph No. 25, 1955.

Kuper, Hilda. *The Swazi: A South African Kingdom.* Fort Worth: Harcourt Brace, 1986.

Lee, Richard B. *The Dobe Ju/'hoansi.* Fort Worth: Harcourt Brace, 1994.

Lever, Janet. *Soccer Madness: Brazil's Passion for the World's Most Popular Sport.* Prospect Heights, IL: Waveland, 1995.

Parman, Susan. *Scottish Crofters: A Historical Ethnography of a Celtic Village.* Fort Worth: Harcourt Brace, 1990.

Schaffer, Matt, and Christine Cooper. *Mandinko: The Ethnography of a West African Holy Land.* Prospect Heights, IL: Waveland, 1987.

Tonkinson, Robert. *The Mardu Aborigines: Living the Dream in Australia's Desert.* Fort Worth: Harcourt Brace, 1991.

Turnbull, Colin. *The Mbuti Pygmies: Change and Adaptation.* Fort Worth: Harcourt Brace, 1983.

Underhill, Ruth M. *Papago Woman.* Prospect Heights, IL: Waveland, 1979.

Vogt, Evon Z. *The Zinacantecos of Mexico: A Modern Maya Way of Life.* 2d ed. Fort Worth: Harcourt Brace, 1990.

Weiner, Annette. *The Trobrianders of Papua New Guinea.* Fort Worth: Harcourt Brace, 1988.

Williams, Melvin D. *Community in a Black Pentecostal Church.* Prospect Heights, IL: Waveland, 1984.

Wong, Bernard. *Chinatown: Economic Adaptation and Ethnic Identity of the Chinese.* Fort Worth: Harcourt Brace, 1982.

Landmark Anthropological Studies

Bourdieu, Pierre. *Outline of a Theory of Practice.* Cambridge: Cambridge University Press, 1977.

Chapple, Eliot D. Culture and Biological Man, Fort Worth: Holt Rinehart Winston, 1970.

———*Culture and Biological Man.* Fort Worth: Holt Rinehart Winston, 1970.

Desmond, Adrian, and James Moore. *Darwin.* New York: Time Warner, 1991.

Fried, Morton H. *The Evolution of Political Society.* New York: Random House, 1967.

Goffman, Erving. *The Presentation of Self in Everyday Life.* New York: Doubleday, 1959.

Gould, Stephen Jay. *Ontogeny and Phylogeny.* Cambridge, MA: Belknap, 1977. *Mismeasure of Man; Time's Arrow,* and others, and collected essays beginning with *Ever Since Darwin.*

Hall, Edward T. *The Silent Language.* New York: Doubleday, 1959.

Harrison, G. A., J. M. Tanner, D. R. Pilbeam, and P. T. Baker. 3d ed. *Human Biology.* Oxford: Oxford University Press, 1988.

Lakoff, George, and Mark Johnson. *Metaphors We Live By.* Chicago: University of Chicago Press, 1980.

Lévi-Strauss, Claude. *The Savage Mind.* Chicago: University of Chicago Press, 1966.

Lovejoy, Arthur O., and George Boas. *Primitivism and Related Ideas in Antiquity.* Baltimore: Johns Hopkins University Press (1997 reprint, first edition 1935).

Needham, Joseph et al. *Science and Civilization in China.* Multi-volume series. Cambridge: Cambridge University Press, 1954 and continuing.

Powdermaker, Hortense. *Stranger and Friend.* Prospect Heights, IL: Waveland, 1966.

Wolf, Eric R. *Europe and the People Without History.* Berkeley: University of California Press, 1982.

Index